Understanding Bitcoin

Cryptography, engineering, and economics

PEDRO FRANCO

WILEY

Dedicated to Alvaro, Rafael, Luis, and Nayra

Contents

About the Author

Pedro Franco was born in Astorga, Leon (Spain). He holds a MSc in Electrical Engineering from ICAI, a BSc in Economics, and an MBA from INSEAD. Pedro has been a consultant with McKinsey and Boston Consulting Group and a researcher with IIT prior to gaining more than 10 years of experience in financial markets holding Quant and Trading positions in Credit, Counterparty Risk, Inflation, and Interest Rates. He has created various mathematical libraries for financial derivatives, and managed teams of software developers.

The author can be contacted at pfrancobtc@gmail.com.

Acknowledgments

Thanks to Juan Ramirez for helping me gather the courage to write this book.

Thanks to Jon Beracoechea, Manuel Castro, and Robert Smith for exhaustively reviewing an early version of the book and providing many excellent suggestions. Thanks also to Eli Ben-Sasson, Alejandro and Alvaro Franco, Jeff Lim, Jan Pelzl, Stefan Thomas, Evan Schwartz, Rodrigo Serrano, Alena Vranova, and Bob Way for reviewing parts of the book and providing insightful comments.

Finally, thanks to my family for their patience and support; without them this book could not have been written.

Foreword

I have been hoping for some time for a good book covering the technology and ideas behind Bitcoin to be written.

There is certainly a wealth of information about cryptocurrencies, but the field advances rapidly and it is sometimes difficult for the non-initiated to understand the fundamentals and catch up with new developments. This book takes readers to a thorough understanding of the current state-of-the-art cryptocurrencies' technology, as well as its future economic and technological implications, without assuming any previous knowledge of the many fields than constitute Bitcoin. This is an enabling book that empowers the reader to participate in and contribute to this great adventure.

The book clearly exposes many concepts previously mainly known to insiders of the cryptocurrencies' world. It covers a wide range of topics, from the economics or the basic technology (such as elliptic curve cryptography, Merkle trees or the blockchain) to advanced cryptographic concepts (such as non-interactive zero-knowledge proofs), and explores many applications based on these ideas (such as multi-signature wallets or fully anonymous payment systems). All this is accomplished in a book that is very approachable and comprehensible.

Readers new to Bitcoin will surely be surprised by the ingenuity of the technology and the broad range of applications it enables. Those familiar with Bitcoin will find many sections, such as the sections on economics or advanced applications of cryptocurrencies, informative and thought provoking.

I believe Pedro's book will be well received in the business and financial community as well as by the general public, spreading the knowledge about Bitcoin and contributing to this technology crossing the chasm to the early majority.

Jeff Garzik
Bitcoin Core Developer at BitPay, Inc.

Fascinating! We're back to the dialogue form...

- What is Bitcoin?
- It's a digital currency.
- Yeah, I get that, but who is behind Bitcoin?
- Nobody.
- What do you mean by nobody? Somebody must be controlling it!
- Nobody is controlling it, it is an algorithm.
- What? You mean like Terminator? So you say the world is going to be taken over by machines?
- Well, not the world, but maybe some businesses.
- Right... (rolling her eyes) But who controls the algorithm? Some mad scientist?
- It's an open source project.
- An open what?
- Yes, free code. You can download it from the internet and do with it whatever you want.
- So you don't have to pay for the "program"?
- Well, it's free as in freedom, not free as in beer. *Stallman*
- What does beer have to do with it?
- The code is not only free in the sense that you can use the program free of charge. It is also free in the sense that you can take the code, modify it, and release a program of your own with it.
- Wait a second! If I can do that then I can make my own bitcoins. What value does a bitcoin have then?
- No, you cannot mint your own bitcoins. What you can do is invent your own currency. And then you have to somehow make it gain acceptance...
- Oh, but this surely is the end of Bitcoin. If you can make as many currencies as you want, none of them would have any value.
- Currencies have value because of social convention. Bitcoin has value because people are willing to give value to it.
- I don't think you are right. Euros or dollars have value, everybody knows that.
- Well if bitcoins do not have value I will gladly accept your bitcoins (smiling).
- Bitcoins are not backed by anything so they cannot have value.
- Neither euros, dollars nor Bitcoin are backed by anything. You can say that all of them are the result of consensual hallucination. They have value because people give value to them. There is not much difference between them in this regard.
- I don't think so. You can buy things with euros or dollars, but what can you buy with bitcoins?

Line from Neuromancer!

- You can buy almost anything with bitcoins. There are companies that will gladly accept your bitcoins in return for regular currency that you can use to buy anything. Converting bitcoins to sovereign currencies is just a technical interface and many companies provide this service. Besides, you can do things with bitcoins that you cannot do with sovereign currencies.
- Like what?
- For example, you could launch a crowd-funding campaign, just creating a special type of Bitcoin transaction.
- That sounds cool.
- There are many more applications that were impossible until now, such as a car which reads its ownership from the cloud. If you want to buy the car, you just pay the owner with bitcoins and the car knows automatically you are its new owner because it can look it up in Bitcoin's database. And there might be more applications to come that nobody has thought of yet, as was the case (and still is) with the internet.
- I guess I did not think of it that way.
- As they say, a currency is just the first application. The technology allows transferring value securely and in a decentralized way and this can lead to many new cool applications.
- I'm intrigued, I'd like to learn more.
- Great! I believe I have the right book for you...

who?

Preface

Opinions about Bitcoin are highly polarized between enthusiasts and skeptics. The author believes that the point of view of the skeptics is easier to grasp for someone not familiar with Bitcoin's technology. The objective of this book is to present the technology and arguments from both sides of the divide so that readers can form an informed opinion of their own.

What drives the passion of the enthusiasts is that Bitcoin is a technological breakthrough that creates many new and interesting applications. As is often the case with brand new technologies, many future applications of the technology might not be envisioned today. Who could have imagined the success of video streaming services or social networks in 1994? Enthusiasts feel the technology will yield many unforeseen applications for many years to come. The fact that most of these applications are intertwined with monetary economics makes it even more interesting.

The economic and technical aspects of Bitcoin are so intertwined that, in the opinion of this author, they should be tackled together. Arguing about one of them without understanding the other would be like trying to run a car with only one pedal: just pressing the gas or the brake pedal. Sure, the driver could descend a mountain with only the brake pedal, but then she could not go much further. Similarly a driver with only the gas pedal could probably ascend a mountain, but she would be better off not trying to descend it. This book covers the technology behind Bitcoin, ranging from cryptography to software engineering to monetary economics.

References to Bitcoin's source code are scattered throughout the text, especially in the technical sections. These references are intended as clues for readers interested in the implementation of the Bitcoin protocol, but can be safely skipped by other readers.

This book is divided into three parts. The first part serves as an introduction to Bitcoin's technology and philosophy (Chapters 1 and 2). This part will also cover the economic arguments both in favor of and against Bitcoin (Chapter 3) and some business applications (Chapter 4). This part is designed for the time-constrained readers who are mostly interested in the business and economic impact of Bitcoin's technology.

The second part covers in detail how Bitcoin works, starting with public key cryptography (Chapter 5), transactions (Chapter 6) and the blockchain (Chapter 7). The last two chapters expand on related topics: wallets (Chapter 8) and mining (Chapter 9). In this line, two additional great resources for developers are the Developer Guide (Bitcoin Foundation, 2014a) and the Reference Guide (Bitcoin Foundation, 2014b) maintained by the Bitcoin Foundation, and the forthcoming book by Andreas Antonopoulos (Antonopoulos, 2014).

The third part completes the cryptocurrencies landscape. First, digital currency technologies preceding Bitcoin are discussed (Chapter 10). Then alternative cryptocurrencies based on Bitcoin (alt-coins) are covered (Chapter 11) and new applications of cryptocurrencies beyond payment systems are explored (Chapter 12). Most of the action in the cryptocurrencies community is focused on these new applications and Chapter 12 will introduce several of the brand new projects that are being built. Bitcoin is not anonymous, and Chapter 13 explores techniques that can be used to de-anonymize users, as well as technologies that are being built to enable users to counter these techniques and enhance their privacy. The chapter concludes with an introduction to the technology, based on zero-knowledge proofs, to create fully anonymous decentralized digital currencies. The book concludes (Chapter 14) with a discussion of some additional technical topics and the latest developments being discussed in the community.

An earlier version of this book has been registered in the blockchain. The hash of this earlier version is

1324585ce12bdf2c16995835e1ba1a04246592e7755c6c1933419fe80f97f10e

and was registered in the blockchain in transaction

e144275426185d0a0b85e7bdcfdfbbaa6f7f750a522007aeaae6f0f8708838bb.

The blog for this book can be found at understandingbitcoin.blogspot.com.

Madrid, July 2014

PART
One

Introduction and Economics

CHAPTER 1

Foundations

There has been ample media coverage of Bitcoin, and many public figures have been compelled to state their opinion. As Bitcoin is a complex topic, covering cryptography, software engineering and economics, it is difficult to grasp its essence and implications with only a superficial look at it. Thus some commentators might not have a clear picture of how it works and the implications. It is the goal of this book to equip the reader with the knowledge to evaluate the merits of this technology.

Figure 1.1 summarizes some misconceptions around Bitcoin.

Bitcoin is a decentralized digital currency. This means there is no person or institution behind it, either backing it or controlling it. Neither is it backed by physical goods, such as precious metals. This might seem counter-intuitive at first glance: how could it exist if no one controls it? Who created it then? How did the creator lose control over it?

The answer to this seeming paradox is that Bitcoin is just a computer program. How exactly this computer program works is the subject of the second part of this book. The program has a creator (or creators) but his identity is unknown as he released the Bitcoin software using what is believed to be a pseudonym: Satoshi Nakamoto. Bitcoin is not controlled in a tight sense by anyone. The creator did not lose control of it because he

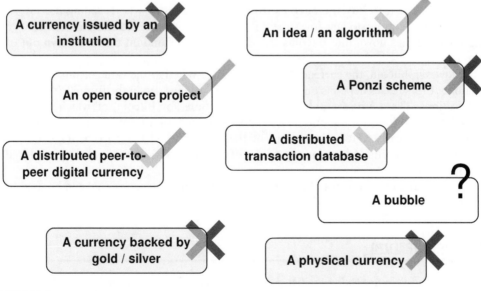

FIGURE 1.1 What Bitcoin is (and isn't)

(she?, they?) never owned the code. The code is **open source** and thus it belongs to the public domain, as will be further explained in section 1.2.

One of the most innovative features of Bitcoin is that it is **decentralized**. There is no central server where Bitcoin is running. Bitcoin operates through a peer-to-peer network of connected computers. Bitcoin is the first digital currency built in a decentralized way, a technological breakthrough. The decentralized nature of Bitcoin will be further explored in section 1.1.

Bitcoin creates its own currency called bitcoin, with a small b. The creation of a currency is integral to how the system operates, as it serves two simultaneous purposes. First, it serves to represent value. Second, issuance of new bitcoins is used to reward operators in the network for securing the distributed ledger. These two functions cannot be unbundled without significantly changing the design.

The heart of the Bitcoin network is a database holding the transactions that have occurred in the past as well as the current holders of the funds. This database is sometimes called a ledger, because it holds the entries representing the owners of the funds. Bitcoin is not the first distributed database to be created. However, the requirements of a financial database are different from those of other applications, such as file sharing or messaging systems. In particular, financial databases must be resilient against users trying to double-spend their funds, which Bitcoin solves elegantly. This is explored in the following sections and in Chapter 2.

Some critics have argued that Bitcoin is a **Ponzi scheme**. **It is not.** In a Ponzi scheme there is a central operator who pays returns to current investors from new capital inflows. First of all, in Bitcoin there is no central operator who can profit from the relocation of funds. Second, there is no mechanism to deflect funds from new investments to pay returns. The only funds recognized in the Bitcoin protocol are bitcoins, the currency. Transfers of bitcoins are initiated by the users at their will: the protocol cannot deflect funds from one user to another. Third, a new investment in Bitcoin is always matched with a disinvestment. Investors who put money into bitcoins usually operate through an exchange where they buy the bitcoins from another investor who is selling her investment. There is simply no new investment flowing into bitcoins: the amount of sovereign currency that has flown into bitcoins exactly matches the amount that has flown out of bitcoins.

However, bitcoin, the currency, can be a bubble. Whether the value of bitcoin crashes, holds, or increases depends on whether bitcoins will be used in the future for different applications. There are several interesting applications for Bitcoin, of which the most straightforward (but not the only) are to serve as a medium of exchange and a store of value. It is too early to tell whether any of these applications will become important in the future. The merits of bitcoins as medium of exchange and store of value are explored in Chapter 3.

Finally, Bitcoin is not just a currency but a whole infrastructure that can be used to transfer value digitally: see section 1.4 and Chapter 12.

1.1 DECENTRALIZED

Most currencies in use today are fiat currencies, where the currency is issued by the government and its supply managed by a central bank.

FIAT MONEY

Most currencies today (Euro, US Dollar) are fiat money. Fiat money does not have intrinsic value, as it is not backed by anything. It is called fiat money because there is a government decree ("fiat") declaring the currency to be legal tender. The acceptance of fiat money depends on expectations and social convention. If confidence in a currency is lost, usually because of irresponsible monetary policy, fiat money can stop being accepted.

Experience has shown that leaving monetary policy in the hands of governments is usually not a good idea, as governments could have an incentive to increase the monetary supply to solve pressing short-term financial problems. This behavior can lead to high inflation and a loss of confidence in the currency.

The conventional solution is to entrust monetary policy to a semi-independent central bank. The central bank is tasked with managing the monetary policy, usually with the goals of economic growth, price stability, and, in some cases, stability of the financial system.

Bitcoin is based on a peer-to-peer network of computers running the software. These computers are called nodes. Participants in the network might be running nodes for different reasons: for profit as in the case of miners (Chapter 9), to manage full-node wallets (Chapter 8), to collect and study information about the network (Chapter 13), or simply as a social good.

Bitcoin's decentralized nature contrasts to the structure of fiat currencies. Central banks make monetary decisions after evaluating evidence gathered from the evolution of the economy. In a decentralized system such as Bitcoin, discretionary decisions are not possible. The original creators of the system have to take most of the decisions upfront at the design phase. These decisions have to be carefully balanced, and take into account the incentives of the different users, otherwise the decentralized system is doomed to fail. In Bitcoin the monetary policy follows a simple rule: the final monetary base is fixed at around 21 million bitcoins and new bitcoins are minted at a planned schedule and paid to users who help secure the network. This serves the double purpose of providing the bitcoins with value due to their scarcity and creating incentives for users to connect to the network and help secure it by providing their computational power.

Control in a centralized system is usually concentrated in an institution or a small group of key people. Thus changes in a centralized system are relatively straightforward to decide and implement. Control in a peer-to-peer network is more subtle: changes in a peer-to-peer network have to be agreed by a majority of the peers at least. But even then, if a strong minority does not agree to a change, implementing the change can be technically challenging as the network runs the risk of a split.

One advantage of the decentralization of power is that changes that are contrary to the interests of most users would be rejected. In contrast, in centralized systems sometimes the outcomes are adverse to most of the participants, as in a currency debasement by excessive printing which usually leads to high inflation.

Another feature of decentralized systems is their resilience. Decentralized systems are robust against attacks either by insiders or by external forces. This feature might have been critical for the existence of Bitcoin. Earlier centralized attempts to create digital currencies (section 2.1) were forced down by governments. However, to force down a decentralized system, all individual users must be forced down, which is a much harder task. Bitcoin's peer-to-peer nature makes it censorship-resistant, claim its supporters.

The technology to securely (cryptographically) transfer value digitally had been available many years before the creation of Bitcoin (Chapter 10). However, it had always required the creation of a centralized trusted party. Bitcoin not only does not require a central trusted party to operate, but it is also designed to resist the attacks of malicious participants in the peer-to-peer network. As long as these malicious participants do not control a majority of the network these attacks will not succeed (section 7.5).

The main technological breakthrough accomplished by Bitcoin is solving the double-spending problem in a distributed financial database. A double-spend attempt occurs when a user tries to spend some funds twice. All financial systems must reject these attempts. This is relatively straightforward in a centralized system, as transactions are recorded in a central database and future spending attempts are checked against this database first. In a decentralized system, many copies of the database are shared among the peers, and keeping a consistent state of the database is a difficult computational problem[1]. In the context of Bitcoin the problem is how the network can agree on the state of the distributed database when messages between the nodes can be corrupted and there might be attackers trying to subvert the distributed database. Bitcoin gracefully solves this problem (section 2.3 and Chapter 7).

1.2   OPEN SOURCE

Bitcoin is open source software. **Open source** software makes the source code available for anyone to use, modify, and redistribute free of charge. Some well-known open source software products include the Linux and Android operating systems or the Firefox web browser. A large portion of the internet infrastructure runs on less known (but no less important) open source software. The goal of open source is to make software development similar to academic peer-reviewed research. By publishing the source code for anyone to see and check, open source aims to increase the quality of the software.

The difference between open source software and proprietary software lies in their licenses. A proprietary software license grants the right to use a copy of the program to the end user. However, ownership of the software remains with the software publisher. In contrast, an open source license grants the user the right to use, copy, modify, and redistribute the software. The copyright of the software remains with the creator, but the creator of an open source software transfers the rights to the user as long as the obligations of the license are met.

Another difference between proprietary and open source programs is that proprietary programs are usually distributed as compiled binaries. This means that the software is usually distributed in machine language. Users willing to gain knowledge on what the software is doing must interpret the machine code in a time-consuming process called reverse engineering (Eilam, 2005). Most proprietary licenses forbid the use of these reverse

---

[1] This computational problem is called the Byzantine Generals' problem, introduced in Lamport et al. (1982).

engineering techniques. Thus under a proprietary license the user is usually not allowed to understand or seek knowledge of what the software is actually doing. In contrast, open source software is always distributed with a copy of the source code. A user who wants to understand what the software is doing can just read the source code. Cryptographic open source software has the advantage that it allows users to check that the code does not contain any backdoor or security vulnerabilities[2].

It is unlikely that Bitcoin could have been released under a proprietary license. Had Bitcoin been released as closed-source, its creator could have easily inserted code that deviated from the specification: say, creating new bitcoins and sending them to an address controlled by him. Most users presumably would not have accepted decentralized cryptographic financial software distributed as a compiled binary and with a proprietary license. It is telling that most competing cryptocurrencies (Chapter 11, section 12.7), have either been launched using an open source license or have switched to an open source license.

Open source licenses grant the user the right to use, copy, modify, and redistribute the software. Different licenses may impose different obligations on the users. Broadly speaking, open source licenses belong to one of two families:

- **"Copyleft."** These licenses impose the obligation to distribute derived works under the same license. If a user of the software makes modifications to it, she is obliged to release the modified software under the same license. This is referred to as the share-alike requirement. Thus "copyleft" licenses preserve the open source nature of the software as it is modified. An example of a "copyleft" license is the **GNU Public License (GPL)**.
- **"Permissive."** These licenses impose very few restrictions on the redistribution of the software, usually just that the derived software acknowledges the original software and retains the copyright notice. Proprietary software that incorporates software released under an open source permissive license retains its proprietary nature as the license usually only requires that the proprietary software includes the copyright notice. Several common open source licenses belong to this family, such as the BSD license, the MIT License or the Apache License. Bitcoin was released under the MIT license.

Proprietary software requires that the company issuing the software maintains and updates it. In contrast, open source software acquires a life of its own once released. It usually does not matter if an original creator decides to stop working on an open source project, as other developers could take it over. For this reason it does not matter who Satoshi Nakamoto is, or that he has moved on. Open source projects are resilient: even if some developers are forbidden or discouraged to work on a project, other developers from all around the world can take over.

---

[2] This should not be interpreted that open source code does not contain security flaws or backdoors. Indeed, many security flaws have been found in open source projects (Green, 2014b; Poulsen, 2014). Open source advocates argue that it is more difficult to include flaws and backdoors into open source programs because there is a higher level of scrutiny, and that these flaws are typically discovered and repaired sooner than similar flaws placed in proprietary software (Raymond, 2001).

Under an open source license it is legitimate to start a new independent software project from a copy of an original project. This process is called **forking**. The threat of a fork can often keep the developers of an open source project honest. If the developers of a project introduce changes that are detrimental to the users of the software, anybody can create a fork, undo those changes and continue the development. Users will most likely follow the fork without the undesired features. Thus forking can be seen as a kill switch that prevents developers from evolving a project against their users. Most large open source projects are rarely forked[3]. Bitcoin is somewhat special in this respect, as it has been forked many times by developers wishing to test new concepts. This has given rise to many alternative cryptocurrencies called alt-coins. Alt-coins will be covered in more detail in Chapter 11.

Open source advocates argue that companies releasing proprietary software often lose the incentive to innovate once a product has achieved a dominant market position. Many software markets behave like natural monopolies where a product with first mover advantage can capture a large market share. Thus innovation in many software categories is low, these advocates suggest. In contrast, if an open source software captures the majority of the market this does not bring about the end of innovation, as anybody can keep on adding improvements to the software. Thus the pace of innovation in open source software can be higher than in closed source software.

One problem facing many open source projects is the **tragedy of the commons**. Although many people benefit from an open source project, few developers might have an incentive to contribute to it. Many open source projects face difficulties in getting appropriate funding or development time. There have been some indications that Bitcoin could be facing this problem (Bradbury, 2014b).

An exposition of the merits of open source software can be found in Raymond (2001).

1.3   PUBLIC ASSET LEDGER

The heart of Bitcoin is a distributed database that holds a copy of the common asset ledger. As this database is distributed, each participant in the network (a node) keeps a copy of it. Copies of this database kept by the different nodes are consistent by design.

On the other hand, every user is in control of her own funds, through a cryptographic private key. When a user wishes to spend some funds, she must use this private key to sign a message that states who she wishes to send the funds to as well as the amount to send. The user broadcasts this signed message to the network, and every participant in the network receives a copy of it. Then each node can independently verify the validity of the message and update its internal database accordingly[4].

---

[3] Most projects are really forked many times by individual users wishing to tinker with them or test new features. However, forks of large open source projects that split the developer base, such as the LibreOffice fork from OpenOffice (Paul, 2011), are rather rare.

[4] The process is actually more involved to prevent double-spending attacks where a user sends different messages to different parts of the network. How Bitcoin prevents double-spending attacks is the subject of Chapter 7.

In traditional financial systems, value is represented in ledgers (databases) managed by financial institutions. Users must place trust in these financial institutions that these databases will not be subverted either by insiders or by outside attackers. The protocols and procedures that safeguard traditional financial databases are not generally revealed to the public. In contrast, Bitcoin makes the database public and creates an open source software protocol to secure it. This protocol is designed to be resilient against attackers participating in the network. Bitcoin users do not need to place trust on any entity: the system is said to be trust-less.

All the financial information flowing through the Bitcoin network is public, except the identities behind the transactions. Bitcoin does not use personal information to identify the holders of funds, but Bitcoin addresses. Addresses are long strings of seemingly random letters and numbers, such as "13mckXcnnEd4SEkC27PnFH8dsY2gdGhRvM". Bitcoin is like making everybody's bank statements public online, but with the identity blacked out (Back, 2014b).

Although in principle there is no way to associate addresses to identities, there are many techniques to analyze the information flowing through the network and acquire different grades of knowledge about Bitcoin addresses and the users behind them (Chapter 13).

Bitcoin is not anonymous, and it can sometimes be less anonymous than the traditional payment systems. In the traditional payment system, for instance, an employer does not gain knowledge of where an employee spends her wage, although the employee's bank has that information. If an employee were paid in bitcoins, her employer could see where she spends the money simply following the trail of transactions emerging from the address where the wage was sent to. The employee could follow some practices to hide this trail of transactions (Chapter 13).

In other cases, this transparency can be an advantage. One such example is the case of public entities where a transparent destination of funds could help increase the quality of the administration and help avoid corruption. In the case of commercial enterprises some level of transparency can be beneficial, for example financial statements that could be verified against the public ledger. There has been some technological progress towards achieving different levels of transparency in a public ledger system (section 8.5).

1.4   IT'S NOT ONLY THE CURRENCY, IT'S THE TECHNOLOGY

Transfer of value has traditionally been a slow and highly manual process. In essence, Bitcoin is a protocol to create distributed consensus. This protocol allows transferring value securely in a trust-less way: it is an open platform for money. But it is not only restricted to money: Bitcoin and similar protocols can transfer any digital asset (Chapter 12). The technology is cheaper and faster than most of the alternatives, creating opportunities for new applications.

The digital transfer of value enables the adoption of smart contracts. **Smart contracts** are contracts that do not require human interpretation or intervention to complete. Their settlement is done entirely by running a computer program. Smart contracts are math-based contracts, as opposed to law-based contracts. A trust-less digital transfer of value opens the door to new applications that make use of smart contracts.

One such application is autonomous agents. Autonomous agents should not be confused with artificial intelligence. Autonomous agents are just straightforward computer programs, created for a specific task. One example is a computer program running in the cloud that rents storage space and offers end users file-sharing services. Up until now computer programs could not hold value: a computer program presumably could not open a bank account in its name. With the introduction of Bitcoin, computer programs can control their own funds and sign smart contracts with cloud service providers to rent cloud storage and computing power. Similarly a storage agent could enter into smart contracts with its end users. The storage agent can settle these smart contracts, making bitcoin payments to the cloud provider and receiving bitcoin payments from its end users (Garzik, 2013a). A more extensive discussion of autonomous agents can be found in section 12.4.

Autonomous agents are just one example, and many more innovative ideas are being devised (Chapter 12). Some of these ideas may turn out not to be practical, but maybe a few could become mainstream. A decentralized system is an ideal test ground for these technologies, as innovators do not need the approval of anybody to try out their ideas: a decentralized system enables **permissionless innovation**.

Bitcoin is an API (Application Programming Interface) for money and bitcoin the currency is just the first application. Bitcoin could be used as an open platform for the exchange of value in much the same way that the internet is an open platform for the exchange of information. It can be used as a protocol on top of which applications can be built, much like email, web browsing, or voice-over-IP are built on top of the TCP/IP protocol. This is where most of the excitement around Bitcoin and related technologies comes from. Regardless of whether bitcoins have a future as currency, the technology has shown that many applications are now possible and innovators will continue to push forward with new ideas. Bitcoin could become a platform for financial innovation.

One of Ronald Coase's most important economic insights in *The Nature of the Firm* (Coase, 1937) was that one factor that contributed to the creation of firms was high transaction costs. If there were no transaction costs, an entrepreneur could contract any good she needs in the open market, and this would be efficient, as an efficient market would always achieve the best price for that good. However, transaction costs, such as information gathering, bargaining, policing the contract, keeping secrets and so on, can be a significant portion of the total cost of contracting out to the market. For this reason, it might be cheaper for an entrepreneur to hire some employees to produce the goods internally, thus starting a corporation. Transaction costs are also at the root of public goods and government action.

Bitcoin's technological breakthrough creates an opportunity to lower the costs of entering and upholding contracts, say through smart contracts. More efficient contracts thus have the potential to change corporations and government action.

CHAPTER 2

Technology (Introduction)

Until the introduction of Bitcoin, transmitting money digitally had required the mediation of a third party. The main breakthrough of Bitcoin has been to allow digital payments with no trusted third party. This chapter serves as an overview of the technology behind Bitcoin.

2.1 CENTRALIZED DATABASE

The most straightforward way to try to create digital value is to assign value to a certain data pattern, basically a string of zeroes and ones. The problem with this approach is that digital information is easy to replicate at basically no cost. This leads to the double-spend problem, exemplified in Figure 2.1. Say Alice has a digital coin, represented by the binary number 01000101. She could transfer this value to Bob, by sending him a message with this number, so that Bob had a copy of the number and thus the value. The problem is obviously that nothing prevents Alice from sending this same number to another user or indeed to many other users.

So digital value cannot be represented simply as a number because digital data is very easy to replicate many times and thus knowledge of the number does not have any value. As common sense suggests, for something to have value it must be scarce. The challenge then is how to create scarcity using digital technologies that allow the perfect copying of information.

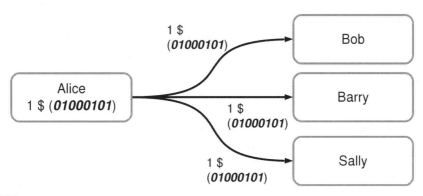

FIGURE 2.1 Double-spending problem

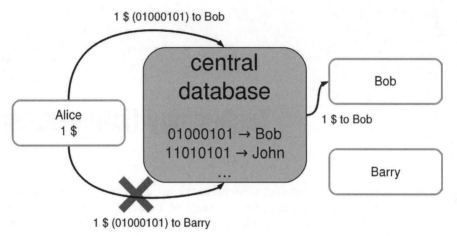

FIGURE 2.2   Central counterparty holding a centralized database

The next step towards building a digital payment system is to create a central database, holding a list of the users and the funds held by any of them. This system is shown in Figure 2.2.

Now if Alice wants to transfer 1 unit of the currency, say a token, represented by the number 01000101 to Bob, she contacts the server running the central database and directs it to transfer this token to Bob. The server updates the database, and the token now belongs to Bob. If Alice tries to double-spend the token 01000101, sending it to Barry this time, she would have to again connect to the central server and direct it to send the token to Barry. However, upon checking the database, the server sees that the token 01000101 does not belong to Alice any more, and thus she is not authorized to spend it.

A central database solves the double-spend problem. However, there are issues associated with a central database. For a start, all users must have previously registered with the central server in order to operate. Thus the central database knows the identities of all the users and collects their financial history[1]. A central database is also an easy target to attack, either by insiders or by outsiders. If an attacker gets control of the central database, she could change the ownership of any funds, thus stealing them from their legitimate owners. Or she could create new funds (tokens) and assign them to herself.

Perhaps the main drawback of a central server is that it constitutes a single point of failure, as portrayed in Figure 2.3: the payment system can be easily taken down by shutting the central server.

Some early digital payment systems were based on the idea of a central database holding the positions of all the users. Two famous examples are e-gold and Liberty Reserve. E-gold ceased operations in 2009 (Wikipedia, 2014h), and Liberty Reserve in 2013 (Wikipedia, 2014i).

Figure 2.4 shows the analogy between BitTorrent and Bitcoin. Both are systems where the coordination of information is done in a decentralized way. In BitTorrent (the

---

[1] Technology exists to implement a payment system based on a central server where users retain their anonymity. This technology is based on blinded signatures and is the subject of section 10.1.

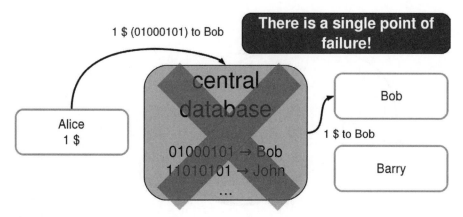

FIGURE 2.3 Central counterparty single point of failure

BitTorrent	**Bitcoin**
• It is a protocol for p2p file-sharing • Protocol released in 2001 • In 2009 accounted for > 40% of internet traffic • It is a distributed database of files accessed through "torrent" descriptor files • Users can contribute to the database directly (by seeding)	• Distributed p2p cryptocurrency • The open-source project was announced in 2009 • At the beginning of 2014 it had a capitalization of several billion USD • A distributed database holds all the transactions since inception • Users (nodes) contribute directly to the database

FIGURE 2.4 Analogy between BitTorrent and Bitcoin

protocol) any user can create a torrent descriptor and seed the file into the network. Other users in possession of the torrent descriptor can then connect to the network and retrieve the file (Wikipedia, 2014d). Bitcoin's ledger database is distributed and maintained by many computers called nodes. Bitcoin users can send new transactions to this distributed database, where they are recorded. Both systems are resilient, even in scenarios where a large portion of the network is forced down.

2.2 ADDRESSES, TRANSACTIONS

At the center of the Bitcoin network is a decentralized ledger that contains the balance of every Bitcoin user. Bitcoin identifies users by large strings of letters and numbers such as "13mckXcnnEd4SEkC27PnFH8dsY2gdGhRvM". The address is the public part of a public–private cryptographic key[2]. The private part of the key is under the

---

[2] Bitcoin addresses are not exactly public keys, but are derived from public keys (section 5.6).

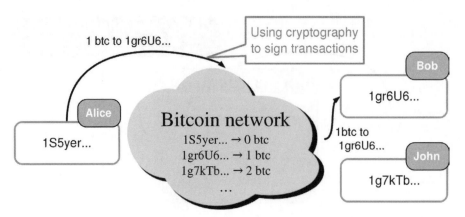

FIGURE 2.5   User sending funds. State of the database after the transaction has settled

control of the user. Figure 2.5 shows how a user (Alice) sends some funds to another user (Bob): Alice uses her private key to sign a message saying "I want to send 1 bitcoin to 1gr6U6..." that she sends to the network. Note that Alice does not identify the user she wants to send funds to, just the address to receive the funds. Thus Alice must find out Bob's address through other means.

Upon receiving Alice's message, nodes in the network follow these steps:

- They verify that the signature is correct. If it is not they reject the message.
- They check that the sending address has enough funds to honor the transaction. If there are not enough funds credited to the address, the transaction is considered invalid.
- Finally, they update the database, subtracting the funds from one address and crediting them to the other.

An important detail is that nodes in the network do not know the identities of either Alice or Bob, as users are identified only by their addresses. Bitcoin users are identified by a pseudonym: Bitcoin provides pseudonymity.

Another important detail is that addresses are not granted by the network. They are created inside the users' devices when it runs the Bitcoin software that generates the cryptographic public and private keys. As the public and private keys are intimately related (Chapter 5), they have to be generated jointly and locally on the user's device. The address generation process is straightforward and can be performed almost instantaneously by any device such as a laptop or a smartphone. There is also no restriction on the number of addresses that a user can create. Indeed, it is recommended that users generate many addresses to enhance privacy (Chapter 13).

No prior registration is necessary to use Bitcoin. In fact, new users do not even have to communicate their addresses to the network to be able to receive funds. A user, say Bob, can generate an address and communicate this address to Alice through other means, such as an email or the pairing of two smartphones. Alice can now send funds to Bob's address and the network would accept the transaction even though it has never encountered that address before.

In a centralized system the funds are held by a central entity, which also holds the means to control those funds, say by changing the registries in the ledger. In contrast, in a decentralized system, the private keys that give access to the funds are solely in the hands of the end users.

Addresses, public–private keys and transactions are discussed in more depth in Chapters 5 and 6.

2.3 DISTRIBUTED DATABASE, THE BLOCKCHAIN

Bitcoin's distributed database is called the **blockchain**. Transactions are grouped in blocks of transactions roughly every 10 minutes. These blocks of transactions are then recorded one after the other in a chain of blocks, hence the name blockchain. This may seem a strange way to record information, compared to, say, a regular relational database. The blockchain was designed to be resilient in the presence of attackers in the network. Blocks are linked to create a record of the history of transactions that cannot be altered. The link between blocks is a cryptographic link that cannot be forged unless the attacker has vast computational resources at her disposal. The blockchain is discussed in greater detail in section 7.4.

Aside from the blockchain, nodes keep an additional database called the Unspent Transaction Outputs cache (UTXO) (Chapter 6). The UTXO is a ledger that records the funds available for every address, in essence working as a cache for the blockchain. As new transactions come, the UTXO is updated: funds from the sending addresses are subtracted and added to the receiving addresses. The UTXO is more similar to the central databases at the heart of most centralized systems. Figure 2.6 shows a, sometimes useful, abstraction for Bitcoin: a distributed ledger with entries for the funds available

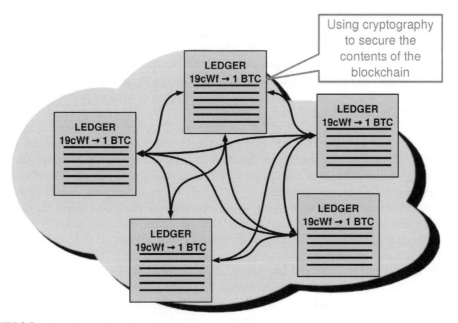

FIGURE 2.6 Bitcoin as a distributed ledger

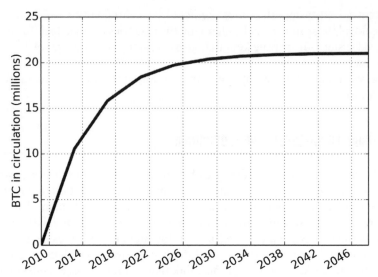

FIGURE 2.7 Bitcoin issuance theoretical schedule

to every address, which roughly corresponds to the UTXO. Every node in the network holds a copy of the distributed ledger. Furthermore, copies of the ledger are consistent across nodes, and new transactions have the same effect in all these copies.

Bitcoin achieves consensus in the distributed database using several cryptographic constructions. The details can be found in Chapter 7, but roughly speaking, consensus is secured applying large amounts of computational power. This computational power serves the purpose of providing protection against attacks and is rewarded with the issuance of new bitcoins. The protocol encodes a schedule of new bitcoin creation, and all the newly created bitcoins are distributed among those who secure the blockchain, called **miners**. Miners compete to create blocks of transactions that are appended to the blockchain. A miner who creates one of these blocks is granted the **block reward**, consisting of a certain number of newly minted bitcoins. A native currency is essential to the design of Bitcoin, as the issuance of new currency is used to pay for the cost of securing the distributed ledger.

Figure 2.7 shows the schedule of bitcoin creation. The pace of new issuance is halved roughly every four years, so that eventually the total number of bitcoins will reach a total of roughly 21 million. The number of bitcoins in circulation, as of the time of writing, is around 13 million. Bitcoins' value stems from their scarcity, as the number of bitcoins that will eventually be issued is fixed.

Miners also collect fees from the transactions that are published in the blockchain. Fees are still a small fraction of total miners' compensation, currently below 1% of their total compensation. It is expected that as the issuance of new bitcoins shrinks, transaction fees will take over as the principal compensation to miners.

During the end of 2013 and beginning of 2014 there has been an investment boom in Bitcoin mining equipment. It is estimated that over USD 200 million were invested in Bitcoin mining equipment in 2013 (Luria and Turner, 2014). This investment rush has been fuelled by the increase in the price of bitcoins and by technological evolution in mining equipment (Chapter 9). This investment trend will likely ease in time, barring another large increase in the price of bitcoin, with the future decrease in issuance of new bitcoins and the mining technology catching up with state-of-the-art semiconductor process technology.

An attacker who wished to subvert the distributed database to perform a double-spending attack must enter a race with legitimate nodes[3]. The result of this race is determined by the amount of computational power. A straightforward attack would require a computational power as large as the power of the legitimate network. That is, the attacker would need to control more than 50% of the *combined* power of the network. This type of attack is called a 51% attack. Other types of attacks, requiring somewhat lower fractions of computational power, are possible. In any case, an attacker would have to devote a significant investment to be able to mount an attack against the blockchain.

2.4 WALLETS

The software that helps a user manage her funds is called a wallet. The functions of the wallet software are to hold (securely) the user's private keys, create transactions that are sent to the network, and collect incoming and outgoing transactions to show the balance of available funds to the user. As a user can own many addresses, most software wallets are ready to manage multiple addresses, aggregating the funds across them.

All wallet software can create new addresses, for instance when it is run for the very first time. To create a new address a key generation algorithm is executed (Chapter 5). Creating a Bitcoin address is straightforward and instantaneous.

The wallet software also implements the cryptographic protocol to sign a transaction with the private key. Private keys are usually kept in the device. Losing these private keys prevents a user from accessing the funds. The funds are still in the distributed ledger, but without the private keys there is no way to correctly sign a transaction to spend them and therefore they are considered to be lost. Thus it is highly recommended that backups of the private keys are created. Most wallet software assists the user in creating digital backups.

Another risk for wallets is for an unauthorized person, say a attacker, to get hold of the private keys. If an attacker gains access to the private keys, she can send the funds in the associated addresses to some addresses under her control. Thus it is important to properly secure the private keys stored in devices connected to the internet. Many wallets offer encryption of the private keys[4] before they are stored locally. This decreases the convenience for the user, who has to type the password to decrypt the private keys before using them, such as when sending a transaction. However, if the device is compromised, the attacker would only be able to get a copy of the encrypted private keys. She would then have to brute-force them, a time-consuming process, especially if the encryption password is well chosen. Technologies to securely handle private keys are explored in more depth in Chapter 8.

---

[3] A resourceful attacker could perform a double-spending attack over accounts under her control, but she cannot change the balances of other accounts, as these are protected by public-key cryptography.

[4] Using a symmetric cypher (section 8.1).

Private keys could also be kept on physical media—such as a piece of paper—or digital media not connected to the internet. This is called cold storage, as the private keys are not accessible from the internet and are thus safe from electronic attacks. These keys can be subject to physical theft, though, and must be secured appropriately.

Some wallet implementations run a full Bitcoin node. A full node keeps a complete copy of the distributed database, the blockchain. These wallets have the advantage of not having to rely on any third party server, at the cost of having to store and process the whole transaction database.

Lightweight wallet implementations are also available. These lightweight wallets rely on third party nodes to feed them the information they need, such as the balances for the addresses in the wallet. They also rely on third party nodes to relay the transactions created by the wallet. Lightweight wallets are more suitable for devices with limited memory and processing/battery capabilities, such as smartphones. The technology behind lightweight wallets is explored in more depth in section 8.8.

It is recommended that a wallet with an open source implementation is used (section 1.2). A proprietary source wallet can constitute a security risk, if the author of the wallet decides to include a backdoor into the binaries[5]. There are several open source implementations of both full node wallets and lightweight wallets.

A third type of wallet is web wallets. In a web wallet the funds are transferred to a third party, often a website, which then manages the funds on behalf of the user. The user experience is similar to that of existing online banking services. Web wallets offer convenience for their users, as the service takes charge of managing the private keys. However, the user is open to the web service stealing her funds, or the service being attacked and robbed. In both cases, the user could lose all her funds, as the private keys are entirely controlled by the web wallet service. Following many episodes of theft or attacks on these services (McMillan, 2014), there have been calls to use already available technology (multisignatures) to create web wallet services where the service operator (or an attacker) cannot take control of the client's funds. These technologies are explored in sections 8.3.

2.5   THE DIFFERENT MEANINGS OF BITCOIN

Bitcoin is an overloaded word, as it can mean several things:

- The **protocol**. The protocol is the specification of how to construct the distributed database (the blockchain), how to parse it, how transactions should be assembled, what constitutes a valid transaction, and so on.
- The **network**. This is the peer-to-peer network to which nodes connect. Nodes in this peer-to-peer network exchange messages containing new blocks being added to the blockchain and new transactions being published.

---

[5] A backdoor can also be included into the binaries of an open source wallet, and these binaries offered as a download in a website. However, in the case of an open source wallet, the user always has the option of downloading the source code, reviewing it, and compiling it herself (or paying someone to do it for her).

- The **currency**. A bitcoin, usually spelled with lower case "b", is a unit of the native currency of the Bitcoin network. There will be a total of roughly 21 million bitcoins issued. Although bitcoin is the main unit of account, each bitcoin is divisible to 100,000,000 pieces, called **satoshis**[6].
- The **open source implementation**. This is the original open source project, written in C++, implementing the protocol. The project was recently re-branded to **Bitcoin Core**, in part to avoid confusion between the different meanings of Bitcoin. Both the source code and complied binaries can be freely downloaded from bitcoin.org/en/download.

Bitcoin Core is a single computer program but it includes two different services:

- **Bitcoin Core Wallet**, also known as **bitcoin-qt**, is the default implementation for a wallet. The wallet is a full node wallet as it requires a full node to run. Bitcoin Core Wallet presents a GUI to the user using the qt framework, hence the name bitcoin-qt.
- **Bitcoin Core Server**, also known as **bitcoind**, implements a network node. It can be run in headless mode, i.e. without a graphical user interface, as a daemon, hence the name bitcoind. Bitcoin Core Server is used to connect to the Bitcoin network, interchange messages with it, interpret the blockchain, handle new transactions in the network, and so on.

There has recently been some interest in the community in dividing the Bitcoin Core project into two separate standalone programs, as the target users for the wallet and the node software have been diverging.

---

[6] Further divisibility could be achieved with a change in the protocol. Currently the protocol represents amounts using 64-bit integer numbers that hold the amount of satoshis. To achieve further divisibility, the protocol could be changed to another representation. Note that this change would require coordination of all users of Bitcoin to upgrade their software.

CHAPTER **3**

Economics

Different types of money have been used through the history of humanity (Szabo, 2005). In principle Bitcoin could serve as money as it satisfies the technical properties of money: it is durable, divisible, fungible, easy to transport, and impossible to counterfeit. Modern mainstream economists (Mankiw, 2003) usually assign money three functions:

- **Medium of exchange**. Money can be exchanged for goods and services.
- **Store of value**. Money can be used to transfer purchasing power from the present to the future.
- **Unit of account**. Goods and services are quoted in terms of the money unit.

A lot of the economic debate has centered on whether Bitcoin is or is not a currency. Bitcoin critics argue that Bitcoin does not serve the three functions of money and thus does not conform to the definition of money. Bitcoin supporters reply that an asset does not have to fulfill the three functions of money to be valuable, and call this argument the "money or nothing" fallacy (Graf, 2013). Moreover, there is some economic evidence (Koning, 2013) that the traditional three functions of money can be unbundled.

Bitcoin as a currency is more readily accepted by economists of the Austrian School (Graf, 2013; Šurda, 2012). The Austrian School is a school of economic thought originated in Vienna in the late 19th century whose method is rooted on the analysis of the actions of individuals. Some of the most controversial contributions of the Austrian School are:

- Austrian School economists believe money emerges from the competition between several mediums of exchange. The most accepted of these competing mediums of exchange emerges as money. Other mediums of exchange can co-exist and these are called secondary mediums of exchange or sometimes quasi-money. In contrast, mainstream economists believe it is governments that create demand for fiat money by declaring it legal tender, meaning it must be accepted as payment to settle all debts, public and private.
- Austrian School economists believe that an increase in the money supply or an expansion in credit will inevitably lead to price increases and economic instability. Thus inflation for Austrian School economists is not an increase in the prices of goods and services, but merely an increase in the money supply.
- Austrian School economists believe deflation can be caused either by technological progress or by a decrease in the monetary supply. Only the second cause is considered problematic, as deflation arising from technological progress is not harmful for

economic growth. Thus Austrian School economists advocate a fixed money supply. This view is not shared by mainstream economists, who believe that the economy has significant price rigidities, such as sticky wages, that prevent it from reaching an equilibrium. Mainstream economists believe a small amount of inflation helps grease the wheels of economic growth.

■ Austrian School economists believe business cycles are created by banks issuing excessive credit through fractional reserve banking[1]. which leads to a misallocation of economic resources and the consequent reversal causing a recession. While mainstream economists believe there is little to do during expansions and much to do during contractions (increase the monetary supply, increase government spending), Austrian School economists believe there is little to do during contractions (just let the economy filter out the excesses by itself) while action must be taken during expansions (limit the increase in the monetary supply).

None of these ideas are considered valid by mainstream economists. Less controversial is the Austrian theory on the creation of money introduced in **Mises' regression theorem**. Under Mises' regression theorem, the value of a currency stems from the fact that users assume it will keep its value with the passing of time. A currency has value today because holders expect to be able to use it tomorrow in exchange for goods or services. The value of a currency today was carried on from yesterday's value. Going back through time, at some point the currency must have been pegged to some valuable commodity from where it took its value. Thus fiat money's current value had its roots in commodity money, i.e. money backed by a commodity, such as precious metals.

Many Austrian School economists are in favor of the role of Bitcoin as a currency. However, some have criticized Bitcoin on the grounds that it is at odds with Mises' regression theorem, as it does not have its origin in commodity money.

On more practical grounds, some criticism of the role of Bitcoin as a currency has been put forward by several research groups (Normand, 2014; Natham, 2014; de Vries et al., 2014; Bennenbroek, 2014).

However, a consensus seems to be emerging among economists that Bitcoin is a good medium of exchange, a risky store of value and a poor unit of account (Dourado, 2014). The following three sections explore in further detail how well cryptocurrencies fulfill the three functions of money. The last sections of the chapter address the topics of volatility, deflation, and regulation. It should be kept in mind that most of the arguments in this chapter and the following apply equally to any cryptocurrency other than Bitcoin.

3.1   MEDIUM OF EXCHANGE

Bitcoin is already accepted by tens of thousands of businesses. Thus there seems to be a consensus, even among critics, that Bitcoin can serve as a medium of exchange. Figure 3.1 presents the number of transactions per day. Bitcoin has showed a steady increase in the number of transactions, but at less than 100,000 transactions per day it is still considerably below other payment methods.

---

[1] Under fractional reserve banking, only a fraction of customer's deposits are kept in reserve, and the rest is lent.

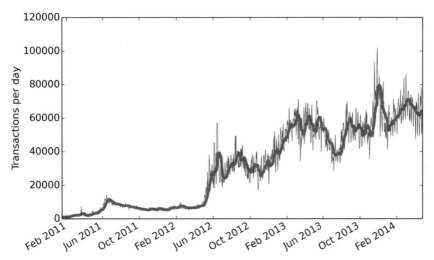

FIGURE 3.1 Transaction per day (with 14-day moving average). Data from <u>blockchain.info</u>

Most economists agree that Bitcoin still has a small user base, and that to become a universal medium of exchange, it has to achieve critical mass. Critical mass is the point where the benefits to new users exceed the cost of adopting the new technology. For some technologies, such as a digital currency, the benefits to a new user increase with the number of other users that have already adopted the technology, as there are more opportunities to transact. Thus the total benefits to all users increase quadratically with the number of users. This is known as the network effect (Varian, 2003). Once a technology reaches the critical mass and passes it, positive feedback kicks in and the adoption of the technology becomes explosive. See section 11.9 for a more extensive discussion of the network effect.

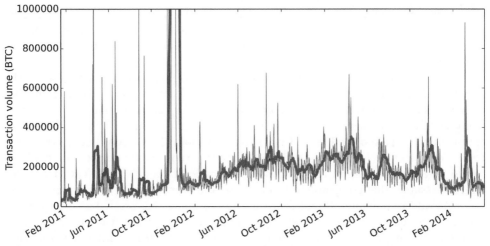

FIGURE 3.2 Estimated daily transaction volume in bitcoins. Data from <u>blockchain.info</u>

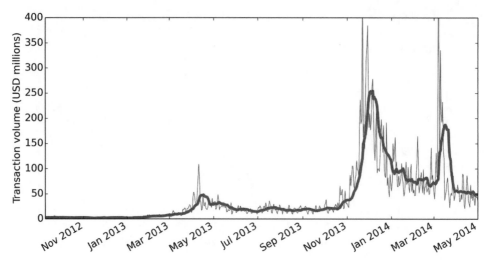

FIGURE 3.3 Estimated daily transaction volume in USD. Data from <u>blockchain.info</u>

Figure 3.2 shows the estimated daily transaction volume in bitcoins, and Figure 3.3 shows the corresponding estimated daily transaction volume in USD. As of the time of writing, and according to this data, the critical mass for the widespread adoption of Bitcoin as a medium of exchange does not seem to have been reached yet. Supporters claim that the growth of Bitcoin naturally follows several cycles. The last cycle crossed the critical mass point for technologically savvy early adopters at the end of 2013 (see Figure 3.3), and a natural period of consolidation followed. These supporters argue that entrepreneurs are building the infrastructure that will allow regular users to take advantage of Bitcoin, thus creating the foundations for the next growth wave.

However, critics reply that several internet heavyweights may build digital payments infrastructure. This could lead to a standards war (Varian, 2003), where Bitcoin, an open source project, would have to compete with companies with great financial muscle. If the result of this hypothetical standards war were to favor one of these large commercial enterprises, economic theory suggests Bitcoin (or other cryptocurrencies) could be crowded out of the market. Critics also argue that Bitcoin would not be able to compete with other emerging, or established, payment systems due to the large costs of running the mining infrastructure.

Figure 3.4 shows the total miners' revenue as a percentage of transaction sizes. The compensation to miners has oscillated in the 1% to 5% range, comparable to the fees applied to credit card transactions. Most of this revenue—currently above 99%—comes from the issuance of new bitcoins to reward miners. Only a small fraction comes from transaction fees paid by end users. Critics (de Vries et al., 2014) argue that, as the block reward decreases over time, this cost would have to be covered by transaction fees. This would take the transaction fee to levels comparable to today's credit card fees. This analysis assumes that compensation to miners would remain constant. However, there is some evidence (Chapter 9) that compensation to miners has created a gold rush and poured large sums of investment into the mining industry. Under this optic, compensation to miners might be overestimated due to the block reward, and the network could stabilize at lower compensation levels to miners.

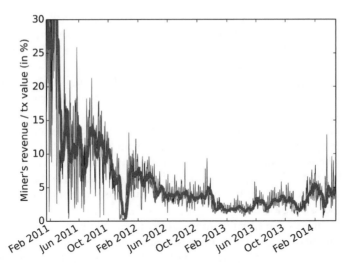

FIGURE 3.4 Miners revenue/transaction value, including 14-day moving average. Data from blockchain.info

3.1.1 Pros

This section will present some advantages of Bitcoin as a medium of exchange[2], in no particular order.

Bitcoin users are **not at risk of security breaches**. This contrasts with the loss of traditional financial information when a retailer is compromised (Krebs, 2014). A compromise of a retailer that uses Bitcoin payments can lead to financial loss for the retailer, if the attacker gets access to the retailer's private keys. However, the compromise does not threaten the user's funds, as Bitcoin users are in control of their private keys. Critics of Bitcoin reply that web wallets and exchanges are equally prone to security breaches, and that there is no recourse for final users when these breaches occur.

Bitcoin's transaction **fees are lower** than credit cards' fees. Critics reply that once all costs are added, such as theft protection and compliance/regulatory costs, Bitcoin does not hold a significant cost advantage.

Merchants using Bitcoin are **protected from charge-back fraud**, i.e. a customer looking for a retraction of a payment once the good has been delivered. Critics argue that this is a double-edged sword, as the ones who are subject to fraud risk are the customers. Bitcoin supporters counter that charge-backs, as currently implemented in credit card transactions, can be imitated using escrow transactions (sections 4.5 and 6.3).

Bitcoin transfers are almost **instantaneous**, compared to bank transfers that can take several days to settle. However, other payment methods, such as credit cards, present transaction settlement times comparable to Bitcoin's.

---

[2] Alternatively, some of these characteristics could be viewed neither as pros or cons, but simply as features, and the same could be said about the classification in pros and cons in the following sections.

No base fees are collected using Bitcoin, unlike credit cards[3]. This could **enable micropayments**, especially if new technologies to handle micropayments (section 12.3) are adopted by users. Micropayments could allow content providers, such as newspapers or video on demand, to charge for smaller slices of content.

Bitcoin and related technologies enable the **transfer of any digital asset** aside from currency. Furthermore, new protocols (section 12.7) open the door to the execution of more involved contracts and related applications.

Bitcoin is a **push payment system**, similar to cash, where the user has to proactively generate the transaction. In contrast, other payment systems such as credit cards are pull systems, where users authorize a retailer (often revealing sensitive information), and then the retailer pulls the payment from the user's account. Push payment systems can have advantages in reducing fraud or unwanted purchases as users are in control of the purchasing process (Brown, 2014c).

Bitcoin's payments can either be more anonymous or less anonymous than traditional payment methods (Chapter 13). **Increased anonymity** comes from the use of pseudonyms. Decreased privacy comes from the fact that if an attacker could de-anonymize the address corresponding to a user, then the attacker could have access to the user's complete financial information[4].

Bitcoin is a new payment system, independent from the traditional financial sector, and this could provide resilience to the economy in case of a crisis, as it creates a parallel payment system.

3.1.2 Cons

Similarly, drawbacks of Bitcoin as a medium of exchange, in no particular order, follow.

Most users of Bitcoin would end up using intermediaries, either because of convenience or because they find the technology too daunting. In this case the new technology would be mainly used by companies, and there will be **no significant decrease in costs**.

Bitcoin is **illiquid** compared to fiat currencies, as attested by the volume of foreign exchange markets for crosses such as the EUR/USD or GBP/USD, which are up to three orders of magnitude larger than Bitcoin's exchange turnover. Also, already established **fiat currencies have large network externalities** that preclude competition from alternative currencies.

Bitcoin **transactions do not offer a credit option**, as opposed to credit cards, where this credit option is built in by default. Bitcoin supporters argue that this service could easily be added to Bitcoin transactions by web wallet providers, or better still by existing financial institutions who already have experience managing consumer credit.

Regulations, such as the IRS ruling classifying Bitcoin as a capital asset (section 3.7), can greatly increase the **reporting and compliance costs**, thus hampering the use of Bitcoin as a medium of exchange. Further regulation aiming to protect consumers could even prevent the usage of Bitcoin.

---

[3] This is not strictly true, as there is a minimum transaction fee in the Bitcoin protocol, currently set at 0.00001 bitcoins as of version 0.9.1 of Bitcoin Core. A more detailed discussion of transaction fees can be found in section 9.3.

[4] Although the user, or the user's wallet, can create many addresses, these might be linked together.

Transactions take several minutes on average to be confirmed, i.e. included in the blockchain. Meanwhile, change from an unconfirmed transaction is locked and cannot be used until the transaction is cleared. This can cause inconvenience for a user following a regular shopping pattern, say in a mall. A user spending a transaction output would have to wait for the change of this transaction to be confirmed in the blockchain before being able to spend this change in a following transaction. Wallets can implement solutions to this problem, like spreading large transaction outputs into many outputs of small quantity so they can be readily spent (Chapter 6).

A single currency for the whole world may not be an efficient solution, as the trouble in Europe's periphery attests. Bitcoin supporters reply that it could coexist with local currencies, and even prosper providing a gateway between them.

Bitcoin could face **scalability pressures** if its use is generalized. A more detailed exploration of this topic can be found in section 7.7.

The **technology could be adopted by established companies and governments**. For instance, a government could issue a cryptocurrency fully redeemable for fiat money. If this were to happen, users could switch to this technology, leaving Bitcoin and other cryptocurrencies behind.

3.2 STORE OF VALUE

The main criticism made of Bitcoin as a store of value is its volatility. Figure 3.5 shows the price history of Bitcoin so far. There is some agreement between economists that Bitcoin is viewed more as a risky investment in a novel business model than as a stable store of value. Under this view, the price of Bitcoin follows similar dynamics to that of a start-up. The rational for this investment will be explored later in this section.

There is a tension between the use of bitcoins as a medium of exchange and their use as an investment. Figure 3.6 shows the annual velocity of bitcoins, calculated as the daily transaction volume (times 365) over the existing supply of bitcoins. The velocity

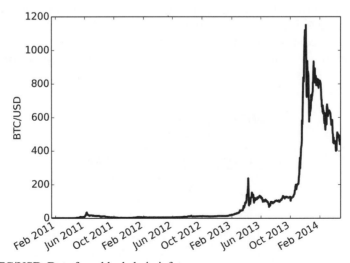

FIGURE 3.5 BTC/USD. Data from blockchain.info

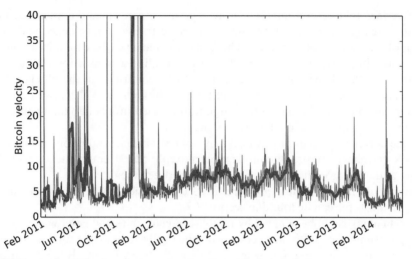

FIGURE 3.6   Annual Bitcoin velocity, using data from blockchain.info

of bitcoin has been in the single digits, comparable to the velocity of fiat currencies in advanced economies (Šurda, 2012) but much lower than the velocity of other digital currencies.

The low turnover of Bitcoin might be explained by hoarding. **Hoarding** refers to the fact that a large portion of the bitcoins in circulation are kept by individuals as an investment. There is evidence (Ron and Shamir, 2013) that the majority of the bitcoins are kept on "dormant" accounts. Furthermore, the ownership of bitcoins is highly concentrated in the hands of very few people, mostly early adopters, as Table 3.1 shows.

The hoarding effect could also be measured using coin-days destroyed. The **coin-days destroyed** in a transaction are computed by multiplying the amount spent by the period since those funds were last spent. For example, if a user receives 100 bitcoins, and keeps them for 100 days before spending them, this last transaction will destroy $100 \cdot 100 = 10,000$ coin-days. Figure 3.7 shows the accumulated coin-days destroyed compared to the accumulated coin-days created. Note that coin-days are created with the passing of time and with the issuance of new bitcoins, thus its parabolic increase. Roughly half of

TABLE 3.1   Bitcoin wealth concentration. Data from Wile (2013)

Number of users	Percentage
47	28.9%
880	21.5%
1,000	24.8%
1,000,000	20.7%
Lost	4.1%

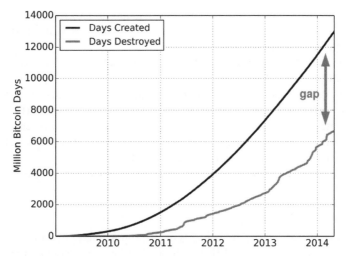

FIGURE 3.7 Cumulative coin-days destroyed. Data from <u>blockchain.info</u>

the coin-days created have been destroyed: the difference between the two is a measure of hoarding.

The store of value and medium of exchange functions of a currency are complimentary: nobody would use bitcoins as a medium of exchange if they do not have any value. Conversely, nobody would use them as a store of value if they did not have any use. Bitcoin would have to balance these two uses for the system to grow. If bitcoins are hoarded excessively, this could lead to their being perceived as hard to get and thus losing their appeal as a medium of exchange.

3.2.1 Bitcoin as Investment

The risk/reward profile of investing in Bitcoin resembles an investment in a high-risk start-up more than an investment in a stable store of value. The advantages of Bitcoin with respect to investments with similar risk/reward profiles are its liquidity and its availability for anybody to invest. An additional advantage of Bitcoin as an investment is its low correlation with other assets.

The "Bitcoin start-up" is a new payment system and the associated products that could be launched using it (Chapter 12). Bitcoins are just the tokens that give access to this system. The greater the volume of funds using the system, the greater the value of these tokens. A market for these tokens has developed, where participants demand the tokens either to perform transactions or speculate on the future value of the tokens.

Once a stationary state is reached there is less incentive for speculators to hold the bitcoins. On the other hand, if the value is stable, there would probably be more demand to use it as a store of value.

As with early stage start-ups, there is some probability that Bitcoin will grow to capture a significant market share of the payments market and there is some probability that it will fail and the value of the investment will go to zero. Some possible scenarios under which the start-up would fail and the price could collapse to zero are:

- A serious security flaw is found. The security flaw has to lead to massive hacking, otherwise a slow deployment of the solution to the flaw could provide a smooth transition (section 14.6).
- An attack undermines the trust in the technology. This could lead to users leaving in a self-reinforcing negative loop.
- A competing technology, say an alt-coin (Chapter 11), a meta-coin (section 12.7) or a payments platform from a big internet player, replaces it. Under this scenario most of the investment in the ecosystem is preserved because it can be easily re-purposed to the substituting technology. However, the value of bitcoins would collapse as users and companies leave them for the new network.
- Bitcoin would lose its value in a world with no electricity and network connectivity.

3.2.2 Pros

Bitcoin **avoids confiscation, capital controls or disproportionate taxation**. In contrast, fiat currency or precious metals could be confiscated either physically or through an order to the financial intermediary holding them. A user who owns bitcoins cannot be denied access to the funds, as long as she has access to a device connected to the internet and keeps a copy of the private keys.

There are **no storage costs**. Bitcoin users incur the costs of setting up and properly securing a wallet (Chapter 8), but once this initial set-up is complete, there are no additional costs to storing bitcoins.

Bitcoins are **easy to transport**. Private keys can be carried in storage media such as a USB flash drive or uploaded to the cloud. In contrast, both fiat currencies and commodities can be cumbersome to transport, especially in large quantities.

The **scarcity is fixed by an algorithm**. Bitcoin documentation stipulates that to change the monetary supply of bitcoins, the consensus of every bitcoin-holder is required, and that even if all Bitcoin users unanimously decide to implement such a change the resulting currency could not be called Bitcoin, as it deviates too much from the original design (Bitcoin wiki, 2014r). Therefore no central authority can decide to debase the currency. Critics argue that changes to the money supply of Bitcoin could be done through a majority decision (Natham, 2014) and that the people involved in this decision are not monetary experts. This is in contrast to most fiat currencies, where there is usually a central bank entrusted with the task of preserving a relatively stable value for the currency. Some Bitcoin supporters do not agree that central bankers have done a good job, because they have unnecessarily inflated the money supply.

Bitcoin uses **cryptographic security**, as opposed to physical security in the case of precious metals, or institutional security in the case of fiat currency.

Bitcoin provides **automatic record keeping**. Records are automatically produced, as all transactions are recorded in the blockchain.

Bitcoin is **deflationary**, given its fixed money supply. Moreover, the constant loss of private keys leads to an actually decreasing monetary supply. A deflationary currency is considered harmful by mainstream economists, as it increases the burden of debts that are usually denominated in nominal terms, and also due to price/salaries rigidities of the economy. However, Austrian School economists, including some Bitcoin supporters, consider that a fixed monetary supply is not necessarily harmful, as deflation would be produced by technological progress.

Bank instruments	Cash / Metals	Bitcoin
• Pay interest (of an inflationary currency) • Counterparty risk (deposit insurance, but also deposit haircuts* possible) • Risk of taxation / confiscation • Risk of currency debasement	• Cost of forgone interest • Anonymous • Risk of theft / loss • Cumbersome to move in large quantities • Risk of currency debasement (cash)	• No interest (but currency is deflationary) • Pseudo-anonymous • Risk of theft / loss • Easy / fast / cheap to move in large quantities • High price volatility • Does not carry legal tender status

* A haircut is a reduction in the notional of a deposit

FIGURE 3.8   Bitcoin as a store of value compared with other assets

Figure 3.8 summarizes some advantages and disadvantages of Bitcoin as a store of value compared with other alternatives. Bitcoin attributes are very different from those of the alternatives, and this could make Bitcoin attractive for some users or applications.

3.2.3   Cons

Bitcoin's source code is open source, thus it can be **easily** and legally **replicated**, opening the door to many **substitutes**. Critics argue that many cryptocurrencies will be created, competing with each other in a race to the bottom that will end in hyperinflation and collapse. This view assumes that all cryptocurrencies achieve the same level of acceptance. Proponents of Bitcoin reply that cryptocurrencies are subject to network effects, due to infrastructure investment, marketing, mind-share and liquidity. Bitcoin currently holds the lead due to its first moving advantage, but if other cryptocurrencies were to replace it in the future, the network effect would favor the leading cryptocurrency, as the market tends to gather around this leading cryptocurrency due to the network effect. The issue of alternative cryptocurrencies is discussed in more detail in section 11.8.

Critics argue that Bitcoin cannot be used as a store of value because of its **volatility**. Contrary to fiat currencies, there is no authority, such as a central bank, to ensure the stability of its value. Thus the price of bitcoin could be subject to self-fulfilling dynamics, where an incident could feed back on itself, becoming a full-blown confidence crisis.

There is **no control over the money supply**. The money supply can be changed through a majority process, first through the open source project, and then through miners and users agreeing to the change.

Holding bitcoins is not a good protection against inflation because if the price of bitcoin relative to fiat rises as a consequence of inflation, the **gains would be taxable**. Bitcoin proponents argue that this is true for most assets, and in any case holding bitcoin would constitute a partial hedge against an inflationary increase in the money supply of fiat currencies.

Cryptocurrencies do not have **legal tender status**. In contrast, fiat currencies usually have legal tender status, meaning all debts can be settled with them in their respective countries.

Governments could ban the use of cryptocurrencies. Governments may want to ban cryptocurrencies for several reasons, such as preventing illicit uses of cryptocurrencies, or enforcing currency controls. Bitcoin supporters reply that due to the distributed nature of cryptocurrencies, it is not clear how to enforce such a ban. However, a ban to the gateways of the system, such as exchanges or payment processors, could be feasible.

Bitcoins have **no physical backing**. Therefore there is **no intrinsic value** to support them. Supporters of Bitcoin reply that most of gold's value is not intrinsic value but monetary value, and the same would apply to Bitcoin. Some supporters argue that the intrinsic value of Bitcoin rests in the proof-of-work performed by miners.

For commodities, such as gold, the marginal cost of production acts as a support for price levels: when the price of the commodity decreases below the marginal cost of production, mining capacity is taken out of the market, leading to a lower supply, which in turn increases the price. Bitcoin **does not have a marginal cost of production**[5] to stabilize its price, and thus down-trends in its price could be more acute.

In contrast to bank deposits, there is **no deposit insurance** for Bitcoin users. Bitcoin supporters reply that deposit insurance is not needed if good security practices are followed by issuers and services such as exchanges and wallet providers (section 4.5).

3.3   UNIT OF ACCOUNT

Bitcoin is generally considered not to be a good unit of account. Although bitcoins can be exchanged for many products and services, few of these get their prices quoted in bitcoin directly. Bitcoin is not a good unit of account due to its high volatility. Bitcoin supporters argue that if the price of bitcoin stabilizes then more and more merchants would start quoting their prices in bitcoins.

Critics argue that bitcoin is also not a good unit of account due to the lack of a Bitcoin economy. Only a few products very targeted to Bitcoin enthusiasts, such as mining equipment (9.1) or hardware wallets (8.2.4), quote their prices in bitcoins.

Bitcoin supporters argue that if applications based on autonomous agents[6] (section 12.4) were to take hold, bitcoins would be in greater demand as they would be the natural unit of account for those agents.

Finally, some economists argue the three functions of money are starting to get unbundled thanks to the introduction of new technologies (Dourado, 2014). Under this view, it would not matter much if Bitcoin were not to fulfill the role of unit of account in the present, provided it were to achieve other functions of money.

3.4   DEFLATION

The path of monetary supply of new bitcoins is programmed into Bitcoin's source code. Figure 2.7 in section 2.3 shows the growth of Bitcoin's money supply through time. The

---

[5] However, mining bitcoins does have costs, such as the electricity spent (Chapter 9).
[6] Autonomous agents are computer programs that can run without human assistance once created. Cryptocurrencies allow these agents to engage in financial transactions on their own.

maximum number of bitcoins issued will eventually reach approximately 21 million. This fixed money supply makes it deflationary.

Furthermore, bitcoins are withdrawn from circulation due to their owners losing the private keys. As of the time of writing, an estimated 4% of bitcoins in circulation have been lost (see Table 3.1). The total amount of lost bitcoins can only grow in the future.

Bitcoin's deflationary model is rejected by mainstream economists, arguing that if Bitcoin were to establish itself as an alternative to fiat currencies, this could prevent central banks from implementing monetary policy, would reduce the revenue generated by governments by the printing of money, and could lead to a destabilization of the financial system following a rush to sell bitcoins.

On the other hand, Austrian School economists generally view Bitcoin's deflationary model as a positive outcome, as it would prevent the credit expansion associated with an increase in the money supply in the Austrian theory of the business cycle.

In a sense, it is still too soon to discuss the impact of Bitcoin's deflationary model in the economy, given that Bitcoin represents only a very small portion of the economy. Bitcoin's deflationary model could have been chosen more as a necessity, to confer bitcoins scarcity value, than as a feature.

Some critics have argued that, under Gresham's Law, bitcoins will be forced out of circulation (Smiling Dave, 2013). **Gresham's Law** states that given several currencies in circulation and a fixed exchange rate between them—say, imposed by a government—people would tend to hoard the undervalued currency, and use the overvalued currency. Thus the undervalued currency would disappear from circulation: "bad money drives out good." If Bitcoin is perceived as good money because of its deflationary bias, but the government forces accepting fiat money as payment, then people will tend to hoard the "good money" and get rid of the "bad money," until the "good money" (bitcoins) stops being in circulation, so the theory goes. This would prevent Bitcoin's function as a medium of exchange, and would lead to its collapse. Critics argue that this explains why bitcoins are being hoarded.

Bitcoin supporters retort that bitcoins can be exchanged for fiat currency through relatively liquid exchanges, not through a forced fixed exchange sanctioned by a government. Thus bitcoin payments would still take place even if bitcoins are perceived to be superior to fiat currencies, because the spent bitcoins could quickly be replenished through an exchange. On the other hand, merchants could offer discounts for payments with bitcoins if they perceive bitcoin to be a better currency and are seeking to keep them.

3.5 VOLATILITY

Figure 3.9 shows the historical volatility of bitcoin using a 6 month rolling window. Bitcoin volatility has been an order of magnitude higher that the volatility of foreign exchange crosses[7], even including emerging markets' currencies.

Bitcoin's volatility is explained by regulatory uncertainty, low liquidity, low market capitalization, limited market access, narrow adoption, and so on. Bitcoin supporters

---

[7] A foreign exchange cross is the price at which one currency can be exchanged for another currency. Some of the most liquid foreign exchange crosses are EUR/USD, USD/GBP and USD/JPY.

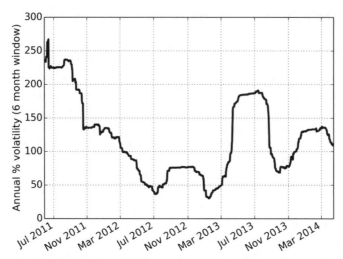

FIGURE 3.9   Bitcoin annual percentage price volatility using a 6-month rolling window. Using bitcoin price data from <u>blockchain.info</u>

argue if some of these factors evolve positively, volatility will likely decrease (Garzik, 2013b).

Bitcoin proponents also argue that volatility should not be considered a barrier for the adoption of Bitcoin as a medium of exchange, as payment processors protect merchants and users from this volatility (section 4.3).

Some proposals put forward to reduce Bitcoin volatility are:

- Create a feedback loop in the Bitcoin algorithm such that if the price of bitcoin increases then more bitcoins would be "printed" and given as a reward to miners, and similarly if bitcoin price decreases then less bitcoins would be printed. The difficulty lies in how to insert a verifiable bitcoin price data stream into the blockchain. If the data is introduced by miners, they have an interest in the creation of new bitcoins and thus an incentive to cheat (Buterin, 2013j).
- Adjust the amount of funds in every wallet according to the purchasing power of bitcoins (Ametrano, 2014). If the purchasing power of one bitcoin raises—say because it appreciates against fiat currencies—the amount of funds in every wallet would be decreased by the protocol in such a way that the purchasing power of one bitcoin would remain stable. Implementing this scheme also requires feeding data of the purchasing power of bitcoins into the blockchain, a task that could be performed by miners. One practical obstacle to this proposal is that miners have an incentive to cheat when publishing bitcoin prices—see Ametrano (2014) for a proposed solution to this problem.
- Entrust Bitcoin's monetary policy to a human[8]. Instead of leaving the pace of money supply increases in the hands of an algorithm, put it in the hands of a Bitcoin central banker.

---

[8] Some have even proposed retired central bankers to perform this role (Irwin, 2013).

None of these proposals seems likely to be implemented, as they would completely change Bitcoin's nature. However, proposals such as these might get implemented in alternative cryptocurrencies.

3.6 EFFECT ON THE FINANCIAL INDUSTRY AND MONETARY POLICY

Bitcoin advocates argue that it lowers the barriers to entry to the financial sector. Traditionally competitors new to the financial sector needed a large capital base and compliance with costly regulations. The introduction of Bitcoin has allowed small start-ups to enter the financial sector, for example payment processors, exchanges, or remittance providers. This can increase the competitive pressure and force margins down. Bitcoin could also increase the pace of innovation, and force financial institutions to overhaul their infrastructure to reach the security level provided by state-of-the-art cryptographic technology.

Another risk to current financial institutions is disintermediation if users prefer to store a larger percentage of their savings in cryptocurrencies. This could gain strength following an increase in deposit taxes, the failure of a large financial institution or if governments decide to apply haircuts on deposits.

There has been some debate about whether fractional reserve banking is possible with Bitcoin. **Fractional reserve banking** alludes to the fact that banks keep only a fraction of their customer's deposits in reserve, lending the rest. Fractional reserve banking contributes to increasing the monetary supply through the money multiplier effect[9]. Although nothing prevents an institution from practising fractional reserve banking with bitcoins, it is not clear that users would favor such an institution.

However, counterparty risk[10] to the institution practising fractional reserve remains. Moreover, there is no deposit insurance or lender of last resort in Bitcoin that can limit this counterparty risk. Thus critics of fractional reserve banking argue that it does not make sense for users to trust their funds to such an institution (Rochard, 2013). Some Austrian School economists have argued that some failed exchanges were operating under fractional reserve banking, and these examples should prevent other institutions

---

[9] When the central bank mints 100 new monetary units the recipient of the funds will deposit them with a bank. That bank will lend a percentage of the funds as a new loan, say 90% if the bank is forced to keep a 10% reserve on deposits. This new loan will find its way back to the financial system, presumably deposited with another bank. This new bank would in turn lend out 90% of the deposited funds (81 monetary units) as a new loan. The process will continue indefinitely. Summing up all the new deposits created:

$$90 + 81 + 72.9 + \ldots = \frac{100}{0.1} = 1000.$$

The original money issued has multiplied through the effect of fractional reserve banking. The **money multiplier** depends on the level of reserves required by the monetary authority. In this example the required deposit reserve is 10% and thus the money multiplier is

$$10 = \frac{1}{0.1}.$$

[10] Counterparty risk is the risk that the bank defaults and is not able to repay its deposits.

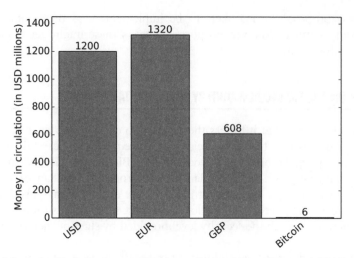

FIGURE 3.10   Money in circulation versus Bitcoin market cap, from Normand (2014), all figures converted to USD

from operating under fractional reserve banking in the cryptocurrencies space (Howden, 2014; Šurda, 2014). Or, more precisely, these examples should encourage users to not trust these companies.

On the other hand, a cryptocurrency could be created where a monetary authority manages the money supply and acts as a lender of last resort. Such a cryptocurrency would presumably have to compete with existing cryptocurrencies for market share. Bitcoin advocates argue that in such a scenario one advantage of Bitcoin, or similar cryptocurrencies, could be "keeping the monetary authority honest."

The monetary base of Bitcoin is still very low, compared to those of established fiat currencies. Figure 3.10 shows the amount of money in circulation (bills and coins) for USD, EUR, and GBP compared to Bitcoin's market capitalization. Bitcoin's size is two orders of magnitude smaller than established currencies.

Digital currencies are still believed to be too small to have an impact on central bank policy. Nonetheless, governments and central banks are starting to pay attention (European Central Bank, 2012; Velde, 2013; Elwell et al., 2013).

Figure 3.11 shows the equation associated with the Quantity Theory of Money (see any economics textbook, such as Mankiw, 2003). The quantity equation is used to argue that if both the velocity of money and the real output of an economy is constant, an increase in the monetary supply produces an increase in the price level, i.e. inflation, without any effect on the real economy. Most economists accept that the Quantity Theory of

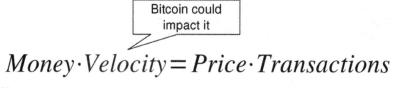

$$Money \cdot Velocity = Price \cdot Transactions$$

FIGURE 3.11   Quantity Theory of Money and Bitcoin's possible impact

Money holds in the long run. However, mainstream economists believe an increase in the money supply can have an effect in the economic activity in the short run.

A recent report (Elwell et al., 2013) has explored the possible effects of Bitcoin on the US dollar's monetary policy. Using the Quantity Theory of Money it is argued that if bitcoins were widely used, this could lead to an increase in the velocity of fiat currencies, as the need to hold fiat currencies would decrease. Such an increase in the velocity of money could lead to inflation, forcing central banks to decrease the money supply, i.e. implement a tightening of the monetary policy.

On the other hand, some Austrian School economists view the widespread use of Bitcoin and its potential effect on the monetary policy of fiat currencies as a positive event. For these economists, such development would be akin to a return to the Gold Standard.

Finally, some economists argue that Bitcoin and cryptocurrencies in general could increase the resilience of the economy as they create an alternative payment system that could be useful in case of turmoil or malfunctioning of the existing financial structures.

3.7 REGULATION

This section is a review of the regulatory landscape of Bitcoin and digital currencies in the US[11]. A review of the regulatory framework of other countries can be found in Law Library of Congress (2014). Cryptocurrencies' regulation is a very broad topic and this section is only a short review. A more detailed exploration of Bitcoin regulation can be found in Brito and Castillo (2013).

Regulation already exists in most countries covering digital money. This regulation was enacted to cover virtual goods such as prepaid cards, frequent flyer air miles, or online games' currencies. Bitcoin and other cryptocurrencies are in principle covered by these regulations. However, these regulations might not cover all aspects of Bitcoin, and for certain use cases there might be a regulatory gray area.

The issuance of legal tender is a government monopoly in the US. However, the issuance of private currencies is permitted under the law, as long as the private currencies do not resemble the US dollar (Brito and Castillo, 2013). Under this view, Bitcoin should not be considered illegal.

A money transmitter is a business that transfers funds from one person to another. Bitcoin itself is a decentralized network, and thus cannot be classified as a money transmitter. However, some businesses involved in Bitcoin, such as exchanges or payment processors, generally fall under the definition of **money transmitters**. Money transmitters are required to obtain a license in every state in which they operate. This forces businesses to seek a license in each state[12]. The goal of these licenses is to protect consumers, as traditionally money transmitters have not operated under deposit insurance.

Money transmitters are also subject to the Bank Secrecy Act, and thus fall under the supervision of FinCEN, the Financial Crimes Enforcement Network. The goal of

---

[11] The material in this section, and in the rest of the book, is intended for general information purposes only and does not constitute investment, legal or tax advice.

[12] The state of New York has been considering creating a **BitLicense** specifically for businesses involved in cryptocurrencies (Brito et al., 2014).

FinCEN is to detect and prevent money laundering and financing of illegal activities. Businesses registered with FinCEN are required to implement **Know Your Customer (KYC)** and **Anti-Money Laundering (AML)** procedures. These rules force businesses to identify their customers and monitor their transactions, reporting on suspicious ones.

Critics argue that compliance with these regulations can add a considerable cost to the operation and that regulation created to protect consumers or to prevent illegal activities could greatly increase the friction without ultimately achieving its goal. Additionally, they argue that laundering money using Bitcoin is very risky given that all transaction records are kept in the blockchain. This could lead to a more efficient implementation of AML rules compared to traditional financial services (Chapter 13).

Recent FinCEN rulings (Rizzo, 2014b) have declared that neither investors nor miners should be considered money transmitters. However, this ruling did not cover web wallet services.

The IRS (Internal Revenue Service) has recently issued tax guidance, determining that cryptocurrencies should be treated as property for tax purposes. Critics have argued that this imposes unreasonable reporting costs for users, making every transaction a taxable event[13] (Santori, 2014). Nonetheless, some developers have rushed to the challenge and have started integrating tax recording capabilities into existing Bitcoin wallets.

Regulations covering financial instruments based on cryptocurrencies, such as derivatives or Exchange Traded Funds (ETFs), are still in the early stages of discussion. New applications of the decentralized technology introduced by Bitcoin, such as distributed exchanges or betting could present a challenge for regulators. A detailed analysis of the regulatory status for these instruments can be found in Brito et al. (2014).

---

[13] It is argued that the IRS could have treated bitcoins as currency, allowing users to ignore small gains and losses when using them.

CHAPTER 4

Business Applications

The first application of Bitcoin is as a cost-effective payment system. This section will present some business models that are being created around this application. The business models introduced in this chapter can be considered the first round of applications in the cryptocurrencies ecosystem. As with every new technology, Bitcoin might spawn innovative ideas which are difficult to foresee, giving rise to newer generations of business models.

An analysis of Bitcoin's impact in the e-commerce payment and money transfer markets can be found in Woo et al. (2013).

4.1 MONEY TRANSFER

The average fee in the remittance market is reported to be in the range of 8% to 9% (World Bank, 2014; Normand, 2014). As of the time of writing, Bitcoin transaction fees are in the order of 0.01% to 0.05% (most of the miners' revenue is due to block rewards). In principle, Bitcoin has a cost advantage compared to current money transmitters. However, there are several factors limiting this theoretical cost advantage:

- A very large portion of the costs of established money transmitters are due to regulatory and compliance costs. These costs are then passed on to consumers, which helps to explain the relatively high fees. New companies offering remittance services using Bitcoin would presumably also have to incur these regulatory and compliance costs eventually.
- Barriers to entry to the remittance market. There might be significant barriers to entry to the remittance market, even for traditional companies (Rizzo, 2014a). One such barrier to entry might be acquiring and maintaining banking relationships, as banks for their part have to incur significant costs related to Anti-Money Laundering (AML) regulations when servicing remittance businesses.
- Transaction costs for Bitcoin are set to rise as the block reward decreases and a larger part of miners' compensation is due to transaction fees.
- Users in the developing world would not have the same access to the technical means to use Bitcoin or other cryptocurrencies (Ersek, 2014).
- Liquidity to convert bitcoin to fiat currencies is very low for many of the currencies in the remittance business. This low liquidity could greatly increase the cost when converting Bitcoin funds to fiat currency in the receiving country. Bitcoin advocates argue that some of the biggest remittance markets have a natural two-way market

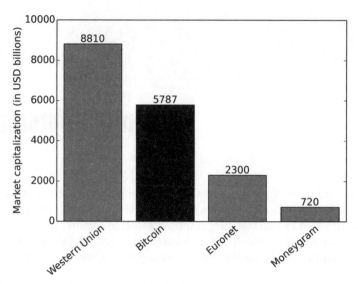

FIGURE 4.1   Money transmitters market capitalization versus Bitcoin. Data retrieved from Google Finance, Yahoo Finance and blockchain.info on May 10th, 2014

between Bitcoin and fiat currency: remittances on one hand and wealth expatriation on the other.

Bitcoin supporters argue that the current regulatory and compliance rules should be adapted to take into account the fact that Bitcoin transactions are kept in a public ledger. A regulatory framework that took into account this transparency could help reduce the compliance costs of money transmitting services.

Figure 4.1 compares the market capitalization of the biggest companies operating in the remittance market with the market capitalization of Bitcoin. It is still an open question whether Bitcoin would see a significant adoption in the remittances market, thus increasing competitive pressure.

A related question is whether a business offering remittance services using Bitcoin technology would be sustainable. Users could dispense with its services if they were to get comfortable with using Bitcoin by themselves, i.e. managing a wallet, converting bitcoin to fiat currency through exchanges and so on.

4.2   EXCHANGES

Exchanges allow users to convert bitcoins (and other cryptocurrencies) to fiat money. Some exchanges allow the conversion of different cryptocurrencies, such as between bitcoin and other alt-coins (Chapter 11).

Exchanges admit different types of orders such as limit orders or market orders. The orders are gathered in an order book that is run through an order matching algorithm. Exchanges collect fees from both parties in the trade. Most exchanges operate continuously, on a 24/7 schedule.

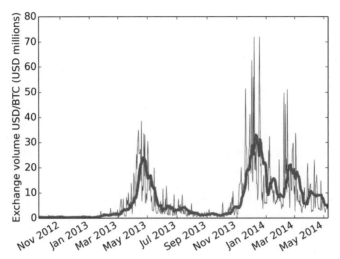

FIGURE 4.2   BTC/USD traded volume. Data from <u>blockchain.info</u>

Figure 4.2 shows the daily traded volume between USD and bitcoin across the largest exchanges. In comparison, daily turnover in global foreign exchange markets was USD 5.3 trillion in April 2013 (Bank for International Settlements, 2013). Thus the liquidity of the Bitcoin market is only a very small fraction of other established financial markets.

The exchange sector is very dynamic, with many small exchanges being created and large ones disappearing. Figure 4.3 shows the evolution of the market share of the largest exchanges for an 8-month period ending in May 2014. As the large swings in market share show, the sector is still in its infancy.

Most of the largest exchanges offer only spot contracts, although there are some exchanges starting to introduce second generation products, such as futures on the BTC/

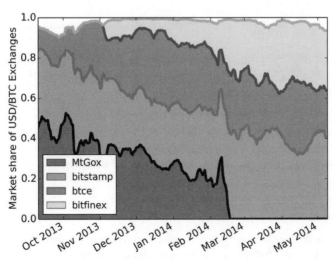

FIGURE 4.3   Exchanges' market share for BTC/USD volume. Data from <u>bitcoinaverage.com</u>

USD rate. Some advocates argue that there might be demand for derivatives based on this exchange rate: miners might want to sell bitcoins forward, while payment processors might want to buy call options or sell put options.

Exchanges usually operate off-blockchain under a trusted third party model. This means that users deposit their funds, either bitcoins or fiat currency, with the exchange. Users hold accounts with the exchange denominated in bitcoins and fiat currency, USD for example. Once an order is crossed, the appropriate accounts are credited and debited, but the funds do not leave the exchange. Only when a customer orders a withdrawal, of bitcoins or fiat, do the funds leave the exchange. Therefore transactions that take place inside the exchange are not recorded in the blockchain. Exchanges usually hold most of their bitcoin funds in cold storage[1] (section 8.2) and keep only a small fraction of their funds in online wallets to cover redemptions.

First-generation web wallets (section 8.3) also operate under a trusted third party model. In both cases users face counterparty risk when depositing funds with these companies, and it is recommended that, if possible, users keep their bitcoin balances in wallets under their own control.

In principle, an exchange could prove the possession of a certain amount of bitcoins by signing an arbitrary message with the private keys associated with the addresses holding those bitcoins, or by transferring their bitcoin reserves from one address to another. Some exchanges have done this in the past to dispel concerns about their financial health. However, most exchanges would presumably rather avoid such a procedure in order not to send clues to their competitors.

The cryptocurrencies community has been coming up with innovative ideas to solve the counterparty risk associated with exchanges and web wallets. The general strategy followed by these proposals is putting users back in control of their own funds (sections 8.6 and 14.5).

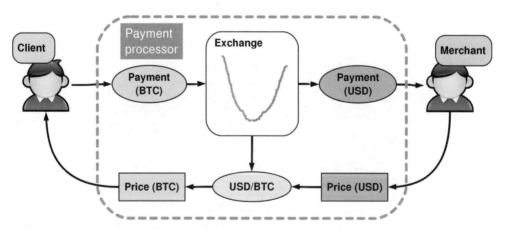

FIGURE 4.4 Payment processor

[1] Private keys hold in cold storage are not accessible from the internet and therefore cannot be intercepted by an attacker. A common cold storage technique is to print private keys on a piece of paper.

TABLE 4.1 Daily transaction volume. Data from Grossman et al. (2014)

Service	Daily Tx volume (USD millions)
Visa	19,000
MasterCard	11,000
PayPal	492
Western Union	225
Bitcoin	68

4.3 PAYMENT PROCESSORS

Payment processors offer solutions to merchants to accept bitcoins as payment. Figure 4.4 shows a stylized representation of the tasks performed by a payment processor. The merchant quotes the prices of its goods or services in USD, these prices are converted to corresponding bitcoin amounts using the spot rate and presented to the client. The client can then pay using her bitcoins. The payment processor converts the bitcoins to USD using an exchange, and returns the USD to the merchant. The merchant receives as payment the quoted price in USD, and the payment processor absorbs the fluctuations of the spot BTC/USD rate. As the settlement period is usually short—in the order of minutes—the conversion risk that payment processors bear is relatively small. Furthermore, the payment processor can achieve economies of scale by grouping market orders.

As of the time of writing, thousands of merchants have signed up with the leading payment processors. The fees charged stand at around 1% (Natham, 2014), which compare favorably with fees of around 2% to 3% for other payment methods such as credit cards. Lower Bitcoin volatility or lower exchange fees could lead to a decrease in payment processor's fees.

Table 4.1 shows the daily transaction volume of bitcoins compared to other payment systems. Bitcoin transaction volumes are still dwarfed by those of other payment systems.

Critics cite several reasons that prevent Bitcoin from effectively competing in the payment processing market:

- Monopolies, either those created by economies of scale or barriers to entry.
- Regulations, such as Know Your Customer (KYC) and Anti-Money Laundering (AML) (section 3.7) would increase the cost of Bitcoin payment processors, limiting their cost advantage.
- Traditional methods provide services that users are willing to pay for, such as chargebacks for fraudulent merchants or credit financing. Bitcoin supporters argue that most of these functions can be offered in the Bitcoin ecosystem (section 4.5).

4.4 WEB WALLETS

Web wallets are companies that hide the complexity of managing a Bitcoin wallet from their users, providing an experience more similar to online banking services. The first generation of web wallets require users to deposit bitcoins with the web wallet service and allow payments to be performed from the provider's website. Web wallets offer their users convenience. However, the users bear a large counterparty risk: the web wallet could be hacked and its funds stolen, or an insider could disappear with them. Web wallets could operate under a fractional reserve model like regular banks, and there are not many tools for their users to monitor their financial health.

Aside from ease of use, web wallets can offer their users other advantages:

- Alert a user that her wallet has been compromised.
- Advise a user against transacting with a merchant with bad reputation.
- Help reduce the risk of address spoofing. When buying goods or services with Bitcoin, users have to send funds to addresses that are usually generated randomly. Because these addresses have no identifying information, they could be spoofed by an attacker. A wallet service can help reduce this risk. This risk is also reduced using the Payment Protocol (section 8.9).
- Connect automatically to the user's bank account.
- Integrate escrow services transparently (section 4.5).

Web wallet service providers could collect revenues by requesting a fee from their users. There is also value to be captured from the data that the service collects from the user's spending habits[2]: a web wallet has an advantage identifying the merchants with whom their users are transacting. The collected information could be used to recommend services to the user or to display better advertisements. Furthermore, in some situations, the wallet service could work with retailers to offer their users promotions, or even sometimes direct users to preferred merchants. The revenue model for this business is similar to the revenue model for other web services, such as email storage, search, and so on.

Web wallets holding their users' funds are considered first-generation services. Users of these first-generation wallet services are subject to considerable counterparty risk. Following several bankruptcies and theft cases at the beginning of 2014, there is a transition to second-generation wallet services that use multisignature technology (sections 6.3 and 8.6). These services use 2-of-3 multisignature addresses where one of the keys is stored in the regular user device, the second key is stored with the web wallet service, and the third key is kept by the user in a secure (offline) place. As the funds are stored in a 2-of-3 address, two of these three signatures are required to make a transaction. Under normal use, transactions are signed by both the local user key and the wallet service key. The wallet service usually requires the user to authenticate, thus providing two-factor authentication to spend the funds. However, the wallet service does not control the funds, it only prevents the user from spending them unless properly authenticated. Thus the web wallet cannot steal the funds. Neither can it require a "ransom" payment to the user to unlock the funds, as the user holds the third key that she could use to unlock the funds.

---

[2] Businesses wishing to collect spending data from users do not necessarily have to provide a web wallet. They could provide the nodes to which a Simplified Payment Verification (SPV) wallet connects. The SPV wallet implementation could be open-sourced to increase user's confidence. On the other hand, most SPV clients use Bloom filters to communicate with the nodes, and wallet information can be somewhat concealed in the Bloom filter. For more details on Simplified Payment Verification and Bloom filters see section 8.8.

There are some companies (Buterin, 2014d) that combine multisignature wallet technology with **machine-learning fraud-detecting algorithms** to assign a **risk score** to each new requested transaction. The algorithm takes into account factors such as the user's spending habits and the owner of the address to which the funds are being sent, in other words, whether it is a reputable company. Depending on this risk score, the service either processes the transaction automatically (for low risk scores), requests two factor authentication or out-of-band confirmation (for medium risk transactions), or even assigns a company representative to manually check the transaction and call the client (for medium- and high-risk transactions).

Regulation is another concern for web wallets. Recent FinCEN regulations (section 3.7) did not address their role. Thus it is not clear whether web wallets services should be considered money transmitters, or if the regulatory treatment for a web wallet depends on whether it holds the private keys, one of the keys on multisignature transactions or no keys at all. If web wallets were declared money transmitters in future rulings, they would be required to seek a money transmitter license.

A related business model is the production of hardware wallets (8.2.4). Hardware wallets could be combined with multisignature web wallet services.

Finally, there is a certain overlap in the functions of exchanges, payment processors, and web wallets that could lead to further integration of these businesses.

4.5 MULTISIGNATURE ESCROW SERVICES

One of the problems with the early use of Bitcoin as a payment method is the irreversibility of payments, in contrast with other electronic payment technologies such as credit cards. These technologies have dispute mediation services built in. Bitcoin does not have dispute mediation services, which can make it cheaper, especially for merchants dealing with charge-back fraud.

However, there are situations where dispute mediation and reversibility of transactions are important. A common example is dispute mediation between a client and an online merchant (Buterin, 2014d). Escrow services provide dispute resolution between two transacting parties using multisignature transactions (section 6.3). First, the client and the merchant choose an escrow service that they both trust. The escrow service provides them with a Bitcoin address whose private key it controls. To make the purchase the client sends the funds to a 2-of-3 multisignature address. The addresses included are those of the client, the merchant and of the escrow service. There are then three possible scenarios:

- If the client receives the goods correctly, she signs a transaction sending the funds in the 2-of-3 multisignature address to the merchant's address, and sends the transaction to the merchant. The merchant can then sign the 2-of-3 multisignature address with its own key and publish it in the blockchain.
- If the goods are not received or are defective, the merchant signs a transaction sending the funds in the 2-of-3 multisignature address to the client's address. It then sends this transaction to the client, who signs it and publishes it in the blockchain, thus receiving back the funds.

- If the client and the merchant do not agree on who should receive the funds, they can request the intervention of the escrow service. In this case, the escrow service decides who should receive the funds, and then signs a transaction returning all the funds to that party except for a commission for itself. The partially signed transaction is sent to the party that the escrow service has decided should receive the funds, who then signs the transaction and publishes it in the blockchain.

Only the third scenario requires the intervention of the escrow service. Thus the escrow service charges only if its assistance is required, targeting the costs on those who use the service instead of spreading the costs among all merchants and users. Credit card processors are good candidates to provide these services, leveraging their expertise in dispute mediation.

4.6   MINING

Miners receive revenues via block rewards and transaction fees. At the current rate of 25 bitcoins per block, the total mining revenue for a year is around 1.3 million bitcoins. Assuming the price of a bitcoin is 500 USD, the annual revenue for the mining industry would total USD 650 million. Mining is therefore one of the biggest businesses in Bitcoin.

Mining is covered in more depth in Chapter 9. Here is only a brief enumeration of different business models in the mining industry:

- Mining equipment manufacturers. These companies design the ASIC (application-specific integrated circuit) processors, subcontract the fabrication to one of the large chip manufacturing companies, and assemble the final product. There are many companies competing in this space. However, once the state of the art in chip manufacturing is reached and mining equipment demand stabilizes, there might be some consolidation. There is also the possibility that a big chip manufacturer may enter the market.
- Datacenters. These are companies renting datacenters hosting mining equipment. Bitcoin mining data-centers have the peculiarity that mining requires higher energy densities than other types of computing such as web servers.
- Miners. They run the ASIC mining hardware, incurring the operational costs and receiving the block rewards. Original miners were enthusiasts, but the sector has professionalized recently with the emergence of ASICs.
- Mining pool operators. Mining pools aggregate the mining power of individual miners to smooth out the rewards from mining, sometimes charging a small fraction of the mining reward for their services.
- Hosted mining, sometimes called cloud mining services or mining as a service (MaaS). The service provider covers all operational costs and rents the mining power in the cloud, offering convenience to users who want to enter the mining business.

It is estimated in Luria and Turner (2014) that 200 million USD were invested in mining equipment during 2013. Assuming the trend at the beginning of 2014 continues, and

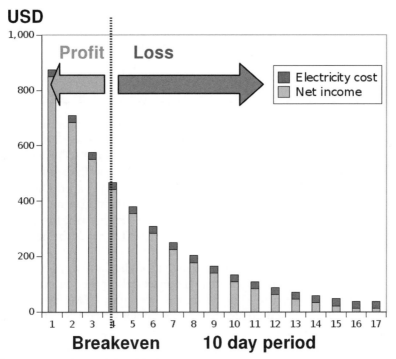

FIGURE 4.5 Cashflows from mining ASIC

15,000 TH/s (tera hashes per second)[3] are added each month, the total investment in mining equipment for 2014 would be USD 180 million[4], assuming mining equipment is sold at a price of 1,000 USD/TH/s. If the price of bitcoin stays constant, the rate of addition to the network will probably level off later in the year 2014 as the economics of adding new hardware worsens with the increased competition. Nevertheless, the incentives to invest in computational power will depend greatly in the price of bitcoins. A more detailed exploration of the economics of mining can be found in Chapter 9.

Figure 4.5 is an illustration of the difficulty of running a cashflow analysis for a mining business. The cashflows in the figure were generated on February 2014, with the data available at that moment. Time is divided into 10-day periods, and figure 4.5 shows the mining revenues and electricity costs; other costs are assumed to be zero. The main two factors determining the merit of the investment are the price of bitcoin and the growth of the total computational power of the network. The price was assumed constant at 650 USD/BTC, the market price at the time of the analysis. The growth of the network hash rate was assumed to be *logarithmic* and the logarithmic growth factor was estimated from the hash rate growth in the previous 5 months. Given the advertised ASIC price at the time, the investment would yield a profit if the equipment were to be received within the following 40 days. If received later, the investment would not reach breakeven.

---

[3] TH/s is a measure of the mining computational power.
[4] This figure does not include additional required investments, such as in datacentres or other infrastructure.

Although this analysis is very rough, it illustrates the difficulty of planning an investment in mining equipment in a period where the technology is rapidly evolving and capacity is being added to the network at an exponential rate.

4.7   ATMS

Bitcoin ATMs allow users to buy or sell bitcoins with cash. The operation of a Bitcoin ATM follows several steps. First, the user scans her identification, and the ATM verifies its validity. Then the user introduces some cash and presents the ATM with a QR code for her public address. This QR code can be generated by a wallet application running in a smartphone or tablet, or it can be printed on a piece of paper. Optionally, some ATMs might generate a paper wallet, that would include the public and private keys for users that do not have a wallet. However, this poses a security risk for the user as the ATM could keep a log of the private keys. Finally, the ATM sends the newly purchased bitcoins to the specified address.

Although Bitcoin ATMs have not been covered specifically in any FinCEN ruling as of the time of writing, most entrepreneurs in the space believe their businesses fall under the money transmitter category. Thus businesses operating ATMs usually register as such. This registration can be burdensome, as some states in the US require the posting of bonds in order to grant a license.

Most ATMs require users to identify themselves, usually scanning some identification such as the user's driver's license or ID. This information is then usually sent to a third party identity verification company[5] that performs a check before allowing the user to operate. Some critics have argued that this does not provide the same level of user identification compared to that of regular bank ATMs.

Exchange rates are usually taken from live quotes on exchanges. On top of the market rate, ATM operators charge a fee in the 3–7% range (Wile, 2014). Some ATMs are one-way and can only be used to purchase bitcoins with cash. More recent machines are two-way and can be used to either buy or sell bitcoins. Companies operating the ATMs are usually connected to an exchange where they can balance their holdings of cash and bitcoins. Businesses also have to manage the logistics of the cash generated/required by the ATMs. In some cases, a banking relation that allows the funneling of cash proceeds to an exchange to buy bitcoins is required.

Early users of ATMs are usually enthusiasts or people attracted by curiosity.

An often-cited use case for Bitcoin ATMs would be for travelers. Travelers could buy some bitcoins in their origin country and exchange them for the local currency of their destination country using an ATM. This would allow them to avoid the usually large retail foreign exchange fees or the fees associated with cashing traveler's checks. Furthermore, travelers could convert excess cash back to bitcoins at the end of their trip.

Finally, supporters argue that ATMs could allow people who are "underbanked," i.e. not covered by traditional baking services, to get access to digital money and participate in e-commerce transactions.

---

[5] Some earlier ATM versions did not record ID information, and this task had to be done manually.

PART

Two

Bitcoin Technology

CHAPTER 5

Public Key Cryptography

Bitcoin is a cryptocurrency. This highlights the importance of cryptography in Bitcoin's design. Without cryptography Bitcoin could not have existed. This chapter serves the purpose of both introducing cryptography and highlighting the main public key cryptography algorithms used in Bitcoin. Additional cryptographic protocols will be introduced throughout the book when describing applications that make use of them. A single chapter does not do justice to the subject, and the treatment here is necessarily shallow and incomplete. Cryptography is a very deep subject, and the interested reader is encouraged to consult a cryptography textbook, such as Paar and Pelzl (2010), Katz and Lindell (2007), or Ferguson et al. (2010).

Cryptography is the science of communicating securely in the presence of adversaries, who can listen in and even control the communication channel. Classical (symmetric) cryptography is concerned with encryption. That is, converting a message to a **ciphertext**. A ciphertext is apparent nonsense to the adversary listening on the communication channel, but the recipient knows how to translate it to the original message.

Cryptographers recommend that the encryption algorithm is made public and that only the encryption key is kept secret. This is known as **Kerckhoffs's Principle**. The rationale behind this principle is that it is easy to make an encryption algorithm that cannot be broken by its creator[1]. But it is very hard to make an encryption algorithm that cannot be broken by anyone in the world. No matter how smart the creator of a cipher is, there is a high probability that there is somebody smarter or more imaginative in the world. Making an encryption algorithm public and subjecting it to the scrutiny of the cryptographic community is a good idea. A motto of Kerckhoffs's Principle could be *make the cryptographic algorithm public, but keep the encryption keys private*.

Most of the early work in cryptography was done on **symmetric ciphers**. A very early example is **Caesar's cipher** (see box). The goal of symmetric ciphers is to encrypt a message to ciphertext using the secret key so that the original message can be recovered only if the secret key is known. A good symmetric cipher must not leak any information about either the message or the secret key. Caesar's cipher can be used as a symmetric cipher, where the secret key is the shift, the number of places shifted in the alphabet. Aside from the fact that the secret key is very small (there are only 26 possible keys, the number of letters in the alphabet), it is not a very good symmetric cipher because it leaks a lot of information about the message. It lets the adversary know the length

---

[1] An exception could be government agencies that can have a group of people devising ciphers and another group trying to break them. This case is not an exception to Kerckhoffs's Principle: the peer review is simply done indoors.

of the message and the frequency of certain letters in the message[2]. This information is enough in most cases to break the cipher. An ideal symmetric cipher is one that produces a ciphertext that is indistinguishable from random noise.

CAESAR'S CIPHER

Caesar's cipher was allegedly used by Julius Caesar to communicate with his generals. Caesar's cipher is a substitution cipher. To encrypt a message each of its letters is substituted by another letter in the alphabet. That is, there is a one-to-one correspondence between the letters of the message and the letters of the ciphertext. The ciphertext is constructed taking the letters of the message and shifting them three places in the alphabet. For instance the word "message" would be encrypted as "phvvdjh". A very entertaining account of the history of cryptography, including Caesar's cipher and other early ciphers, can be found in Singh (2000).

Symmetric ciphers are one of the oldest cryptographic primitives. However, many other cryptographic tools have been devised. Bitcoin originally makes use of three of them:

- **Public key cryptography**. Bitcoin uses public key cryptography to handle transactions. This will be discussed in the rest of this chapter.
- **Hash functions**. Bitcoin uses hash functions to secure the information in the blockchain. This topic will be discussed in Chapter 7.
- **Symmetric key cryptography**. Bitcoin uses symmetric encryption to protect the private keys in a user's wallet. The use of symmetric encryption in the wallet software is not a requirement. However, its use is highly recommended. Symmetric-key cryptography will be covered in section 8.1.

The rest of the chapter will be devoted to public key cryptography. Section 5.1 will introduce public key encryption, the first application of public key cryptography, and then section 5.2 will present digital signatures. The following two sections will introduce two particular implementations of public key cryptosystems: RSA in section 5.3 and elliptic curves in 5.4. Section 5.5 will present two cryptographic tools related to public key cryptography. Finally, section 5.6 will explore the link between public keys and Bitcoin addresses.

    This is a somewhat theoretical chapter, but it is important to understand how Bitcoin handles transactions. It will follow the treatment in *Understanding Cryptography* by Christof Paar and Jan Pelzl (2010).

---

[2] Assuming spaces are removed from the message prior to encryption. If they are not, then even more information is leaked, and breaking the cipher is even easier.

5.1 PUBLIC KEY ENCRYPTION

Public key cryptography was developed during the 1970s by Diffie, Hellman and Merkle (Levy, 2001)[3]. Bitcoin does not use public key encryption algorithms, but a close relative called digital signatures. Nonetheless, this section is devoted to public key encryption because it plays a central role in public key cryptography.

Public key cryptography was developed as a response to an important weakness of symmetric encryption: **key distribution**. When two people use symmetric encryption, they must ensure beforehand that they both share the same symmetric key: they must interchange the keys through a secure channel before using the symmetric encryption system. However, there are many situations where it is not possible to interchange the symmetric key through a secure channel, such as e-commerce. The internet is an insecure channel: traffic can be eavesdropped and even modified in transit. Therefore it is impossible to establish a secure connection through the internet using only symmetric encryption. Public key encryption was developed to overcome this problem (see the SSL and TLS box later in this chapter for an overview of how this process works).

An analogy for symmetric key encryption is that of a safe with one key. This (symmetric) key can be used both to lock the safe (encrypt) and to unlock the safe (decrypt). A similar analogy for public key encryption is that of a safe with a pair of keys. One of the keys, the **public key**, can only be used to lock the safe, while the other key, the **private key**, can only be used to unlock the safe. How does public key encryption solve the key distribution problem? The important point to note is that only the private key (the key that unlocks the safe) must be kept secret. It is perfectly safe, though, to publish the public key (the key that locks the safe), because the wider this key is published, the easier it is for another party to have access to this key and use it to communicate.

Figure 5.1 shows public key encryption in action. In this example public key cryptography is used to encrypt a message. First, the receiver of the encrypted message (Bob) generates a pair of public and private keys, running a **key generation algorithm** (1). The public and private keys are called a **public–private keypair** and are mathematically linked. Every public key protocol has its own key generation algorithm. Some examples will be introduced later in this chapter. The receiver (Bob) sends his public key to the sender (Alice) (2) but keeps his private key secured. After receiving Bob's public key, Alice proceeds to encrypt the message using Bob's public key (3). The result is the encrypted message (ciphertext). This encrypted message is sent over the insecure channel to Bob (4). An attacker eavesdropping the connection can get hold of the encrypted message, but she cannot decrypt it. Only Bob, who has the private key corresponding to the public key, is able to decrypt the encrypted message using the decryption algorithm (5), obtaining the original message (6).

There is a problem with the proposed encryption scheme: the public key is sent over the insecure channel. This opens the possibility of a **Man-in-the-Middle attack** (MitM). Figure 5.2 shows how a Man-in-the-Middle attack works. The attacker (Trudy) controls the communication channel. She can intercept a message flowing through the channel

---

[3] It was revealed in 1997 that researchers at GCHQ (a British intelligence agency) had come up with the idea before. However, it is not clear that the agency recognized the importance of the discovery at the time (Levy, 2001).

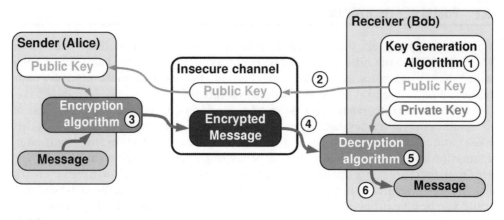

FIGURE 5.1 Public key encryption

and change it before it is received. Trudy takes advantage of her position by intercepting the public key that Bob sends to Alice at the beginning of the communication (2). But she does not forward Bob's public key to Alice, instead she keeps Bob's public key to herself and generates a brand new public–private keypair (3). The keys controlled by Trudy show a dot next to them in Figure 5.2. Trudy then sends her own generated public key to Alice as if it were Bob's public key (4). Later, when Alice wishes to send Bob an encrypted message, she encrypts the message with what she believes to be Bob's public

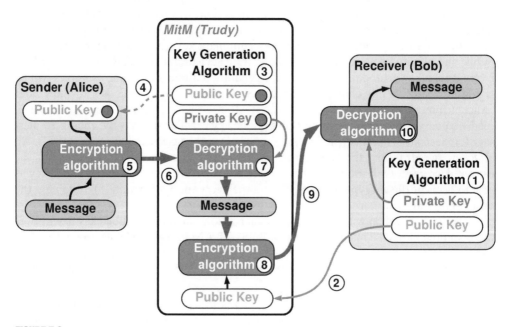

FIGURE 5.2 Man-in-the-Middle attack

key (5). The encrypted message is intercepted by Trudy (6), and because it was encrypted with a public key of her own, she is able to decrypt the message (7). Trudy then proceeds to re-encrypt the message, this time using Bob's public key (8). She then passes this second encrypted message to Bob (9). Bob is able to decrypt the message using his private key (10). Notice that during this attack neither Alice nor Bob have any indication that they are being attacked.

There are several approaches to avoid this Man-in-the-Middle attack:

- Bob and Alice can interchange their public keys using a different, secure channel. The downside to this approach is that this is a similar problem (key distribution) to the problem that public key cryptography tries to solve. However, the **public key distribution** problem is somewhat easier than the symmetric key distribution problem, because to distribute a public key, only authentication is needed. To securely distribute a symmetric key, both authentication and privacy are needed. This means that public keys can be distributed by publishing them widely in a tamper-proof medium, say, a newspaper.
- **Web of trust**. This is the method used by PGP and GPG[4]. In a web of trust, users cryptographically sign the public keys of other users they know and trust, for instance because they have met face to face in a key-signing party. Every user keeps a **keyring**, a set of other users' public keys. A user can cryptographically sign the public key of other users that she knows, i.e. whose public keys are in her keyring. If a user wishes to communicate with someone she does not know, she can ask any of her trusted friends (a copy of whose public keys she has in her keyring) to send her a signed public key of the user she wishes to communicate with.
- **Public Key Infrastructure (PKI)**. PKI assumes there is a central authority, called the **Certificate Authority (CA)**. Everybody has a copy of the CA public key, and trusts the CA. Every user generates a public–private key pair and presents the CA with her public key. The CA verifies the identity of the user and then signs her public key. When Alice wants to communicate with Bob, she sends her **certificate** to him, which comprises her public key and the CA signature for that public key. Bob then checks that Alice's public key is properly signed by the CA, i.e. that the certificate is valid. This is the approach followed by SSL and TLS, the world's largest cryptographic deployment (see box below).

---

[4] PGP, Pretty Good Privacy, and GPG, GNU Privacy Guard, are computer programs that, among other things, use public key cryptography to allow users to communicate privately. They can be used on top of email and other communication protocols to encrypt their contents.

SSL (SECURE SOCKETS LAYER) AND TLS (TRANSPORT LAYER SECURITY)

SSL and its successor TLS are the most widely used protocols for secured communications on the internet. SSL and TLS work in two steps. First, a symmetric key is randomly generated by one of the two ends, say Alice. Next this symmetric key is encrypted by Alice with the public key of the other end (Bob). The encrypted symmetric key is sent over the internet to Bob. Only Bob has the private key, so only he can decrypt the message and obtain the symmetric key generated by Alice. At this point both Alice and Bob have the same symmetric key. Furthermore no one else has this symmetric key. Therefore, Alice and Bob can initiate a data stream between them and encrypt it with this symmetric key.

   Why use public key cryptography only to generate a symmetric key? Why not use it to encrypt the message directly? Because public key algorithms are much slower than symmetric encryption algorithms by several orders of magnitude. Therefore in SSL and TLS public key cryptography is used to establish session keys, i.e. symmetric keys that will be used during the rest of the connection. How does Bob get Alice's public key? One possibility would be for Alice to send her public key over the internet. But this approach is subject to the Man-in-the-Middle attack, and therefore should be avoided. To solve this public key distribution problem, SSL and TLS employ Public Key Infrastructure (PKI). The public keys of the Certificate Authorities (CAs), called root certificates, are included in the installation of the operating system or bundled with the browsers installed in the computer. The websites that use SSL or TLS present the browser with a certificate, signed by a CA, that includes the public key for that website. Indeed, the SSL and TLS protocols are much more nuanced than this short description. For an in-depth analysis of SSL and TLS, see Oppliger (2009). An analysis of the practical realities of PKI can be found in Ferguson et al. (2010).

5.2   DIGITAL SIGNATURES

A second application of public key cryptography is that of **digital signatures**. The goal of digital signatures is similar to that of handwritten signatures: they ensure that a message was generated by the signer, has not been tampered with and the signature is non-repudiable (the signer of a message should not be able to deny having signed it).

   Digital signatures are used in the Bitcoin protocol. Bitcoin addresses are basically public keys[5]. There is a private key corresponding to each public key, and thus to each Bitcoin address. Public keys can be interpreted as bank account numbers. Private keys can then be interpreted as the signatures that unlock those bank accounts. To spend the bitcoins in an address, a transaction authorizing the spending must be signed with the private key. The wallet software creates a Bitcoin address by running the key generation algorithm, and thus any user can create as many Bitcoin addresses as wanted.

[5] Bitcoin addresses are really the hash of public keys (section 5.6).

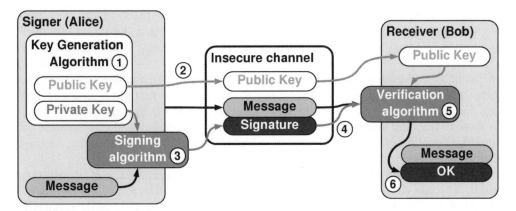

FIGURE 5.3 Digital signatures

Figure 5.3 shows the signature process. First, the signer (Alice) generates a public–private keypair, using the key generation algorithm (1). She sends her public key through the communication channel[6] (2). Next, Alice uses the private key to digitally sign the message (3). It is important that she keeps the private key to herself, not revealing it to anyone. Once the message has been signed, both the message and the signature are sent to the receiver (Bob) (4). Note that the message is not encrypted, but only authenticated. Bob verifies the signature, using Alice's public key (5). If the verification yields a positive result, he knows that the message was originated by Alice (6). Otherwise, he can reject the message as invalid.

Non-repudiation cannot be accomplished using symmetric cryptography. To see why, suppose a symmetric cipher is used to digitally sign a message. Assume that both the signer (Alice) and the receiver (Bob) share a common secret key. Now Alice wants to send a message to Bob, and she uses the symmetric key to encrypt the message. Because the symmetric key is only known to Alice and Bob, Bob knows that the message was created by Alice. However, Bob cannot prove to a third party—say a judge—that Alice sent him the message. There are two potential problems:

- As both Alice and Bob have a copy of the symmetric key, either of them can create an encrypted message. Therefore, Bob is not able to prove that *Alice* signed the message. He can only prove that *somebody* who had the symmetric key produced the message. Because both he and Alice had a copy of the symmetric key, either of them could have encrypted the message. Encryption of a message cannot be used to prove it was generated by Alice.

---

[6] Note that in sending the public key through an insecure communication channel, the Digital Signature procedure is open to the Man-in-the-Middle exploit discussed in section 5.1. The techniques proposed there to avoid this attack (interchange public keys using an off-line channel, web of trust or PKI) are also applicable when using digital signatures. Note also that Bitcoin is not subject to a Man-in the-Middle attack, because the public keys are secured in the blockchain. This will become clearer in Chapter 7.

- Furthermore, to prove that the message was encrypted by the symmetric key, Bob must reveal the key[7]. But by revealing the key to a third party, he allows that third party to sign any message, thus further weakening the security of the signature.

In public key cryptography, the signature binds the sender to the message. Only the signer (Alice) has a copy of the private key, so only she can sign a message with that key. Furthermore, to prove that a message was actually signed by Alice, Bob only has to show to the third party (the judge) the message, the public key and the signature. In summary, public key cryptography solves all the problems and enables secure, binding digital signatures.

A technical point with digital signatures is that the message could be of an arbitrary length. This can be a problem because the algorithms employed by public key cryptography are quite slow. The solution to this problem is to first take the hash[8] of the (arbitrarily long) message, and then sign this hash. The output of a hash function is of the same (shorter) length, independent of the size of the input. Using this hashing step, messages of arbitrary length can be signed explicitly.

A digital signature protocol is the combination of a public-key algorithm with a digital signature scheme. The public-key algorithm provides the underlying asymmetric mathematical algorithm. The digital signature scheme proposes a way to use this asymmetric algorithm to arrive at a workable digital signature.

There are three main *public key families* used in practice:

- **Integer factorization.** These algorithms are based on the difficulty of factoring large integers. The most important example is RSA, introduced in 1977 (Rivest et al., 1978).
- **Discrete logarithm (DL).** Based on the intractability of the discrete logarithm problem on finite cyclic groups. It was introduced in 1976 by Diffie and Hellman for their proposed key exchange algorithm (Diffie and Hellman, 1976).
- **Elliptic curve (EC).** Based on the difficulty of computing the generalized logarithm problem on an elliptic curve. It was introduced in 1985. Despite its technical advantages, adoption has been somewhat limited by the patents covering it.

The main *digital signature schemes* used in practice are:

- **RSA.** The RSA signature scheme is based on the RSA algorithm. It is the most widely used digital signature scheme[9].
- **Schnorr signature.** It is considered the simplest signature scheme that can be used both with discrete logarithm and elliptic curve algorithms. This results in small computational times for signing and verification, as well as smaller signatures. However, as it was encumbered by a patent, it has not been widely used (Schnorr, 1991). The

---

[7] There is a branch of cryptography, zero knowledge proofs, that allows one party to prove to another party that a statement is true without revealing the contents of the statement, that could alleviate this problem. Zero knowledge proofs will be introduced in section 13.5.

[8] Hash functions will be discussed in Chapter 7 in the context of the blockchain.

[9] It is often the preferred signature protocol in X.509 certificates used in TLS.

patent covering the Schnorr signature expired in 2008, which has prompted some calls in the Bitcoin community for a switch to Schnorr signatures.

- **Elgamal signature.** Introduced by Elgamal in 1985, this scheme is applicable to both the discrete logarithm and the elliptic curve algorithms. However, it is not widely used in practice because it is more computationally intensive and its signature bigger than other schemes like Schnorr or DSA.
- **DSA.** It stands for **Digital Signature Algorithm** and was proposed by NIST in 1991 (Wikipedia, 2014g). This scheme is widely used, in part because the patent that covers it was made available worldwide royalty-free.

Bitcoin uses the elliptic curve algorithm with the DSA signature scheme. The following sections will first introduce the RSA algorithm, given its historical and practical importance. The next section will cover the elliptic curve algorithm with the DSA signature scheme.

5.3   RSA

This section is somewhat technical, and the RSA technology is not used by Bitcoin, so it can be skipped by a reader not interested in the technical details of public key cryptography.

RSA stands for Rivest, Shamir, and Adleman. They proposed in 1977 a public-key cryptography scheme based on the difficulty of factoring large integers (Rivest et al., 1978).

Figure 5.4 presents the three main steps to use RSA encryption: key generation, encryption, and decryption. The key generation algorithm follows the steps:

1. Generate two large primes p and q.
2. Multiply the two primes $n = p \cdot q$.
3. Compute Euler's Phi for n. Euler's Phi is the number of integers in the cyclic group $\mathbb{Z}_n$ = {1, 2, ..., n – 1} which are prime to n. It is given by $\Phi(n) = (p - 1) \cdot (q - 1)$.
4. Select an exponent $e \in$ {1, ..., $\Phi(n) - 1$} that is relatively prime to $\Phi(n)$[10]. This exponent will be part of the public key.
5. Compute the private key d as the multiplicative inverse of e modulo $\Phi(n)$, that is: $d \cdot e = 1 \mod \Phi(n)$.

The public key is (n, e), the private key is d. Encryption is straightforward: the ciphertext of a message m is just m raised to the power of the public key e in modulo n arithmetic, that is:

$$c = m^e \mod n$$

The decryption step is also straightforward. To decrypt a ciphertext c, it is raised to the power of the private key d, also modulo n:

$$m = c^d \mod n$$

---

[10] A number e is relatively prime to $\Phi(n)$ if the greatest common divisor between them is 1, that is, $gcd(e, \Phi(n)) \equiv 1$.

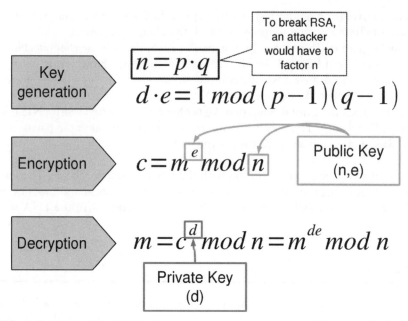

FIGURE 5.4 RSA encryption scheme

A long message m is just a long string of zeros and ones, and can be interpreted as an integer. The number representing the message m must be smaller than the order of the group n. To encrypt a long integer with RSA, n must be chosen to be greater than m. Therefore, although it is technically possible to encrypt long messages with RSA, private and public keys can be very big (of the order of magnitude of the message itself) and the computational cost can become very large. Other public key encryption algorithms, such as elliptic curves, share this problem with RSA. For this reason, public key encryption is commonly used to derive a secret symmetric key, and the message is then encrypted and decrypted with a symmetric cipher using this secret key[11].

In order to break RSA, an attacker has to discover the unique prime factors of n. If an attacker were able to do so, she could run the key generation algorithm to derive d and subsequently easily decrypt the ciphertext. The security of RSA thus depends on the hardness of the factoring problem, whose complexity class is not known. The best currently known algorithm (on regular computers) has a running time exponential in the number of bits. If quantum computers were available, the Shor algorithm could be used. This algorithm is only polynomial in the number of bits. Therefore RSA is not resistant to quantum computers (section 14.6).

For a proof of correctness of the RSA algorithm, as well as many more technical details, the reader can consult Chapter 7 of Paar and Pelzl (2010).

The RSA *signing scheme* is similar to the RSA encryption scheme. Figure 5.5 shows the three parts of the scheme: key generation, signing, and verification. The key

---

[11] A long message m could be split into parts and each of those parts encrypted using the public key. However, this operation is still more computationally expensive than using a symmetric cipher.

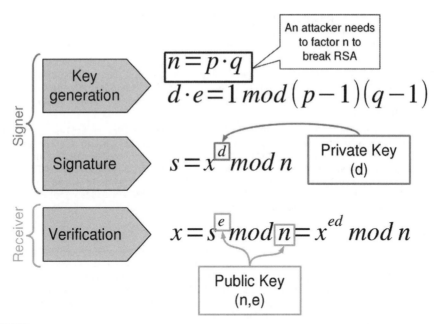

An attacker needs to factor n to break RSA

$$n = p \cdot q$$

$$d \cdot e = 1 \, mod \, (p-1)(q-1)$$

$$s = x^{d} \, mod \, n$$

Private Key (d)

$$x = s^{e} \, mod \, n = x^{ed} \, mod \, n$$

Public Key (n,e)

FIGURE 5.5 RSA signature scheme

generation part is exactly the same as for the RSA encryption scheme. Signing is done raising the message digest[12] x to the power of the private key d:

$$s = x^d \bmod n$$

Verification is done raising the signature s to the power of the public key e and comparing the result to the original message digest x. If they match, the signature is correct.

$$x = s^e = x^{e \cdot d} = x \bmod n$$

The RSA signing algorithm as presented here (called the *textbook RSA algorithm*) suffers from a series of problems that can facilitate successful attacks, such as the existential forgery attack. In an **existential forgery attack**, the attacker could first create a signature s' and then compute the message that generates this signature $m' = (s')^e \bmod n$. The attacker has no control over the value of m' obtained, but she can nonetheless generate a valid message-signature pair. One solution to prevent this attack used throughout this section is to hash the message[13]. Another solution could be to assemble the message m with some structure, such as in $m = m_o \| H(m_o)$, where the original message m_o is concatenated with

---

[12] The message digest is usually computed as the hash of the message, see section 7.1.

[13] The message m is hashed to arrive at $H(m)$. The digital signature is then performed on this hash $H(m)$, obtaining $s = (H(m))^e \bmod n$. An attacker trying to perform an existential forgery attack would create a signature s' and then compute the hash of the message $H(m') = (s')^e \bmod n$.

p

bb28825e31abcf48acf79537d515ce7afdca3971d2893bdee5f44e21befdb8d6be22f427b81eddb
18e1684e39ae7c804c558fe2e96be587107270f1cb99d258531cdf5e2abcc55ab6062e5e1746f1
de1ac37834a602c56603d3155902521aba57007ebf578c24308570d2948da46e51ba3fb0ea07
011d74c3e387d661e05abe5

q

dd820329a37025eef35b156cb4d649d947b55b07a9561e1d0f957c3a50d044400340df2037513
53ae32385ac91652342c686ce2f5fb5513ea1c68199cf212b5e3a86d49ca67acde1b4d313f2282
410d73b260153ce0c85a8934a117226c988a0327eef47b61788df167f5b88929b14f71fe39949f
b4fef2d9f4488c7f8acd627

n

a1f1056d6f374f52876c99eb18f1b9d1296949e470ab0b9e15a57debfa105157ec548375675f59
8327bfadd58fd819209870bd3451821e2aa160b3497102c3e3aef49b1ba1742ad0b41baf5639c
15a87b9385ba55d1ce217dd0da319804abb677dead42a98bbc1dcc8f38d34bf3b270caf61f8371
c311fa656463cb5d6156ac8f1eaa64237fbdfa1ae6188f1f14492371b17dd92f3f5ddd578997aafb
6591d90674955bd9fb5f10dfe5f97fc1935fc847033742c04a52f1f4120c13742dad96676a3471ee
4402675cc8c402e511c7d69f0a7d73f1feb4992bf47013b77033bdd68d8a9bc3cd1ec1d42fc4c25
4d5c4c93d6567c75c1a44bea1eae68ffa66a9de3

e

10001

d

227359ca3c1cb21d467e0e087b980105c41f87feb7114c3967357ba255e25ecbab95171a44d17
e036ed35231da9608526cdb9f04a04a640c81a446bfdaf0d1a78032bd449586570d6b23709b91
51d6e684babe946148a1b89de826c868087df1b851daaced2d1442d9e52627107f8f011dd663a
da5abb5a5f7389df5b9037961cb54df2187a3470524d478ea528ff9ee0dae85ee8b238f0d18da9f
924c1dd0dcd034111ae45318bc5e809ca3571505fbc43f1fb5b0434cb5bed534fe4d998059103a
3e3cdc1af3497aa739f455efd7f3c59c3013d917324263b0a0b084c069ed19dd91666a1c5d0dd6
c81ec97339d28f6ed45b3d012ec9a065de11bdaf2b6591

FIGURE 5.6   Example of a 2048-bit RSA key. All numbers in hexadecimal

its own hash $H(m_o)$, computed using a cryptographically secure hash function H (section 7.1). Note, however, that an existential forgery attack is not applicable to Bitcoin transactions, because, even if successful, an attacker could only create a random transaction which would be rejected by the nodes. The reader can consult Chapter 10 of Paar and Pelzl (2010) for refinements on the RSA signature scheme necessary to use it in practice.

RSA is used in practice with keys of 1024 or 2048 bits. Figure 5.6 shows an example of a 2048-bit RSA key. Modern computer CPUs have 32-bit or 64-bit register sizes, and the operations on 2048-bit numbers as in this example must be split up and performed during multiple clock cycles. This makes operations involving public key cryptography relatively slow.

5.4 ELLIPTIC CURVE CRYPTOGRAPHY

This section is divided in two subsections. The first presents a summary of elliptic curves and their application to digital signatures as used in Bitcoin. The second subsection enters into more details about the mathematics of elliptic curves and could be skipped on a first reading. Elliptic curve cryptography is a much deeper subject than the quick overview presented here and the interested reader is encouraged to consult other references such as Paar and Pelzl (2010) or Washington (2008).

However, for a cryptographically secure hash function (section 7.1), it is computationally infeasible to find a message m′ such that it hashes to $H(m′)$, thus thwarting any existential forgery attack.

5.4.1 Elliptic Curve Summary

Oversimplifying, a cryptographic elliptic curve can be viewed as a very large succession of points. Any point can be reached quickly from a predecessor if the number of steps is known. The elliptic curve protocol starts from a given known point, called the generator. A public key is a point in the elliptic curve. A private key is the number of steps from the generator that must be traversed to arrive at the public key point. Computing the public key given the private key is very fast, thanks to the double-and-multiply algorithm. But the reverse, given the public key finding out the private key, is very difficult. This is known as the discrete logarithm problem. The brute-force algorithm to solve the discrete logarithm problem would traverse the points in the elliptic curve one at a time starting from the generator until it arrives at the desired point. Fortunately this algorithm is computationally infeasible, taking a ridiculous number of years to complete with classical computers[14].

In a nutshell, given the generator of the curve A and a private key d, it is fast to compute the public key $P = d \cdot A$, but the reverse, given A and P compute d, is infeasible with current computers. Any number of messages can be signed if in possession of the private key d. To sign each of these messages a nonce, a random number used only once per private key, must be generated. It is very important that this nonce is never reused. Reusing it just once gives away the private key d and thus the funds in a Bitcoin address.

Symmetric ciphers are more efficient for the same level of security than public key ciphers, both in terms of speed and key sizes. Furthermore, modern symmetric ciphers such as AES are resistant to quantum computing. But as explained at the beginning of the chapter, symmetric ciphers cannot be used for digital signing schemas.

Figure 5.7 shows the key sizes required to obtain a certain security level for various public key cryptography algorithms: RSA, discrete logarithm (DL), and Elliptic Curve

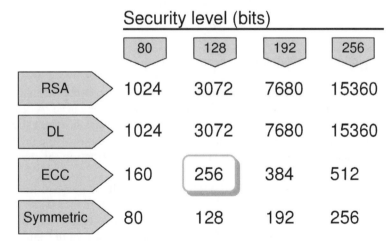

FIGURE 5.7 Key size of several public key cryptography algorithms to obtain various security levels

---

[14] There are known algorithms for quantum computers that can solve the discrete logarithm problem over elliptic curves in polynomial time. This topic will be explored further in Section 14.6.

Cryptography (ECC). The security level is defined as the key length of a symmetric system—such as AES—with the same security. Thus, as the bottom row shows, the key length of a symmetrical cipher coincides with the security level. It should be clear why Satoshi chose ECC: 256-bit elliptic curve digital signatures provide the smallest key sizes for a given level of security, 128 bits[15] in Bitcoin's case. Size is an important factor in Bitcoin, because a large portion of the data that is stored in the blockchain are the ECC signatures for the transactions. If Bitcoin were to use RSA, the size of the signatures would increase by a factor of 12.

5.4.2   Elliptic Curve Theory

Elliptic Curve public key algorithms are based on the generalized discrete logarithm problem on elliptic curves. An **elliptic curve** is a curve in the 2-dimensional plane whose points verify the equation (Weierstrass equation):

$$y^2 = x^3 + a \cdot x + b$$

The points of interest of this curve in cryptography are not the real numbers, but the integers, specifically the integers modulo a prime order p. All operations are performed modulo this p, the *order of the prime field*:

$$y^2 = x^3 + a \cdot x + b \bmod p$$

Note that in this last equation y, x, a and b are all integer numbers modulo the prime order p. All the points $P_i = (x_i, y_i)$ that satisfy this condition are said to belong to the elliptic curve. A **group operation** is defined over this set of points. This group operation is sometimes called addition:

$$P_3 = P_1 + P_2$$

The addition operation has the following geometrical interpretation:

- If the two points are different, the operation draws the line passing through the two points and finds the intersection of this line with the elliptic curve. As this intersection is represented by a cubic equation, the line will always intersect the elliptic curve. The result of the operation is the reflection over the x axis of the intersection between the line and the elliptic curve. The geometric construction for the addition of two different points is shown in Figure 5.8.
- If the two points are the same, then the tangent to the elliptic curve at this point is drawn. The result of the operation is then the reflection over the x axis of the intersection of this line with the elliptic curve. This operation is sometimes called point doubling. The geometric construction for point doubling is shown in Figure 5.9.

---

[15] The 256 bits are halved because of Pollard's *rho* method, whose running time is the square root of the brute-force method: $\sqrt{2^{256}} = 2^{128}$ (5.4.2).

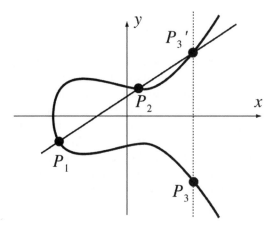

FIGURE 5.8 Elliptic curve addition of two different points

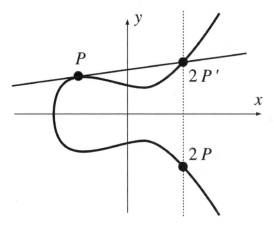

FIGURE 5.9 Elliptic curve point doubling

The equations resulting from these geometrical operations are, for the case of point addition:

$$x_3 = \left(\frac{y_2 - y_1}{x_2 - x_1}\right)^2 - x_1 - x_2 \bmod p$$

$$y_3 = \frac{y_2 - y_1}{x_2 - x_1}(x_1 - x_3) - y_1 \bmod p$$

And for the case of point doubling:

$$x_3 = \left(\frac{3x_1^2 + a}{2y_1}\right)^2 - 2x_1 \bmod p$$

$$y_3 = \frac{3x_1^2 + a}{2y_1}(x_1 - x_3) - y_1 \bmod p$$

Where all operations are performed in modulo p arithmetic, and thus divisions should be interpreted as multiplications by the modular multiplicative inverse. Note that although the equations for the group operations were obtained from a geometrical construction, these equations are evaluated using modular arithmetic, thus losing its geometrical interpretation. One interesting result of elliptic curves is that the points on an elliptic curve with the group operation defined above form an **abelian group**, or commutative group. The group is also a finite **cyclic group**: starting with an initial point in the curve, called a generator, and adding this point successively, all the points in the group are recovered. An abelian group must also include an identity element:

$$P + \infty = P$$

$$P + (-P) = \infty$$

A *point in infinity* (∞) serves as the identity element of the elliptic curve group. Geometrically the point at infinity is placed at infinity in the y axis. The geometrical interpretation of the group operations carry over naturally. As an example, Figure 5.10 shows the geometric construction for the inverse of a point $-P$.

Given a point on the elliptic curve P and an integer d, **point multiplication** is defined as the point T in the elliptic curve which is the result of adding P to itself d times:

$$T = d \cdot P = P + P + \dots + P$$

The **discrete logarithm** operation is the inverse of point multiplication. That is, the discrete logarithm of T with respect to P is the integer d such that $T = d \cdot P$. Point multiplication

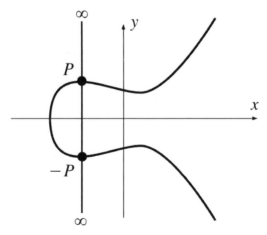

FIGURE 5.10   Elliptic Curve identity element

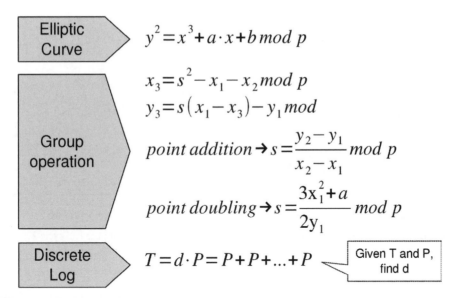

Elliptic Curve

$$y^2 = x^3 + a \cdot x + b \bmod p$$

Group operation

$$x_3 = s^2 - x_1 - x_2 \bmod p$$
$$y_3 = s(x_1 - x_3) - y_1 \bmod$$

$$point\ addition \rightarrow s = \frac{y_2 - y_1}{x_2 - x_1} \bmod p$$

$$point\ doubling \rightarrow s = \frac{3x_1^2 + a}{2y_1} \bmod p$$

Discrete Log

$$T = d \cdot P = P + P + ... + P$$

Given T and P, find d

FIGURE 5.11   Elliptic curve math

is a fast operation using the **double-and-add algorithm**[16]. This algorithm is polynomial in the number of bits of d. The discrete logarithm problem, however, is infeasible, taking an exponential time in the bits of d. Elliptic curve cryptography exploits these facts, much in the same way that RSA exploits the fact that integer factoring is a hard computational problem.

Figure 5.11 shows a summary of the maths involved in elliptic curve cryptography. Figure 5.12 shows a toy example of the elliptic curve group defined by the curve $y^2 = x^3 + 2x + 3 \bmod 263$, with generator $A = (200, 39)$. The second point in the group is given by $A + A = 2A$, the third point by $A + A + A = 3A$ and so on. There are 270 points in this elliptic curve group. The graph on the right shows all the points in the group. Geometrically, the 270 points in the elliptic curve group are distributed in a hard-to-predict fashion over the square (263, 263). They do not resemble a smooth curve.

Given a starting point A, it is computationally fast to advance d positions in the sequence of points using point multiplication $T = d \cdot A$. However, given a point T in the group it is very difficult to know how it has been reached, i.e. the number of elements in the sequence from the generator to this point. One would have to visit points in the curve one by one to discover the number of steps taken to reach the destination point,

---

[16] In the double-and-add algorithm the number d is first represented in binary format. The algorithm proceeds from the most significant bit to the least significant bit, keeping an intermediate result. The intermediate result is initialized to P. At each step the intermediate result is doubled first and then, if the current bit is 1, P is added to it. A more complete description of the double-and-add algorithm applied to elliptic curve point multiplication, together with a numerical example, can be found in Paar and Pelzl (2010).

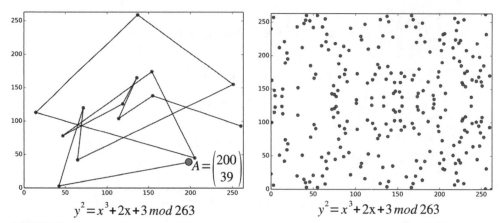

$$y^2 = x^3 + 2x + 3 \, mod \, 263 \qquad\qquad y^2 = x^3 + 2x + 3 \, mod \, 263$$

FIGURE 5.12   An example of a toy elliptic curve with 14 steps (left) and with the full cycle 270 steps (right)

requiring an exponential number of steps[17]. This is the hardness of the discrete logarithm problem.

Before using an elliptic curve algorithm, the parameters of the elliptic curve must be chosen. These parameters are a and b, the coefficients of the curve, p, the order of the prime field and A, the generator or starting point in the elliptic curve. Given these parameters, n, the number of points in the elliptic curve group can be computed by Hasse's Theorem (Paar and Pelzl, 2010).

Choosing the parameters of an elliptic curve is a non-trivial task. There are several standards that determine the parameters of the elliptic curve, with the goal of security[18]. Satoshi chose the parameters of the standard **secp256k1** for Bitcoin. These parameters are shown in Figure 5.13, which compares them to the parameters used in the toy example of Figure 5.12[19]. This comparison gives an idea of the intractability of the discrete logarithm problem for an elliptic curve used in practice.

The best known algorithms to break the elliptic curve discrete logarithm problem take steps proportional to $\sqrt{2^n} = 2^{n/2}$ where n is the number of bits of the key. secp256k1 uses 256-bit keys, so the number of steps needed to break it is 2^{128}. A common implementation of an elliptic curve computation takes 1 million CPU cycles. The CPUs available at the moment have clock speeds of around 3GHz. Thus a single computer is able to

---

[17] There are more efficient algorithms to solve the discrete logarithm than the brute-force algorithm described here, such as Pollard's ρ method or Shank's baby-step giant-step (Paar and Pelzl, 2010; Washington, 2008). However, all these methods still require a number of steps exponential in the size of the key, although the required steps for these methods are roughly the square root of the steps required for the brute-force method.

[18] There is some controversy over the parameters of elliptic curves, due to the suspicion that some government agencies were involved in weakening a standardized random number generator based on elliptic curves (Green, 2013). However, the parameters of this elliptic curve are different from the parameters of the elliptic curve used in Bitcoin.

[19] The notation 0x indicates that the number following is expressed in hexadecimal.

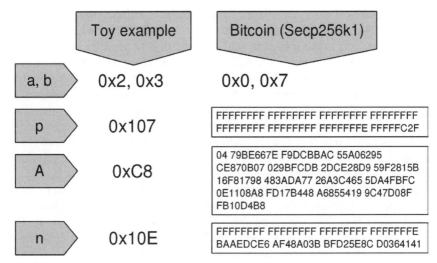

FIGURE 5.13 Parameters in secp256k1 vs toy example. All numbers in hexadecimal

process $2^{11.55}$ elliptic curve computations per second. Elliptic curve can be broken then in $2^{116.45}$ seconds using a single CPU, or about $2^{91.54}$ years, i.e. 3,599,861,590,422,752,58 3,114,293,248 years give or take some years. Throwing a million CPUs at the problem would reduce the time by a million, leaving it at 3,599,861,590,422,752,583,114 years, or roughly 260,859,535,537 times the age of the universe.

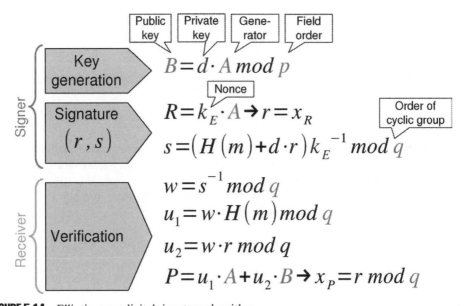

FIGURE 5.14 Elliptic curve digital signature algorithm

On more practical grounds, Figure 5.14 introduces **elliptic curve digital signature algorithm (ECDSA)**. ECDSA is the combination of elliptic curves with the DSA digital signature scheme, and is the signature schema used in Bitcoin. First, note that the parameters of the elliptic curve a, b, the order of the prime field p and the generator A are those given by the standard (secp256k1). Given these parameters, the order of the cyclic group q is given by Hasse's Theorem. First a private key is generated, choosing a random integer d less than q, the order of the cyclic group. It is crucial that the private key d is generated by a good random number generator.

The key generation part of the algorithm computes the public key B from the private key d using $B = d \cdot A \bmod p$, where A is the generator of the group. This step is fast, using the double-and-add algorithm.

To sign a message, first an **ephemeral random number** k_E is generated. As will be shown shortly, it is also important that this number is random, and that it is only used once, i.e. k_E is a **nonce**. The signature consists of a pair of two integers (r, s). The first number in the signature, r, is computed as the first coordinate of the point in the elliptic curve $R = k_E \cdot A$, while the second integer, s, is computed as:

$$s = \frac{\left(H(m)+d \cdot r\right)}{k_E} \bmod q = \left(H(m)+d \cdot r\right)k_E^{-1} \bmod q$$

where m is the message, $H(m)$ is the hash of the message and k_E^{-1} is the multiplicative inverse of k_E. The hashing step is important, to obtain an integer lower than q. The pair (r, s) is published as the signature.

The verification consists of several steps:

$$w = s^{-1} \bmod q$$

$$u_1 = w \cdot H(m) \bmod q$$

$$u_2 = w \cdot r \bmod q$$

$$(x_P, y_P) = u_1 \cdot A + u_2 \cdot B$$

$$x_P = r \bmod q$$

If after these steps $x_P = r \bmod q$, the signature is verified. The interested reader can consult Paar and Pelzl (2010) for the proof of correctness. Note that the signature generated by ECDSA, the pair (r, s), is quite compact.

Let's stress again the importance that the ephemeral random number k_E is not reused. If it were reused in two different signatures:

$$s_1 = \left(H(m_1)+d \cdot r\right)k_E^{-1} \bmod q$$

$$s_2 = \left(H(m_2)+d \cdot r\right)k_E^{-1} \bmod q$$

An attacker could subtract s_1 and s_2, to recover k_E:

$$s_1 - s_2 = \left(H(m_1) + d \cdot r\right)k_E^{-1} - \left(H(m_2) + d \cdot r\right)k_E^{-1} \bmod q = \left(H(m_1) - H(m_2)\right)k_E^{-1} \bmod q$$
$$\Rightarrow k_E = \left(H(m_1) - H(m_2)\right)/\left(s_1 - s_2\right) \bmod q$$

Thus k_E could be discovered by dividing $H(m_1) - H(m_2)$ by $s_1 - s_2$, all of which are known to the attacker. Once k_E is known, d can be computed:

$$d = (s_1 \cdot k_E - H(m_1))/r \bmod q$$

The lesson is that reusing the ephemeral random number k_E just once gives away the private key. This can be problematic for a Bitcoin address, because giving away the private key means losing control over the funds hold in that address. During the summer of 2013, it was discovered that the random number generator used in several Bitcoin Android wallets reused numbers. This led to bitcoins being stolen from several addresses (Buterin, 2013b).

5.5 OTHER CRYPTOGRAPHIC PRIMITIVES

This section introduces two algorithms related to public key cryptography whose applications will be addressed later. The first is blind signatures, which saw their first application in David Chaum's ecash (10.1). The second, Shamir secret sharing, can be used to divide the private keys associated with a Bitcoin address and distribute this information among several participants (section 8.6).

5.5.1 Blind Signatures

A **blind signature** is a cryptographic primitive introduced by David Chaum in 1982 as the base for a new anonymous payment method (Chaum, 1982).

David Chaum introduced the following analogy for blind signatures: assume an envelope with both a piece of paper—say a contract—and carbon paper inside it. The envelope is sealed and sent to the signer. The signer cannot see what is inside the envelope without breaking the seal. The signer signs the envelope, and thanks to the carbon paper, the contract inside the envelope gets signed too. The signer returns the envelope to the sender, who opens it and extracts the carbon-signed contract.

Blind signatures can be created using different public key schemes. David Chaum proposed using the RSA scheme. Other implementations are possible such as those based on the Diffie–Hellman key exchange scheme (Laurie, 2008) or elliptic curves. This section will present blind signatures in the RSA scheme as introduced in Chaum's original implementation.

In a simplified RSA signature algorithm, a signer generates a private key d and the corresponding public key (e, n) (section 5.3). The signer can sign a message m by computing the signature s:

$$s = m^d \bmod n$$

And anyone can verify the validity of this signature using the signer's public key e to compute:

$$s^e \bmod n = m^{e \cdot d} \bmod n = m \bmod n$$

The main goal of blind signatures is to get the signer to correctly sign the message m without getting any knowledge of it. To achieve this, the message is first blinded with a blinding factor. First a random number r is generated[20] and the blinding factor b is computed as $b = r^e \bmod n$. Next the message is blinded by multiplying it by the blinding factor $m_* = b \cdot m \bmod n$. The blinded message m_* is sent to the signer, who then signs it, producing:

$$s_* = m_*^d \bmod n = b^d \cdot m^d \bmod n = r^{e \cdot d} \cdot m^d \bmod n = r \cdot m^d \bmod n$$

The user can then divide s_* by r to retrieve $s = m^d \bmod n$, a correct regular RSA signature for the message m.

Blind signatures provide *unlinkability*: the signer cannot link a signed message to a user, even if presented with the unblinded signature. The proposed application of blinded signatures was an untraceable payment system (section 10.1). The blind signature technology can be also applied to voting systems, as noted in Chaum (1982).

As in RSA signatures, blind signatures produced using this implementation suffer from existential forgery attacks. See section 5.3 for some possible solutions.

5.5.2   Shamir Secret Sharing

Shamir secret sharing, introduced in Shamir (1979), is a cryptographic algorithm that divides a secret, i.e. a number, into several parts, giving each participant in the scheme one of them. The original secret can be assembled with the collaboration of the participants. The algorithm can be structured so that only a subset of the participants is required to reconstruct the original secret.

Shamir secret sharing can be applied to a private key p: this private key is divided into n pieces, in such a way that it can be recovered from any k pieces, but it is not possible to recover from $k - 1$ pieces. This scheme is often referred to as a (k, n) **threshold scheme**. The original implementation proposed by Shamir is based on polynomial interpolation. A polynomial of order $k - 1$ is defined by k distinct coefficients $a_0, ..., a_{k-1}$. In Shamir secret sharing scheme a polynomial of order $k - 1$ is created:

$$a_0 + a_1 \cdot x + a_2 \cdot x^2 + a_3 \cdot x^3 + ... + a_{k-1} \cdot x^{k-1}$$

The secret is the independent coefficient a_0. Each participant in the scheme is given a different point in this polynomial. Only when k of the participants cooperate can the correct polynomial be found and thus a_0 retrieved. If less than k participants cooperate, they cannot determine the polynomial and therefore cannot retrieve the secret a_0.

A nice property of elliptic curves is that if a (k, n) threshold scheme with polynomial interpolation is set up with the private key, the public key can be recovered from k of the n pieces exactly in the same way as the private key. Sum and multiply operations performed on the private key mirror directly into the same operations performed to the public key, i.e. the point in the elliptic curve.

---

[20] This random number must be securely generated, i.e. if a pseudo random number generator is used it must be ensured that it uses enough entropy.

Shamir secret sharing scheme can be useful to protect a cold-storage private key (section 8.2) against physical security breaches. This scheme can be used to divide the private keys and put the pieces in separate cold storages. This is sometimes referred to as **fragmented backups**. Note that a similar function can be performed by multisignature transactions (6.3).

5.6 BITCOIN ADDRESSES

A Bitcoin address is a representation (a hash) of the ECC public key. Figure 5.15 shows the steps to take to arrive at a Bitcoin address from the public key. Bitcoin uses OpenSSL[21] to perform the elliptic curve cryptography. OpenSSL represents the points in a elliptic curve using 65 bytes. The first byte is used to store the type of point in the elliptic curve. A value of 0x04 indicates that the point is uncompressed. A value of 0x02 or 0x03 indicates that the point is compressed. Whether this byte takes the value 0x02 or 0x03 depends on the parity (even or odd) of the omitted coordinate (y coordinate). An uncompressed point means that both the x and the y coordinates of the point are stored. A compressed point means that only the x coordinate of the elliptic curve point is kept: the y coordinate is backed out from x and the elliptic curve equation[22]. Following the leading byte are the two coordinates (x, y) of the elliptic curve point, in case of an uncompressed point, or the x coordinate for compressed points. Bitcoin uses an elliptic curve of 256 bits length, so each coordinate would take 256 bits = 32 bytes of space. An uncompressed point takes a total of 65 bytes = 1 byte for the type, and 32 bytes for each of the two coordinates.

The next step in Figure 5.15 is to hash the OpenSSL representation of the elliptic curve point, first using SHA256 and then RIPEMD160. The first hash function, i.e. the SHA256 produces a hash of 256 bits = 32 bytes. The second hashing function, RIPEMD160 produces a hash of 160 bits = 20 bytes. Satoshi chose this second hashing to reduce the size of the address, making transactions smaller, while keeping a reasonable bit size that makes collisions unlikely[23].

Finally the checksum (cs in Figure 5.15) is computed as the SHA256^2 of the result of the RIPEMD160 hash. Only the first 4 bytes of this hash are kept as a checksum. The purpose of this checksum is similar to the purpose of control digits in bank accounts or credit cards: to avoid transcription errors that would send funds to erroneous addresses. Bitcoin wallet software checks that the checksum of an address is correct before sending funds to that address. If a digit from a Bitcoin address were erroneously typed or copied, the wallet would catch the error and avoid sending funds to this address[24]. Sending funds

---

[21] OpenSSL is an open source cryptographic library that implements the SSL and TLS protocols. It is widely used by a large portion of the software that powers the internet.

[22] Compressing elliptic point curves following this procedure was covered by a patent (Bernstein, 2014).

[23] A collision of a hash function would result in two different keys being translated to the same address. Following the birthday paradox, a collision between two Bitcoin addresses would be found every 17,097,220,342,995,209,945,088 addresses, with a 0.01% probability of collision.

[24] Even if the wallet were to fail to catch the error and the transaction is somehow sent to the network, the nodes in the network would detect the invalid address and would drop the transaction.

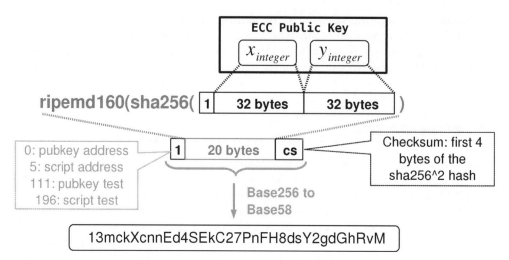

FIGURE 5.15 Address generation

to an address not linked to a known private key makes the funds unreachable, and therefore can be considered lost.

In the next step creating a Bitcoin address, a byte string is prepared to be encoded in Base58. This byte string starts with a byte indicating the *type of address*, followed by the 20 bytes result of the RIPEMD160 hash and finishing with the 4 bytes of checksum. The value of the type of address determines the beginning of the address once encoded in Base58. The type of address can take the following values[25]:

- **0** (decimal) for a **public key address** in the main net. This will result in an encoded address starting with *1*.
- **5** (decimal) for a **script address** in the main net. This will result in an encoded address starting with *3*. Script addresses will be discussed in section 6.6.
- **111** (decimal) for a public key address in the testnet[26]. This will result in an encoded address starting with *m* or *n*.
- **196** (decimal) for a script address in the testnet. This will result in an encoded address starting with *2*.

The last step of the procedure is to encode with Base58. **Base58** is a binary-to-text encoding algorithm that translates binary data to a text format. Base58 is similar to Base64

---

[25] A full list of the address prefixes can be found in Bitcoin wiki (2014l).

[26] Testnet is an alternative blockchain, used exclusively for testing. Testnet uses the same software that the main Bitcoin network but a different blockchain with a different genesis block and different tokens. Tokens for testnet can generally be freely obtained. The testnet has two main goals. First, to test new Bitcoin Core releases or features planned to be added to Bitcoin Core. Second, developers can test their products, such as wallets, in the testnet. If an application runs in the testnet it should run in the main net.

encoding[27]. Base64 uses the characters A–Z, a–z, 0–9 and the symbols + and /. Base58 uses the same characters, except for the symbols + and / and 0, O, I and 1. This avoids confusions, because in some fonts 0 and O and I and 1 have similar, even sometimes identical, representations. To encode a byte string, it is interpreted as a big integer, and successively divided by 58. The remainders at each step of this division are encoded as a character. All this procedure results in Bitcoin addresses that are between 27 and 34 characters long[28]. It is important to note that the characters in an address are case-sensitive.

The hashing of the ECC key makes it somewhat more resistant to attacks with quantum computers. Note, however, that this only applies to addresses whose outputs have never been used. As explained in more detail in Chapter 6, the ECC public key of an address is published in every transaction that spends an output from that address. Once an output from an address has been spent, the ECC public key is published in the blockchain, thus making the address susceptible to attacks by quantum computers. This reason, together with privacy reasons which will be explored in Chapter 13, argue in favor of not reusing addresses. Many wallet implementations generate a new address for the change of every transaction, see Chapter 6 for an explanation of change addresses.

This chapter has been quite theoretical. The role of public key cryptography in Bitcoin will become clearer in the next chapter.

---

[27] Base64 encoding is widely used in the internet when faced with the problem of transmitting binary data using a medium designed for text. This problem arises for example when sending a binary attachment to an email. Base64 ensures that the binary data remains intact during the transmission.

[28] The address can result in a variable length because leading 0 bytes are represented as a character 1. For details on Base58 encoding, see Bitcoin wiki (2014c).

CHAPTER 6

Transactions

Bitcoins do not reside in user's computers. They are entries into a distributed database called the blockchain, which will be explored in Chapter 7. Unlike centralized digital currencies, Bitcoin's blockchain does not store accounts and balances. The blockchain stores transactions.

Transactions are composed of a list of **transaction inputs (TxIn)** and a list of **transaction outputs (TxOut)**. Each transaction output (TxOut) holds two pieces of data: an amount and the recipient address[1]. The address is derived from the public key, as explained in section 5.6. Thus only the owner of the private key can unlock the funds stored in the TxOut. To unlock the funds, the owner of the private key must sign a transaction sending the funds to a new Bitcoin address.

A transaction input (TxIn) holds a reference to a previous transaction output, and a signature that proves that the funds in the previous TxOut it references can be spent[2]. This signature must be done with the private key associated with the public key in the Bitcoin address. If the signature does not match, the transaction is deemed invalid and dropped by the network.

A transaction groups several TxIns and TxOuts (at least one of each). The purpose of a transaction is to distribute the funds from the inputs to the outputs. Inputs in a transaction reference outputs in previous transactions. These outputs must not have been spent, otherwise the transaction is invalid.

For the transaction to be valid, the sum of the amounts of the inputs must be greater than or equal to the sum of the amounts of the outputs. The difference between the inputs and the outputs, if there is any, is the **fee** of the transaction. The transaction fee is collected by the miners that include the transaction in a block (Chapters 7 and 9).

Outputs in the blockchain can be spent only once, and they must be fully expended. If the amount of the outputs is greater than the amount to be spent, the transaction generates change. The sender of the transaction can collect this change by including a **change address** as an additional output to the transaction. The fact that the change address is usually controlled by the sender of the transaction can be actively used by data mining algorithms applied to the blockchain (Chapter 13). The address origin of the funds can be used as the change address in a transaction, but it is recommended to

---

[1] More precisely a TxOut holds a mathematical puzzle that must be solved to spend the output, as explained later.
[2] There is an additional piece of data in a TxIn: a sequence number. More on the sequence numbers later in section 6.5 and in Chapter 12.

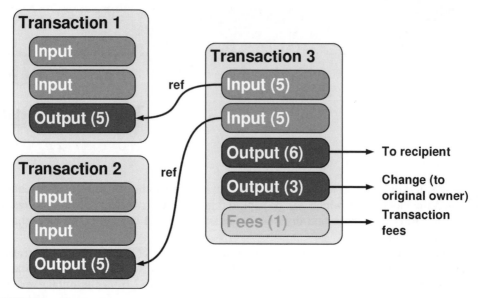

FIGURE 6.1   Transaction

generate a brand new change address for every transaction in order to increase privacy. To what extent this practice is effective will be discussed in Chapter 13.

Figure 6.1 represents an example of a transaction. In this example, the sender wants to send 6 mili-bitcoins to the recipient. However, the sender does not have at her disposal any transaction output with a balance of exactly 6 millibitcoins. She only controls two outputs with a balance of 5 millibitcoins each. Thus she creates a transaction[3] grouping these two outputs, and sends 6 millibitcoins to the recipient. She includes an output to an address under her control to receive the change for the transaction (3 millibitcoins). She leaves 1 millibitcoin as a fee for the miners[4]. Before sending the transaction into the network, she has to sign the two transaction inputs, to prove that she controls the addresses referenced by them.

The transaction is then sent to the network. The first node in the network that receives the transaction verifies that it is a **valid transaction**. If the transaction is correct, the node relays it to other nodes in the network. To verify that a transaction is valid, a node follows these steps:

- It checks that the previous outputs referenced by the transaction exist, and that they have not been spent. The node carries this check by consulting the Unspent transaction outputs cache (UTXO), introduced shortly.

---

[3] In reality the wallet software keeps track of the available outputs to spend, and selects them appropriately. This process is transparent for the user, who is shown a total amount of bitcoins available. Recent versions of several wallets, including Bitcoin Core Wallet, give users more control over which addresses to use in a transaction. These features are called **coin control**.

[4] This fee gives an incentive to the miners to include the transaction in the next block, speeding up confirmation of the transaction. This will become clearer in Chapter 7.

- It checks that the sum of the values of the inputs is greater than or equal to the sum of the outputs. That is, it checks that the transaction is not spending more than the available inputs. The difference between the sum of the value of the outputs and the sum of the value of the inputs is considered to be the fee left for the miner, and it is included in the coinbase transaction (section 7.4).
- It checks that the signatures for each of the inputs are valid, i.e. that each of the inputs is signed with the private key corresponding to the public key associated with the address it references. The process of signature checking is somewhat involved, and will be explored in sections 6.2 and 6.5.

Satoshi forced that a transaction output should be spent fully, because it is computationally more efficient. Bitcoin's software maintains an **unspent transaction outputs cache** (UTXO). The UTXO is a database containing only the unspent transaction outputs. The UTXO is very useful as it can be used to quickly check if new transactions are valid[5]. When a new transaction arrives, its inputs are looked up in the UTXO. If all the inputs are found there then the inputs correspond to valid previous outputs, and the transaction continues to be evaluated. If any of the inputs are not found in the UTXO, the transaction is not valid and can be discarded.

How the blockchain works will be explained in detail in Chapter 7. For the time being, assume that transactions are grouped into blocks that are confirmed together, i.e. are included in the blockchain at the same time.

Figure 6.2 shows the UTXO in action. Initially there are four unspent transactions in the network (0-1 to 0-4) and the UTXO holds these four TxOuts. In the next step a block is created that includes three transactions. The three transactions spend the four TxOuts in the UTXO, thus removing them. But the new transactions in the block also

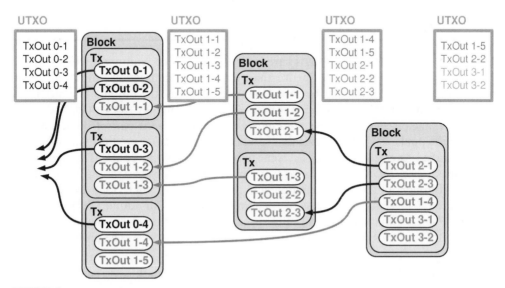

FIGURE 6.2 Unspent Transaction Outputs Cache (UTXO)

---

[5] The UTXO uses the **CCoinsViewCache** class, found in `coins.h`.

introduce give new outputs (1-1 to 1-5) and these outputs are included in the UTXO. The next block spends three of the five TxOuts in the UTXO (1-1 to 1-3) and adds three new TxOuts (2-1 to 2-3) and so on. With the arrival of each new block, outputs that are spent are removed from the UTXO, and new outputs created by the transactions in the block are added to the UTXO. The advantage of keeping a UTXO is that it is much smaller than the whole transaction database (the blockchain). This allows nodes to keep the UTXO in RAM, which considerably speeds up checking the validity of new transactions. Coming back to the question of where the bitcoins reside, it could be said that *bitcoins reside in the unspent outputs of transactions in the blockchain.*

There are uses for Bitcoin transactions aside from transferring value between addresses. Some of these will be introduced in Chapter 12. Most of these uses rely on the ability to store arbitrary data in the blockchain. Once the data is in the blockchain, its existence and validity is secured by the computational power of the Bitcoin network, much in the same way that bitcoins are secured. One way to store data in the blockchain is to use the recipient address as a data field. Say, to secure the data "Thisblobofdata", a transaction could be sent to the address *1Thisblobofdata*[6]. The private key associated with this address is not known. Thus any funds sent to this address would be lost. Understandably, the users of these types of transaction would want to spend as small an amount as possible, say 1 satoshi. The problem is that these outputs are included in the UTXO, and are never deleted from it, because they are unspendable. As a response to this practice, the developers of Bitcoin decided to introduce a minimum threshold amount below which a transaction is assumed unspendable. A transaction output below this threshold is called a **dust transaction**, because it is like dust that accumulates in the UTXO. The threshold is set currently to 546 satoshis (0.0000546 bitcoins), computed as the amount of an output whose minimum fee would amount to 1/3 of its value[7].

6.1 TRANSACTION SCRIPTS

Up to this point transaction outputs have been assumed to be sent to a Bitcoin address. However, the protocol is more flexible than this. Every transaction output creates a mathematical puzzle that must be solved in order to spend the output. The puzzle to unlock the funds and the solution to the puzzle are represented by two **scripts**. The script that creates the puzzle is called *<scriptPubKey>*, because it is the part of the script that contains the public key[8]. The puzzle that solves the *<scriptPubKey>*, thus unlocking the funds, is called *<scriptSig>*, because it is the part of the script that contains the signature. The names *<scriptPubKey>* and *<scriptSig>* are the names for these scripts in the source code and throughout the documentation, and this convention will be followed here.

Figure 6.3 presents the process of spending an output. An output (TxOut) creates a *<scriptPubKey>* that must be solved to spend the funds contained in that output. The input (TxIn) that tries to spend that output defines a *<scriptSig>*. The protocol checks

---

[6] This is a simplification, because a Bitcoin address is converted to Base58, so the data to include in the blockchain would not be human readable.

[7] For more details see "dust" comment in `core.h`.

[8] As will be seen later in the chapter, the *<scriptPubKey>* can contain other things besides the public key.

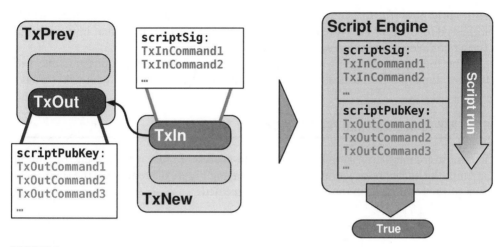

FIGURE 6.3 Scripting

that the *<scriptSig>* solves the mathematical puzzle created by the *<scriptPubKey>*. To do this, the protocol creates a full script by concatenating the *<scriptSig>* with the *<scriptPubKey>* and runs the whole script. If the final result evaluates to true, then the input is considered valid. If the script fails midway or if the end result does not evaluate to true, the input of the transaction is invalid and the whole transaction is rendered invalid and dropped[9].

The scripting language is *stack-based*[10]. Commands, represented by their **opcodes**, either place data on the stack or operate on data on the stack.

Functions that operate on the stack can only take their arguments from the top of the stack (popping the stack) and place their results on the top of the stack (pushing the stack). *<scriptSig>* pushes data to the stack[11], while *<scriptPubKey>* is a mixture of data to be pushed to the stack and functions that pop data from the stack to evaluate. This will be clear later in this chapter when the details of the scripts for the most common transactions are explored.

The scripting language in Bitcoin is quite flexible and powerful, but is *not* **Turing-complete**[12]. It was decided that way to avoid attacks on the network. If the scripting language were Turing-complete an attacker could craft a *<scriptPubKey>* that never finished, say because it enters an infinite loop. This would cause the nodes in the network that evaluate this script to stall and could bring the network down. For this reason it was decided that the scripting language would not contain loops. Nevertheless, the scripting language is

---

[9] If a transaction is rendered invalid by a node, it is not included in the block that the node is mining, and furthermore is not sent to other nodes. The transaction is just dropped from the list of pending transactions that the node maintains and is forgotten (section 7.4).

[10] Bitcoin scripting language is similar to a language called Forth.

[11] A transaction whose *<scriptSig>* includes any command (aside from data that is pushed to the stack) is considered non-standard, and will be dropped by most of the nodes in the network (6.7).

[12] Roughly speaking, a Turing-complete language can be used to instruct a computer to solve any computation problem.

sufficiently powerful to allow for a wide range of applications. Some of these will be addressed in Chapter 12. Note that there are alternatives to Bitcoin that implement full Turing-complete transaction systems, such as Ethereum (section 12.7.3).

The following sections will introduce several types of transactions possible with Bitcoin, starting with the most common. This material is based on Bitcoin wiki (2014v).

6.2 PAY-TO-ADDRESS AND PAY-TO-PUBLIC-KEY TRANSACTIONS

The most common transaction type is **pay-to-address**. Figure 6.4 represent the output and input of such a transaction. The accompanying Figure 6.5 represents the stacks after each of the commands in the <*scriptSig*> is executed.

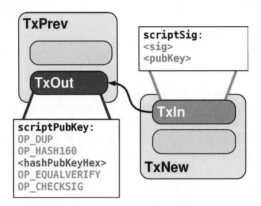

FIGURE 6.4   Pay to Bitcoin address transaction

Stack	Command
	`<sig>` `<pubKey>`
`<sig>` `<pubKey>`	`OP_DUP`

`<sig>`
`<pubKey>`
`<pubKey>`
	`OP_HASH160`

`<sig>`
`<pubKey>`
`<pubKeyHash>`
	`<hashPubKeyHex>`

`<sig>`
`<pubKey>`
`<pubKeyHash>`
`<hashPbKeyHex>`
	`OP_EQUALVERIFY`

`<sig>` `<pubKey>`	`OP_CHECKSIG`
1	

FIGURE 6.5   Stack for a pay-to-address script

The script engine evaluates first the *<scriptSig>* of the input. This *<scriptSig>* just places two pieces of data into the stack. As the stack is LIFO (last in first out), the data that the *<scriptSig>* first pushes into the stack will be needed the latest in the evaluation of the script. The first element to be pushed is *<sig>*, the signature of the (hash of the) new transaction (TxNew) with the private key corresponding to the public key *<pubKey>*. The second element to be pushed to the stack is the public key *<pubKey>* itself. Note that *<pubkey>* is not the Bitcoin address, but the elliptic curve public key from which the Bitcoin address derives (see Figure 5.15 for the relationship between the two).

With the *<scriptSig>* in place in the stack, the protocol now evaluates the *<scriptPubKey>* of the output. OP_DUP is a command that duplicates the last element of the stack, *<pubKey>* in this case. Next is OP_HASH160, a command that computes the Bitcoin address from the EC public key (again see Figure 5.15). The next command in *<scriptPubKey>* places *<hashPubKeyHex>* onto the stack. This is the Bitcoin address that the creator of the output decided to send the funds to. The next command in *<scriptPubKey>* is OP_EQUALVERIFY. This command checks that the last two elements on the stack are equal. If they are not, the transaction is tagged as invalid. After this verification, the two elements are retired from the stack.

The last command, OP_CHECKSIG checks that the transaction signature is correct. First, it hashes TxNew[13] and checks that *<sig>* is the correct signature for this hash. If the signature is correct the transaction is valid, and the script engine yields true. Otherwise the script engine yields false and the transaction is rejected. The process of signing a transaction has more options that will be explored in section 6.5.

In summary, the creator of the output transaction puts in the following condition to spend the output: the new transaction must be signed with the private key associated with the Bitcoin address *<hashPubKeyHex>*. The input that spends this input must provide two elements:

- An EC public key *<pubKey>* that when hashed corresponds to the address *<hashPubKeyHex>*.
- A signature *<sig>* of the whole transaction with the correct private key. This signature proves ownership of the Bitcoin address. Note that the transaction is hashed before signing it with the private key, as discussed in 5.2.

A **pay-to-public-key** transaction is similar to a pay-to-address transaction, but instead of including the address in the *<scriptPubKey>*, the EC public key itself is included. The *<scriptPubKey>* and *<scriptSig>* of a pay-to-public-key transaction are:

```
scriptSig: <sig>
scriptPubKey: <pubKey> OP_CHECKSIG
```

Note that after the *<scriptSig>* and the *<scriptPubKey>* are placed on the stack, the contents of the stack equal those of the last step in Figure 6.5.

---

[13] Before computing this hash, *<scriptSig>* is substituted by *<scriptPubKey>* from TxOut of TxPrev. Otherwise the hash could not be computed as the signature of the hash is included in *<scriptSig>*, which is itself part of the hash. This substitution breaks this circularity, allowing the transaction to be signed.

Pay-to-public-key transactions have the potential disadvantage that the funds are not resistant to quantum computers (section 14.6). Furthermore, the EC public key is bigger than an address, making the spending transaction bigger[14]. Thus it is rarely used in practice.

6.3   MULTISIGNATURE (M-OF-N) TRANSACTIONS

The Bitcoin protocol allows for transactions that require several signatures to be spent, called **m-of-n multisignature transactions** (Andresen, 2011). The *<scriptPubKey>* of these transactions specifies the n public keys. The spender of this output must provide signatures for at least m of these public keys. The *<scriptPubKey>* of a multisignature transaction is:

```
m <pubkey1> ... <pubkeyn> n OP_CHECKMULTISIGVERIFY
```

When executing this script, first the *<scriptSig>* is pushed onto the stack[15]. Then the *<scriptPubKey>* is pushed. The *<scriptSig>* of a valid multisignature transaction includes m valid signatures. The scripting engine then evaluates the command OP_CHECKMUL-TISIGVERIFY by comparing the first signature provided by *<scriptPubKey>* with the first public key in *<scriptSig>*. If they match, it proceeds to check the second signature in *<scriptPubKey>* and so on. If any of the signatures does not match, it tries with the next signature from *<scriptPubKey>* in line. Note that the scripting engine does not come back to check previously checked *<scriptPubKey>* signatures. Therefore the signatures in *<scriptSig>* must be ordered with respect to the signatures in *<scriptPubKey>*, otherwise the scripting engine will render the transaction as invalid.

It is possible that the same wallet has all the signatures that would unlock a m-of-n transaction. However, this would defeat the purpose of a multisignature transaction. It is more common that different parties to a transaction posses the different private keys to unlock the output. In this case, the transaction must be signed by all parties before it is released to the Bitcoin network. The process is as follows: the unsigned transaction is created by a party (it could be one of the signing parties). Then the unsigned (partially signed) transaction is passed around offline (meaning offline of the Bitcoin network) and signed by all the parties. Once the signature process is complete, the transaction is published in the Bitcoin network.

It is also possible to combine multisignature transactions with regular transactions, to create, for instance, a transaction that must be signed by a locking party and m-of-n other parties. The *<scriptPubKey>* for such a transaction would be:

---

[14] Although the transaction that spends this transaction output it is smaller as it does not have to include the EC public key in its *<scriptSig>*.

[15] The *<scriptSig>* of a multisignature transaction must push a OP_0 operation before pushing the public keys. OP_0 is required because there is a bug in the implementation of OP_CHECKMULTISIGVERIFY that makes it pop an extra element from the stack.

```
<pubkey> OP_CHECKSIGVERIFY
m <pubkey1> ... <pubkeyn> n OP_CHECKMULTISIGVERIFY
```

Uses of multisignature transactions include:

- **Three-party escrow**. Multisignatures allow entering into a contract with a non-trusted party. First, a mediator is agreed between the two parties. Second, the sender sends the funds to a multisignature output that requires 2-of-3 signatures. The three public keys included in the *<scriptPubKey>* are those of the sender, the receiver, and the mediator. If after some time the sender and the receiver agree that the transaction should proceed, they both can sign the transaction without the need to involve the mediator. However, if the sender and the receiver don't agree that the transaction should proceed, the mediator is brought in and decides who should receive the funds. Suppose the mediator decides the sender should receive the funds back. In this case the mediator and the sender can both sign a transaction unlocking the funds and sending them back to the sender. This escrow technology opens the door to safe (for the buyer) e-commerce transactions with Bitcoin.
- **Wallet protection service**. The user sets up a wallet by sending the funds to a 2-of-2 multisignature output. One of the two private keys resides in the user's computer. The other key is kept by the wallet service provider. To spend the funds from this wallet, the user first signs the transaction and the wallet software in the computer sends the partially signed transaction to the wallet service provider. The wallet service provider then contacts the user through a different channel (2-factor authentication). After the user is authenticated through this second channel, the provider signs the transaction with its private key and publishes the transaction. Note that the user should require the provider to send its private key for safekeeping, or better use 2-of-3 multisignature transactions (section 4.5), otherwise the wallet service provider could hold the user ransom, and require a bribe to unlock the funds.

The number of signatures available for a multisignature transaction is currently limited to 3. This is due to the current limitation of *<scriptSig>* to 200 bytes. This restriction is set to be lifted in future versions of the protocol to 500 bytes, allowing for a larger number of signatures.

Several uses of multisignature transactions will be reintroduced in Chapter 12 in the context of advanced contracts.

6.4   OTHER TRANSACTION TYPES

If a transaction has an empty *<scriptPubKey>*, anyone can spend it with the following *<scriptSig>*:

```
OP_TRUE
```

That is, the *<scriptSig>* just puts the value 1 into the stack, so the transaction is correct. As anyone can spend this transaction, the first person to spend it will be the miner that is including it in the block, so these transactions can be considered equivalent to fees for the miners. As this type of transaction is not standard, nodes running Bitcoin Core will not rely it[16].

Another example of a non-standard transaction is the one encoded in the following *<scriptPubKey>*:

```
OP_RETURN <additional data>
```

The OP_RETURN renders the output unspendable. Additional data can be included in the *<scriptPubKey>* after the OP_RETURN command. This type of transactions are called provable prune-able or unspendable. The reason is that, because nobody can spend these transactions, the output can be removed from the UTXO. These transactions were introduced in version 0.9 of the protocol as a way to solve the issue of users trying to insert random data into the blockchain. The main advantage of this transaction type is that it does not clutter the UTXO with unspendable transactions when inserting data into the blockchain. A more complete explanation of the various ways of inserting data into the blockchain will be explored in Section 12.6.

There are many more commands available to include in a transaction *<scriptPub-Key>*. A full list can be found in Bitcoin wiki (2014v). Some of these commands are currently deactivated in the code (for instance OP_MUL, OP_DIV, OP_OR). It is possible that some of these disabled commands, or new commands will be added to future versions of Bitcoin if the need arises. However, the process of adding or changing functionality in Bitcoin must be done conservatively, in order not to introduce vulnerabilities or break existing clients.

6.5   TRANSACTION SIGNATURE

To spend the funds stored in a transaction output, the spending transaction must be signed with the private key associated with the address where the funds are stored. Signing a transaction encompasses the following steps[17]:

- A copy of the transaction is made, so that the original is not corrupted.
- The transaction to be signed does not contain the *<scriptSig>*, as the signature is part of the *<scriptSig>*, and therefore the *<scriptSig>* will be assembled after the signature. In place of *<scriptSig>*, the *<scriptPubKey>* from the output it references is copied.
- The whole transaction is then hashed and this hash is signed with the private key corresponding to the Bitcoin address of the output that is being spent.

This section will cover some transaction details this description has glossed over. Figure 6.6 shows additional elements that are included in a transaction.

A transaction has a **lock time** variable, named *nLockTime* in the code. Also, each input in a transaction has a **sequence number**, named *nSequence*. A transaction is only

---

[16] However, a miner encountering this type of transaction would gladly include it in the block it is mining to receive the extra fees.
[17] The code for transaction signing can be found in the function SignSignature in `script.cpp`.

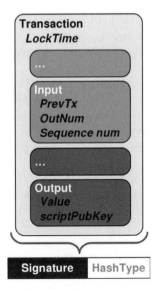

FIGURE 6.6   Elements of a transaction

considered final when its lock time has been reached or when the sequence number of all its inputs are set to the maximum plausible value[18].

The lock time originally allowed the sending of a pending (non-finalized) transaction that could be replaced at a future time. This technique is called **transaction replacement**. The period to replace such a transaction is determined by the value of *nLockTime* and can be specified as either a block number of a time-stamp. If the value of *nLockTime* is lower than 500000000, it is interpreted as a block number[19]. If it is above, it is interpreted as a Unix date[20]. Note that for a transaction to be replaceable the sequence number of at least one of its inputs must be lower than the maximum. Successive versions of a transaction could be broadcast with higher sequence numbers for its inputs. This way a transaction could be modified by the parties involved before being published in the blockchain. A transaction is considered final when the *nLockTime* is reached or all the sequence numbers of the inputs are at the maximum.

Transactions whose *nLockTime* have not been reached or whose sequence numbers have not been set to their maximum are called **unfinalized transactions**. Unfinalized transactions are not included in the blockchain, and are dropped by the nodes that receive them. This was not always the case: before 2010 unfinalized transactions were kept by the nodes, waiting for the lock time to be reached, or for a new substituting transaction that was final (i.e. its lock time was reached or the sequence number of all its inputs were set to the maximum). These unfinalized transactions resided in the unconfirmed

---

[18] Sequence numbers are represented as unsigned integer numbers. The maximum allowed value for an unsigned integer depends on the platform, i.e. 32 bits versus 64 bits, and is referred in the documentation as *UINT_MAX*.

[19] It is estimated that block number 500000000 will be reached in year 11,521 AD.

[20] Unix date is defined as the integer that represents the number of seconds lapsed since 00:00:00 UTC January 1, 1970.

transactions' memory pool or mempool for short (section 7.4). Allowing unfinalized transactions to accumulate in the mempool is a security risk: an attacker could perform a **denial of service (DoS)** attack against the Bitcoin network by filling up the mempool of the mining nodes with time-locked transactions.

Chapter 12 will explore several applications where the ability for several parties to create a transaction and sign it sequentially is important. This functionality is still possible even with transaction replacement disabled: parties can send the partially completed transactions through alternative channels. Using the mempool to store partially completed transactions was a convenience, but most advanced contracts are still possible without it.

Another feature of transactions showed in Figure 6.6 are signature hash types. Every signature in a *<scriptSig>* includes a flag which indicates which inputs and which outputs are covered by the signature. This flag is called the **hash type** of the signature, and can take three values:

- **SIGHASH_ALL**. The signature covers all the outputs. This means that changing any of the outputs will make the transaction invalid. Modifying any output in a transaction would require all the inputs to be signed again, reflecting this change. The interpretation is: "agree to spend the input if everybody else spends theirs and the outputs are the ones specified." This option does not allow other inputs to update their sequence numbers. It is the default option in the protocol.
- **SIGHASH_NONE**. The signature does not include any of the outputs. This means any of the outputs can be changed at will, and the signature will still be valid. The interpretation is: "agree to spend the input if everybody else spends theirs, but do not care about the outputs." This option allows other inputs to update their sequence numbers.
- **SIGHASH_SINGLE**. The signature includes only the output of the same index as the input. That is, if the input is in third position, the signature only covers the output in the third position. The interpretation is: "agree to spend the input as long as my output is the one specified, and do not care about the others." This option allows other inputs to update their sequence numbers.

Signatures have an additional flag, **SIGHASH_ANYONECANPAY**, that can take a true or false value. This flag can be combined with any of the previous three flags[21]. If set to true, the signature only includes the current input. If set to false, the signature includes all the inputs. The interpretation is: "any other inputs can be added to the transaction." This flag is useful, for example in a crowd-funding transaction (12.5.1).

The flexibility of the transaction scripting language, combined with the different ways in which a transaction can be signed and the ability to insert random data into the blockchain, creates many opportunities for innovative types of applications. Some of these will be explored in Chapter 12.

---

[21] All these flags are packed together in an integer variable named **nHashType**. This variable can be found in `script.cpp`. The code that takes out the inputs and outputs not covered by the hashtype prior to signing, can be found in CTransactionSignatureSerializer::Serialize in `script.cpp`.

The scripting language is very powerful but it should be used with great care. It is easy to get some parameters of a script wrong, with disastrous consequences. Here are two examples of real world errors (Shirriff, 2014b). The first mistake created the following *<scriptPubKey>*:

```
OP_DUP
OP_HASH160
0
OP_EQUALVERIFY
OP_CHECKSIG
```

Note that in place of a valid address, a 0 is included, thus making the transaction unredeemable. The second bug in a *<scriptPubKey>* is found in some coinbase transactions:

```
OP_IFDUP
OP_IF
OP_2SWAP
OP_VERIFY
OP_2OVER
OP_DEPTH
```

This script is meaningless and not redeemable. To understand why it was included in some transactions, the trick is to convert the hexadecimal representation of this script to ASCII: the *<scriptPubKey>* then reads literally "script."

6.6 PAY-TO-SCRIPT-HASH (P2SH)

At the end of 2010 there was a push to make multisignature transactions standard to allow for more secure wallets. At this point multisignature transactions, as introduced in section 6.3, were already part of the protocol. In order to use a multisignature transaction the sender of the funds has to create a *<scriptPubKey>* with all the necessary information. This information includes all the addresses and the number of valid signatures required to spend the output. One possibility to make multisignature transactions standard would be to create a new type of address that passes all this information from the recipient of a transaction to the sender, so that the recipient could present the sender this address. But an address containing all this information would be very long. For example, to encode a 2-of-3 multisignature address, the address would be roughly three times that of a regular transaction. Furthermore, as a multisignature *<scriptPubKey>* is bigger than a regular pay-to-address *<scriptPubKey>* it is more expensive to include in the blockchain, requiring bigger fees. These fees are paid by the sender of the transactions, while it is the receiver who selects a multisignature address.

The chosen solution was to create a new type of transaction that encoded the conditions to redeem a transaction in the *<scriptSig>* rather than in the *<scriptPubKey>*. That is, the instructions to spend the output are shifted from the output to the input, or from the sender to the receiver of the funds. This type of transaction is called

pay-to-script-hash, or **P2SH** for short[22]. The main idea behind P2SH is that the script used to spend a transaction resides in the *<scriptSig>* and that the *<scriptPubKey>* just holds a hash of such a script. The hash of the script makes sure the output can only be spent as the recipient of the funds intended.

BITCOIN IMPROVEMENT PROPOSALS (BIPS)

A proposal to change part of the Bitcoin protocol is drafted in a document called a **Bitcoin Improvement Proposal (BIP)**. BIPs are technical documents that are discussed by the Bitcoin developers and the community at large (including miners, companies using Bitcoin services, and so on), usually through the mailing list and the forums. When a BIP is controversial, or there are several incompatible proposals, it is subject to a vote. The participants in the voting are miners, or more precisely mining pool operators. Miners are responsible for rolling out the changes in the protocol. If a significant portion of miners are against a change, they can refuse to roll it out, causing a fork in the blockchain (Chapter 7). For this reason it was decided that sensitive changes to the code should be voted by miners, as they are the ones with the power to make or break such a change.

To vote, miners usually include a string with the result of their vote in the input of their coinbase transaction (coinbase transactions will be covered in section 7.4). Every block mined includes a vote, thus representation is proportional to mining power. The blockchain is observed for a period, for instance 1000 blocks, to recount the votes.

Note the subtle governance of the Bitcoin protocol: developers propose a change to the protocol, but it is miners who vote for or against it. A proposal is accepted if a majority (55% or greater) of the miners accept it. Once a proposal is accepted, it is implemented in the code and distributed. A list of the BIPs and their status can be found in Bitcoin wiki (2014d).

Figure 6.7 illustrates a multisignature transaction encoded both in the original way (on the left) and as a P2SH transaction (on the right). The *<scriptSig>* of the P2SH transaction includes the information of both the *<scriptSig>* and the *<scriptPubKey>* of the original multisignature transaction. The *<scriptPubKey>* of the P2SH transaction is very short: it includes two operators and a 20-byte hash of the script that is included in the *<scriptSig>*. The general layout of the *<scriptSig>* and the *<scriptPubKey>* of a P2SH transaction is:

```
scriptSig: [signature(s)] {script to be evaluated}
scriptPubKey: OP_HASH160 [20-byte-hash of {script to be
   evaluated} ] OP_EQUAL
```

---

[22] There was a lot of debate on how to engineer this type of transaction. Three proposals were made: BIP 12 (a.k.a. OP_EVAL), BIP 16 (a.k.a. P2SH) and BIP 17 (a.k.a. CHV, check-hash-verify). These were put to a vote, resulting in BIP 16 winning (see box).

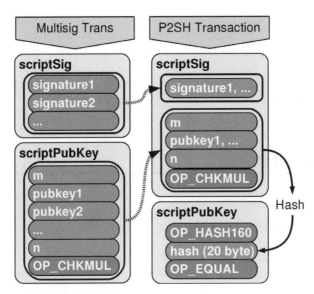

FIGURE 6.7 Pay-to-script-hash transaction

A new type of address was also created, the **script address**. The information encoded in a script address is just the 20 bytes of the hash script. This makes for very compact addresses. The rules to create a script address are similar to those introduced in section 5.6 for regular addresses. However, instead of hashing an elliptic curve public key, as in a regular address, in a script address the script itself is hashed. This hash is prefixed with a value of 5 (decimal) before Base58 encoding. This results in script addresses that start with 3.

The <*scriptSig*> of a P2SH transaction does not allow arbitrary scripts to avoid security problems. Allowing arbitrary code in a <*scriptSig*> could result in Denial of Service (DoS) attacks. An attacker could craft transactions with a <*scriptSig*> that is very costly to evaluate, thus draining the computational (or memory) resources of the nodes, causing the network to slow down, new transactions to be dropped, and so on[23]. Allowing script code in the <*scriptPubKey*> is not so problematic, because the code in the <*scriptPubKey*> is run only when attempting to spend an output: the transaction with this code must be already in the blockchain, and funds have been sent to it. Therefore to perform a DoS attack placing the malicious script in the <*scriptPubKey*>, an attacker must spend funds. Many features in the scripting language are disabled and the Bitcoin developers are cautious when making changes to the scripting language for this very reason.

The only allowable scripts in a P2SH transaction are pay-to-public-key, pay-to-address, and multisignature transactions[24].

---

[23] An example of how such an attack could be done if an arbitrary script is allowed can be found in the source code in `main.cpp`: DUP CHECKSIG DROP ... repeated 100 times ... OP_1.

[24] The function that validates the valid scripts in a P2SH transaction is AreInputsStandard in `main.cpp`.

When using P2SH transactions, a lot of care should be taken because any error could render the transaction unspendable. Also note that the details of the transaction script are not stored in the blockchain initially, only the hash of the script is. Therefore, the creator of the transaction must keep a copy of the script that generates this hash. Losing the copy of the script may not render the transaction unspendable, but can lead to the need for considerable reverse-engineering work to reconstruct it from the hash present in the transaction output.

6.7   STANDARD TRANSACTIONS

As of the time of writing, the Bitcoin implementation defines six types of transaction[25]:

- **TX_PUBKEY** or pay-to-public-key. The <*scriptPubKey*> of this type of transaction is [OP_PUBKEY OP_CHECKSIG].
- **TX_PUBKEYHASH** or pay-to-address. The <*scriptPubKey*> of this type of transaction is [OP_DUP OP_HASH160 OP_PUBKEYHASH OP_EQUALVERIFY OP_CHECKSIG].
- **TX_SCRIPTHASH** or pay-to-script-hash (P2SH). The <*scriptPubKey*> of this type of transaction is [OP_HASH160 <20-byte-hash> OP_EQUAL]. Non-standard transactions placed in the <*scriptSig*> of a P2SH transaction are not allowed.
- **TX_MULTISIG** or multisignature transaction. The <*scriptPubKey*> of this type of transaction is [m sig1 ... sign n OP_CHECKMULTISIG]. A multisignature transaction is considered "standard" if $n \leq 3$ and $m \leq n$.
- **TX_NULL_DATA** also known as OP_RETURN transactions. The <*scriptPubKey*> of this type of transaction is [OP_RETURN <data>].
- **TX_NONSTANDARD** If it is not any of the five previous transactions.

The first five types are deemed **standard transactions**. As of the time of writing, only standard transactions are forwarded or mined by nodes that implement the reference Bitcoin software. To include a **non-standard transaction** in the blockchain, an agreement must be reached with a miner: the non-standard transaction will then be included in the

TABLE 6.1   Types of transaction. Data from webbtc.com on June 17, 2014

Transaction type	Percentage
Pay-to-address	99.062%
Pay-to-pubkey	0.847%
Multisignature	0.056%
P2SH	0.032%
OP_RETURN	0.002%
Unknown	0.002%

---

[25] The transaction type is one of the results of running the function **Solver** in script.cpp.

blockchain when this miner resolves a block. Depending on the hash rate of the miner, this can take a while (Chapter 7).

Table 6.1 shows the occurrence of each type of transaction. Although this chapter has introduced several different types of transactions, most of the transactions are still of the pay-to-address type, and only a small fraction are multisignature, P2SH, or OP_RETURN transactions. However, the new types of transactions are set to become more important in the future, once service providers (such as wallets) start to offer multisignature transactions, or even make them the default.

CHAPTER 7

The Blockchain

The blockchain is arguably the most important innovation introduced by Bitcoin. It is the missing link that makes distributed peer-to-peer digital currencies possible. The blockchain is in essence a distributed database holding all the Bitcoin transactions since the beginning (January 3, 2009) and a method to secure this database.

The blockchain keeps a secure list of all the transactions. However, there are relevant questions, such as whether a particular transaction output is spendable, that the blockchain does not answer directly. Software that uses the blockchain, like mining nodes or wallets, has to parse the blockchain to extract the relevant information. This information extracted from the blockchain is usually fed to a database. For instance, the Bitcoin node software uses LevelDB, a key-value store to keep a copy of the unspent transaction outputs (UTXO). To populate this database, the whole blockchain has to be parsed as explained at the beginning of Chapter 6 (see Figure 6.2).

The blockchain uses **proof-of-work** to secure the distributed database. This means the blockchain is secured against tamper attempts by the computational power that has been applied to create it. An attacker wishing to change the blockchain would have to apply a computational power equivalent to all the computational power spent from that point in time to the present. Furthermore, the attacker would have to outrun the legitimate Bitcoin network, which keeps adding entries to the distributed database. In other words, it would have to catch up, computationally speaking, with the legitimate network to change the information in the database. Attacks to the blockchain will be covered in section 7.5.

Section 7.1 introduces hash functions, the cryptographic primitive used in the blockchain. Section 7.2 presents time-stamping, a way to secure information at a certain point in time. Section 7.3 introduces the proof-of-work concept. Section 7.4 puts together the previous sections, explaining how the Bitcoin blockchain works. The last sections cover particular details of the blockchain, such as double-spend attacks and how to protect against them (section 7.5), how to update blocks quickly (section 7.6), and scalability with an increasing rate of transactions (section 7.7).

7.1 HASH FUNCTIONS

A **hash function** is an algorithm that takes data of arbitrary length as an input and outputs a bit-string of fixed length, named the **hash value**. The hash value is always the same for the same input data. A hash function is a map from the set of input data (of arbitrary length) to the set of hash values, with the particularity that small differences in the input data produce large differences in the result. A common requirement is that hash computation is fast. Hash functions are widely used in computing, for instance to quickly locate data records using hash tables. The size of the hash values is usually smaller than the size of possible input data. Therefore many input data points will share a single hash value.

A good hash function should distribute input values to hash values proportionally, so that every hash value is linked to roughly the same number of possible input values. One way to achieve this proportionality is making the hash value "behave" as randomly as possible. Note that although the hash value "behaves" as though it was random, it is still deterministic: given an input, its hash value will always be the same[1].

Bitcoin uses **cryptographic hash functions** to perform proof-of-work. Cryptographic hash functions (sometimes called secure hash functions) impose additional requirements over regular hash functions:

- **One-wayness (preimage resistance)**. Given the hash value, it must be computationally infeasible to find out the input data. As will become clear later, this is a key property for the application of proof-of-work.
- **Weak collision resistance**. Given an input it is computationally infeasible to find another input with the same hash value.
- **Strong collision resistance**. It is computationally infeasible to find two input data points that result in the same hash value.

Bitcoin uses SHA256^2 as its proof-of-work function. SHA256^2 is the application of the SHA256 hashing function twice. SHA256 is part of a set (SHA-2) of hash functions designed by the NSA and published by NIST in 2001. SHA256 is a hash function of this family whose output is 256 bits long.

Figure 7.1 shows an example of the SHA256^2 hash function. The input value at the top of the figure is the string "This is the message #1". The hash value in hexadecimal

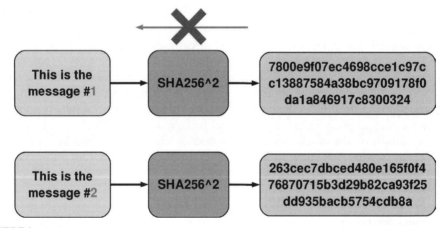

FIGURE 7.1 Hash functions

---

[1] Sometimes hash functions are compared to meat grinders. The analogy works in the sense that it is not possible to revert from the hamburger to the piece of meat. However, the analogy is not so good in stressing that, given the same exact piece of meat, the hamburger must be exactly the same.

is "7800e9f07...". In the lower part of the figure the input value is the string "This is the message #2" and the hash value is "263cec7db...". Note how a change of just one digit in the message leads to a completely different hash value. A good hash function behaves like a random mapping from the input value to the hash value.

SHA256 meets the preimage resistance requirement: given the hash value it is computationally infeasible to recover the message that generated it. Computationally infeasible means that there is no known algorithm that can recover the message within a time that is related polynomially to the size of the input. What this means in practice is that the best known algorithms to break a hashing function, i.e. recover the message given the hash, are brute-force algorithms that take an impractical (exponential) amount of time.

Many cryptographic hash functions, SHA256 among them, are constructed from a simpler primitive called a **compression function**. A compression function operates on an input of a fixed length and produces an output of the same length. The goal of a compression function is to scramble the bits of the input in a deterministic but complicated way to arrive at the output. This is achieved putting the original message through a series of data-shifting and mixing operations with random-like constants[2].

The **Merkle-Damgård construction** is a recipe to build cryptographic hash functions that accept input data of arbitrary length using a compression function as a building block. Merkle and Damgård demonstrated that, if the compression function is collision-resistant, then the whole construction is also collision-resistant. Figure 7.2 shows the general construction. In the case of SHA256, the compression function (labeled f in the figure) operates on 256 bits of data. The compression function accepts two inputs: an intermediate hash value[3] and a block of input data. To compute the SHA256 hash, the input data (also called the message) is first broken into blocks of 256 bits length. The end of the message is padded with zeros and the length of the message (the figure is a simplification, see National Institute of Standards and Technology (2001) for details). The intermediate hash value is initialized to *IHV* (Initial Hash Value). Then the compression function is applied to each message block, using the hash value from the last step as the

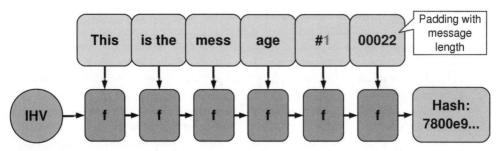

FIGURE 7.2 Merkle-Damgård construction

---

[2] The compression function itself is usually created from a building block which is iterated several times, 64 times in the case of SHA256. The interested reader can find the details in National Institute of Standards and Technology (2001).

[3] The intermediate hash value is used to initialize the internal registers at the beginning of the first round (National Institute of Standards and Technology, 2001).

intermediate hash value into the next step. The hash value yielded by the last step is the SHA256 hash of the whole message.

SHA256, as with most cryptographic hash functions, was designed to be fast on general purpose hardware. Also, because the round of the compression function uses only bitwise operations and additions with 32-bit registers, it is suitable for efficient hardware implementation. This has given rise to the ASIC mining industry, which will be covered in Chapter 9.

PASSWORD HASHING

Many websites face the problem of authenticating users. It is common practice to issue or allow users to choose a user-name and password that will be subsequently used for authentication. Websites could retain this information in clear-text. This is easy to implement: each time a user logs on, the password sent along is just compared with the stored clear-text password. However, this is considered a very bad security practice, because if the website were to be compromised the passwords of all its users would automatically get leaked.

Thus it is recommended that websites do not keep a copy of the clear-text password, but of the hashed password. When the user logs on, the password sent along is hashed, and this hash is compared with the stored hash. If the website gets hacked, then only hashed passwords get leaked. To obtain the clear-text passwords from the hashed passwords, the attacker would have to brute-force the hashes. Brute-forcing is done by trying many possible clear-text passwords to see if their hashes match the desired hash. This is a time-consuming process, but there are some shortcuts. One of these shortcuts is to construct **rainbow tables**. If an attacker wants to crack many passwords at the same time, she could store a list of passwords along with their hashes in a database (called a rainbow table). Once a rainbow table is available, some passwords can be cracked just by searching their hashes in the table.

To protect against rainbow tables it is advisable to salt passwords. A nonce (a random number used only once), called the salt, is stored along with the hash of each password. The **salt** is prefixed to the clear-text password before hashing. This defeats the purpose of rainbow tables. It is still possible to brute-force passwords, but it has to be done one password at a time, worsening the economies of scale of password cracking.

Many standardized hash functions, including SHA256, are fast. This can be a problem for password hashing, because fast hash functions make password cracking easier. One possible solution is to apply the hash function multiple times. For instance, the Linux operating system allows specifying a number of rounds (for instance 50,000) that the hashing function will be applied to a (salted) password prior to storing it in the /etc/shadow file. Using many rounds slows password cracking attempts.

> Another approach to protect against brute-force password cracking is to use a key-derivation function. A **key-derivation function** is a function that intentionally takes a large amount of time to evaluate. As legitimate users only need to perform this computation once when authenticating, its difficulty can be set such that it takes a slightly noticeable time, say half a second, on regular hardware. An attacker trying to brute-force the hash would have to spend half a second for each trial, slowing her down considerably. Examples of key-derivation functions are slow hash functions such as in **PBKDF2** (Kaliski, 2000) or **bcrypt** (Provos and Mazières, 1999) and **memory-hard hash functions** such as **scrypt** (Percival, 2012). Scrypt will be covered in section 11.1 when introducing Litecoin.

The Merkle-Damgård construction is vulnerable to **length extension attacks**. Suppose an attacker does not know the message m, but knows its hash $H(m)$. She could compute the hash of a message $m\|m'$ (where $\|$ denotes concatenation) by using $H(m)$ as the IHV to the hash algorithm and then feeding it m', thus obtaining $H(m\|m')$ as a result[4]. One solution to the length extension problem is proposed in Ferguson et al., (2010): hash twice. That is, apply the hash function again to the hash of the message[5].

It is believed that Satoshi chose SHA256^2 instead of plain SHA256 as a protection against length-extension attacks. It is not clear how to exploit length extension against the proof-of-work, but it seems that Satoshi decided to play it safe. Besides, the main downside of double hashing, namely an increase in computation time, is irrelevant in Bitcoin, because the whole point of the proof-of-work is to make finding the nonce computationally expensive (section 7.3).

7.2 TIME-STAMP

A digital **time-stamp** is analogous to a physical time-stamp, such as a postmark on a letter or a rubber stamp from an official organism. A digital time-stamp proves that certain information—say a digital document—existed at a particular time. It has many applications, such as documenting that a contract between two parties occurred, that a transaction in a website materialized, or indeed that a group of transactions in a digital currency took place.

The information included in a digital time-stamp is usually the hash of the data to secure. Using a hash has several advantages. First, the information to be time-stamped can be kept private and separate from the medium used to secure the time-stamp. Second, a hash is usually significantly smaller than the information that generated it, reducing storage costs. Third, digital signatures usually work best on data of a predetermined size.

---

[4] If the hash of m is padded and the length has been appended to it, the attacker might not be able to compute the hash of an extended message $m\|m'$ but of $m\|padding + length(m)\|m'$. This might still be acceptable for some attacks.
[5] Bitcoin applies the double hashing differently than in Ferguson et al. (2010). Bitcoin computes $H(H(m))$, whereas Ferguson et al. (2010) recommend computing $H(H(m)\|m)$.

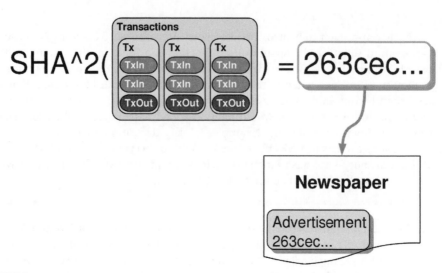

FIGURE 7.3   Time-stamping a group of transactions by publishing their hash in a newspaper

There are several ways to secure a digital time-stamp. A naive method would send a trusted party a copy of the information, and the trusted party would store in a (hopefully) safe place the data received, together with the time of reception. This method is susceptible to the trusted third party losing the database or being compromised. A second method would rely on a trusted third party, called a **Time-Stamping Authority** (TSA) (also called a **digital notary**) to sign with its private key a combination of the data to be secured together with the time when this data was communicated to the authority. This signature would be sent back to the original owner of the data. The security of this set-up rests on the integrity of the TSA. If the TSA decided to collaborate with a cheater, it could time-stamp a document retroactively[6].

A third method to secure a digital time-stamp would be to publish the hash of the data in a public place, such as a newspaper. This is shown in Figure 7.3, where a group of transactions is hashed, and the hash is published in an advertisement in a public newspaper. An attacker wishing to change any of the transactions would have to find a collision with the published hash[7], or alternatively subvert all the papers with a copy of the published hash.

A time-stamping authority could use this idea, publishing for instance a hash of the signature of a time-stamp. It would, however, be costly to publish a hash for every time-stamp. A TSA could achieve economies of scale by "mixing" the hashes of multiple time-stamps before publishing. Combining the hashes of multiple data to be time-stamped can be done efficiently using Merkle trees, covered in section 7.6.

---

[6] The time stamping authority method can be refined to account for a non-trusted TSA (Haber and Stornetta, 1991; Massias et al., 1999).

[7] The attacker would have to find a change in any transaction such that when all the transactions are hashed again, the original hash is recovered. If the hash function is collision-resistant, this attack is computationally infeasible.

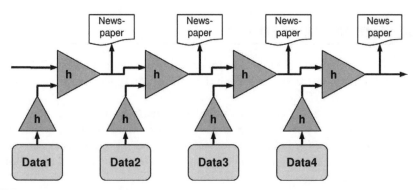

FIGURE 7.4 Linked time-stamping

Figure 7.4 introduces another refinement to further secure digital time-stamps: **linked time-stamps**. The main insight is that if the hash to be published is linked to the previously published hash, this will help further secure the older hash. An attacker who wishes to change some data from the older hash would have to find a *double* collision in the hash function: one collision for the old hash and another for the new published hash. After another step in the chain, the attacker would have to find a *triple* collision. Thus the hash chain increases exponentially the security of older hashes. Although in Figure 7.4 the hash is published at each point in time, hashes could be published with a longer periodicity to save costs.

In summary, a Time-Stamping Authority could work in the following way. First, data to be time-stamped from clients is gathered during a certain period. When the collection period finishes, the data is hashed together using, for instance, a Merkle tree (section 7.6). The resulting hash (root of the Merkle tree) is hashed together with the final hash of the previous time period, and this final hash is published.

A digital currency could use this method to secure transactions. But this requires a central counterparty to gather the transactions and publish them. It would also need a public medium, such as newspaper advertisements, to publish the hashes. The central counterparty would presumably bear the cost of publishing the hashes. This central counterparty running the currency constitutes a central point of trust in the system. However, the main design principle of Bitcoin is distributed trust, and the proof-of-work is the last piece of the puzzle to achieve it.

7.3 PROOF-OF-WORK

Digital services are subject to several types of attacks and abuses against them. One example, denial of service (DoS), occurs when a server is flooded with bogus requests for its services. If the number of bogus requests is greater than the number of requests the server can cope with, legitimate users will be unable to get served, or experience delays. A denial of service attack thus disrupts the regular flow of a server and should be avoided. Another such attack is email spam, where an email account is filled with unsolicited email that usually contains advertising or malware.

DENIAL OF SERVICE (DOS) ATTACKS

Denial of Service attacks are attempts to make a machine unavailable. DoS attacks were featured in mainstream news when the Anonymous collective attacked several websites.

A DoS attack usually enlists many participants in disparate locations. Sometimes an attacker can enlist a botnet[a] under her control to perform the attack. These are called Distributed Denial of Service (DDoS) attacks. DDoS attacks are harder to counter, because the bogus requests come from many IP addresses, making it harder to distinguish attackers from legitimate users.

An account of underground groups on the internet practising DoS for profit can be found in Menn (2010). An account of the adventures of Anonymous, including several of their DoS attacks, can be found in Olson (2013).

---

[a] A botnet is a group of computers under the control of a single (malicious) entity. Computers connected to the internet are usually enlisted to be part of the botnet by infecting them with malware, turning them into zombie computers. The entity controlling the botnet can command them to perform a task, such as reporting login or financial information, participating in a DoS attack, clicking on advertisements on a website (click fraud), serving email spam, or even mining Bitcoins for their controller. This last application was popular for a brief period, but given the advances in mining technology it is not economical any more (Chapter 9).

One possible defense against these attacks is to require the client requesting the service prove that some work has been done, i.e. **proof-of-work**. The proof-of-work could be the solution of a computationally-hard problem, a memory-hard problem, a problem requiring user intervention (such as a CAPTCHA)[8], and so on.

The problem must be moderately *hard to solve but easy (computationally fast) to verify*. A service provider can then pose the problem to anyone who requests the service, and only grant access to those users that pass the challenge. This allows the service provider to identify the users that are willing to pay the price to enter the service. If the proof-of-work is well designed this price will be a minor inconvenience (like a short delay) for legitimate users but an economic deterrent to attackers of the service. Proof-of-work systems can be implemented following two protocols:

- **Challenge-Response**. This protocol assumes an ongoing communication between the client and the server. First the client requests the service, then the server chooses a proof-of-work and challenges the client. The client then has to solve the proof-of-work and send the response to the server. Finally the server verifies that the proof-of-work has been correctly done and then grants the client access to the service. This is

---

[8] CAPTCHA or "Completely Automated Public Turing test to tell Computers and Humans Apart" is a proof-of-work test where the user is presented with hard to read letters that she must type back. It is used to tell apart humans from machines, given that humans are still somewhat better than artificial intelligence algorithms at recognizing characters. However, artificial intelligence is progressing fast, as is the difficulty of the CAPTCHAs.

the model used for example in CAPTCHAs. The advantage of this protocol is that the server can adapt the difficulty of the proof-of-work to the conditions, such as server load.

- **Solution-Verification**. This protocol is asynchronous: solution and verification can be done at different times. Ongoing communication between the server and the client is not required. First, the client creates a proof-of-work problem and solves it: this problem should be different every time and chosen by an algorithm: for instance, the client could use the result of a hash function to generate it. Then the client sends the solution to the server, who verifies it and proceeds accordingly.

To secure the blockchain—the distributed transaction database—Bitcoin requires proof-of-work to be performed on blocks of transactions following the Solution-Verification protocol. Bitcoin uses **partial hash inversion** as the proof-of-work function. Partial hash inversion requires that the hash of a block of transactions matches a certain pattern. The pattern to match is that the hash starts with at least a certain number of 0 bits. This is called hash inversion because the proof-of-work must invert (i.e. match) a certain pattern in part of the hash. It is important that the hash function is preimage-resistant. Otherwise it would not be computationally hard to find a partial hash inversion, defeating the purpose of the proof-of-work.

Figure 7.5 shows partial hash inversion applied to the message "This is the message #". The hash function used in the figure is SHA256^2, Bitcoin's hash function. The partial hash inversion in this example requires that the first 12 bits (3 hexadecimal characters in the figure) are zero. The free variable to solve the partial hash is a nonce appended to the message. To solve the partial hash inversion, a nonce must be found such that the hash of the message and the nonce matches the partial hash, i.e. the hash starts with at least three zero characters. Figure 7.5 increments the nonce until it finds a solution. The solution is found in the nonce value 6193. Although this example starts with a nonce value of 1 and increments it at each step, nothing prevents one from trying nonces at random. For well behaved hash functions, the computational cost of both methods is equivalent.

It is computationally costly to solve the partial hash inversion, because many nonces (6,193 in this case) had to be tried before finding a solution. However, it is computationally cheap to verify that the work has been done, it only requires one hash

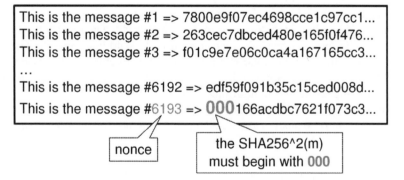

FIGURE 7.5 Partial hash inversion proof-of-work

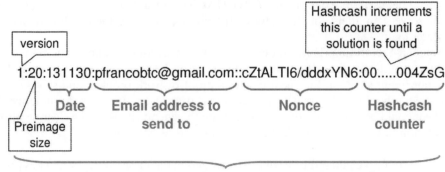

FIGURE 7.6 Hashcash

evaluation[9]. One of the advantages of using partial hash inversion is that the difficulty of the proof-of-work can be easily adjusted by changing the number of 0 bits that the solution hash must begin with.

Bitcoin borrowed the idea of using partial hash inversion as a proof-of-work function from **Hashcash**. Hashcash was introduced by Adam Back in 1997 as a mechanism to put a curb on spam email (Back, 2002). Email is cheap to send, and this has led to the proliferation of spammers. Spammers send millions of unsolicited emails with commercials (or malware). Even though the probability of any single email to have its desired effect on the recipient (i.e. clicking on it) is very small, it is economically profitable for spammers because of the very low cost per email sent. Hashcash proposes to add a token to the header of an email. This token includes a proof-of-work that some computational time has been spent to generate it. The proof-of-work function used in Hashcash is partial hash inversion, using SHA-1 as the hashing function.

Figure 7.6 presents an example of a Hashcash header. The header includes:

- The **version** of the Hashcash protocol, 1.
- The **preimage** size, 20 bits or 5 initial zero characters in hexadecimal. The preimage size indicates the number of initial zero bits for the partial hash inversion.
- The **date** when the email is sent, 131130 or November 30, 2013. The hashcash token is only valid for a certain period.
- The **recipient email address**, pfrancobtc@gmail.com.
- A **nonce** (cZtALTI6/dddxYN6) used only for one email. The logic behind this nonce is to avoid the same hashcash header being used to send many emails. The receiving email server can store the nonces in a cache and if an email arrives whose nonce is found in the cache, the email is dropped. This avoids a botnet master from reusing the same hashcash header in multiple emails.
- The **hashcash counter** (00...004ZsG). Hashcash increments this counter until it finds a value such that the hash of the whole header matches the preimage requirement.

---

[9] The function that checks that the proof-of-work test is correctly passed in the Bitcoin Core source code is called CheckProofOfWork and can be found in main.cpp.

The SHA-1 hash of the hashcash header is shown at the bottom of Figure 7.6. The first 20 bits (5 hexadecimal characters) of this hash are zeros, and therefore the header is valid. The amount of work to solve the partial hash collision problem is exponential in the number of initial zeros, doubling with each additional zero bit. On the other hand, confirming the validity of the hashcash header always takes the same amount of work.

7.4   THE BLOCKCHAIN

Bitcoin combines the ideas behind linked time-stamping and Hashcash style proof-of-work to arrive at a way to secure the distributed database. This is the main innovation introduced by Bitcoin.

The **blockchain** is an *ever-growing chain of blocks*. Each block contains a group of new transactions and a link to the previous block in the chain. New transactions in the network are collected into a block which is appended to the blockchain. Note that old transactions are still in the blockchain: old blocks are never removed from the blockchain, thus the blockchain can only increase in length.

Each block is secured with a partial hash inversion proof-of-work. This is depicted in Figure 7.7, arguably the most important figure in this book. First, each block includes a group of (valid) transactions, the hash of the previous block, and a nonce. The nonce in a block solves the partial hash inversion problem. That is, the nonce is a number such that the hash of the entire block (including the nonce) starts with a certain number of zero bits. In Figure 7.7 the hash of the block 271,076, mined on November 23, 2013, is 0x0000000000000006e1163..., starting with 61 zero bits (or 15 zero characters in hexadecimal representation).

It is easy to adjust the **block difficulty** by increasing the number of starting zero bits. The Bitcoin protocol adjusts this difficulty to target **10 minutes between blocks**. This difficulty adjustment is part of the rules of Bitcoin and it is coded into every Bitcoin client.

The block difficulty is adjusted every 2,016 blocks or roughly every 2 weeks[10]. The adjustment takes into account the change in the computational power of the whole network since the last adjustment, by comparing the time-stamps of two blocks 2,016 positions apart. When mining power is being added to the network, blocks will be mined quicker than the target 10 minute period. The difficulty will be adjusted higher but trailing the growing network power.

If the correction to the difficulty is greater than 4 or lower than 1/4, it is clamped to those values. This helps protect against large swings in the difficulty if the power of the network changes too quickly.

Finding a partial hash collision is done through brute forcing: trying random (or consecutive) nonces until one of them creates the partial hash collision. Thus the time it takes to solve a block is random.

The persons or institutions contributing their computational power to solve the partial hash inversion power are called **miners**. The assistance of the miners is critical to secure the blockchain, and the protocol compensates them with newly minted bitcoins. A **block reward** is the compensation that is paid every time a miner solves the hash inversion

---

[10] It would be exactly two weeks if the difficulty during the 2 weeks was perfectly adjusted to the power of the network, and blocks would get mined exactly every 10 minutes.

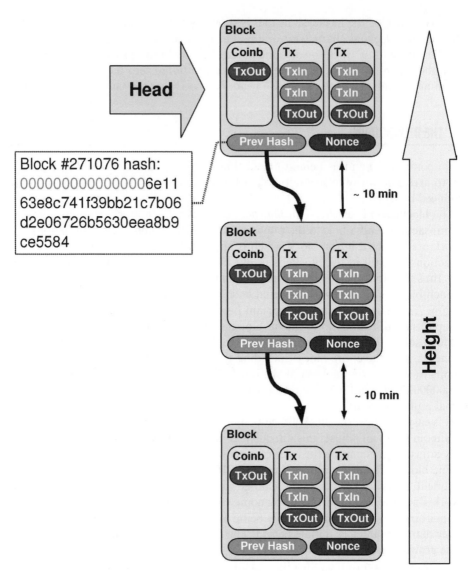

Block #271076 hash:
00000000000000006e11
63e8c741f39bb21c7b06
d2e06726b5630eea8b9
ce5584

FIGURE 7.7 The blockchain

problem. Thus *new bitcoins issued are allocated to the miners that contribute their compu-tational power to secure the blockchain.*

Every block includes a special transaction called the **coinbase**[11]. The coinbase is the first transaction in a block—see Figure 7.7. It has only one transaction input (TxIn), which is not linked to any previous transaction output (TxOut) and does not serve any purpose[12]. On the other hand, the coinbase can have many outputs. The sum of values

---

[11] Technically the coinbase is the only input to the first transaction in a block. Abusing the notation, throughout this book the first transaction in a block will be referred to as the coinbase transaction.
[12] This input can present any value. Some miners use it to publish a message, or to secure data in the blockchain (section 12.6). The coinbase of the very first block by Satoshi has the message: "The

in these outputs equals the block reward, plus the sum of all the fees granted by the transactions collected into the block.

BLOCK DIFFICULTY

The partial hash inversion problem can be understood as finding a nonce such that the resulting hash is lower than a **target hash**. The target hash is a 256-bit number that starts with several zero bits. Internally the Bitcoin client compresses this 256-bit number into a 32-bit unsigned integer, named **bits**. As each block saves a copy of the *bits* integer, this compression saves considerable space in the blockchain.[a]

In the example of Figure 7.7, *bits* has a value of 419892219, or **0x19070bfb** hexadecimal. This gives a target hash of **0x070bfb** $2^{8 \cdot (0x19-3)}$ = 0x00000000000000070b-fb000... where all the last zero nibbles have been omitted. The mined block had a hash of 0000000000000006e1163e8... thus meeting the target.

Sometimes the **difficulty** of mining a block is represented as a floating point number. This floating point number is the quotient of the initial target hash 0xffff $\cdot 2^{208}$ over the current hash target. The difficulty started at 1 at the beginning of the blockchain (January 3, 2009) and it cannot be lower than 1.

---

[a] The *bits* 32-bit value is stored in a variable named nBits, member of the class CBlock-Header. The definition of this class can be found in core.h. The conversion between the full 256-bit hash and the compressed 32-bit is performed in CBigNum::SetCompact and CBigNum::GetCompact, both in bignum.h.

Blocks usually include many transactions aside from the coinbase. But a valid block can be created without including any transaction except for the coinbase. Indeed, this type of block was very common at the beginning of the Bitcoin network, when very few transactions were broadcast. These "empty" blocks help secure the blockchain and award miners the block reward for doing so. Miners can choose which transactions to include in the blocks they mine, and they usually decide to include them based on the fee they pay (section 9.3).

The miner who solves the hashing problem uses the coinbase to pay the block reward to herself. This is why solving the partial hash inversion problem is called **mining**. All miners in the network compete to mine blocks. The **hash rate** of a miner is her computational power, measured in hashes/second. The **network hash rate** is the total hash rate of all the miners in the network, and it stands at around 30,000 TH/s[13] at the time of writing. Mining a block can be compared to a lottery, where the chances of a single miner are proportional to her share of the network hash rate.

The block reward was initially set to 50 bitcoins per block. Every 210,000 blocks, or roughly every 4 years, the block reward is halved. At the time of writing the block reward stands at 25 bitcoins. Figure 2.7 from Chapter 2 shows the total number of bitcoins in circulation assuming each block is mined exactly every 10 minutes. As expected, the

---

Times 03/Jan/2009 Chancellor on brink of second bailout for banks."
[13] That is 30,000,000,000,000,000 hashes/second.

number of bitcoins awarded (the slope in the figure) decreases exponentially, making the total amount of bitcoins in circulation settle to a value of approximately 21 million. This issuance schedule is programmed in the logic of Bitcoin Core[14]. This **currency generation algorithm** is considered immutable by the community. At the time of writing, the total amount of bitcoins in circulation stands at around 12.5 million.

Historically roughly 99% of the compensation of miners has come from the block reward, and only 1% of their retribution from transaction fees. It is expected that over time a larger percentage of the retribution will be due to transaction fees.

The process of solving blocks is called mining in analogy to mining precious metals. Miners are rewarded with new currency. This analogy, although useful, can be carried too far. The block reward is fixed by the protocol and is not affected by the number of miners or the power they contribute. Contrary to precious metals mining, an increase in the mining investment does not increase the number of bitcoins in circulation. New investment in mining increases the total hash rate, thus reducing the share of original miners, keeping the total reward for the network constant[15].

The block preceding a given block is called its **parent block**. Blocks reference their parent block in the blockchain by including its hash in their data structure, as in Figure 7.7. Thus the blockchain keeps blocks in chronological order. The first block in the blockchain is called the **genesis block** and it was created by Satoshi in January 3, 2009. The order of a block in the blockchain, starting from the genesis block is called the **block height**. The last block added to the blockchain is called the **blockchain head**. New blocks are added on top of the blockchain head.

A **fork** occurs when two miners arrive at a new block at roughly the same time. Both blocks solve the partial hash inversion problem, but only one of them can be part of the long-term blockchain. The discarded block is called an **orphan block**. The decision of which branch of the blockchain is the valid one is not taken by any party[16]. Rather the dispute resolves itself organically.

A fork can persist for several blocks, as shown in Figure 7.8. This happens when there is a split in the network, and some miners believe one branch of the fork is the legitimate blockchain, while the others follow the other branch. The protocol determines that *the correct blockchain is the longest one*. So miners have an incentive to stop working in a branch as soon as it is clear that it will be orphaned, because work on an orphaned branch is wasted. Therefore forks resolve themselves quickly, usually in just 1 block. The average number of forks has been around 2%, i.e. on average every 50 blocks there is a fork in the blockchain. Forks of more than one block are very rare.

Transactions included in the blocks of a fork are not lost. When a fork is resolved and a branch of the blockchain is discarded, the transactions in that branch are introduced again into the unconfirmed transactions' memory pool, ready to be included in the next block mined. Some of these transactions might already appear in a block of the

---

[14] The path followed by the money supply is controlled by the variable CMainParams::nSubsidyHalvingInterval in `chainparams.cpp`. This variable determines the numbers of blocks after which the block reward will be halved. It is later used in the function GetBlockValue in `main.cpp` to assign the reward to a block.

[15] There is a temporary increase in the speed at which new blocks are mined until the feedback mechanism catches up and settles the expected time between blocks back at 10 minutes. Thus new investment temporarily accelerates the release of new bitcoins.

[16] An exception was the fork that occurred in March 2013 following the 0.8 release of Bitcoin Core, see box "Forks Due to Changes in the Protocol."

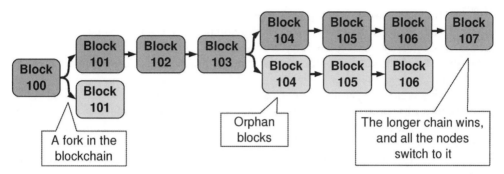

FIGURE 7.8 Dynamics of the blockchain

legitimate branch of the fork. In this case, these transactions are discarded and excluded from the unconfirmed transactions' memory pool.

Every fork resolution produces winners (the miners that solved blocks in the accepted branch) and losers (miners whose solved orphaned blocks). The protocol avoids having a central party or group deciding about the correct branch, in line with the decentralization philosophy of Bitcoin.

The Bitcoin protocol solves a fork in favor of the longest blockchain. **Blockchain length** is measured by the combined difficulty of all the blocks in the chain. If blockchain difficulty were measured by the number of blocks instead, an attacker could generate many "valid" blocks with a lower difficulty than the legitimate blockchain, thus winning the blockchain race by cheating. This is not possible, and an attacker must resort to having a significant percentage of the network hash rate at her disposal to pull off such an attack (section 7.5).

FORKS DUE TO CHANGES IN THE PROTOCOL

Forks can also occur due to differences in the code run by various nodes. One famous example occurred in March 2013 after the release of version 0.8 of Bitcoin Core, which changed the database used for the UTXO from BerkeleyDB to LevelDB. The new version introduced a subtle change in the rules of the Bitcoin protocol (Buterin, 2013a; Andresen, 2013b). This change resulted in a block being recognized as valid by the miners running version 0.8, but invalid for miners running version 0.7 of the software, creating a fork in the blockchain. As there was more computational power running version 0.8, this branch of the blockchain pulled ahead. However, this was leaving miners running the older version behind.

Developers and mining pool operators discussed the course of action, and decided to revert to the branch followed by miners with the older version. Miners and users running version 0.8 downgraded to version 0.7 and reset their blockchains to that branch. Some services had to shut down temporarily while performing the downgrade to protect from possible double-spending attacks.

Forks due to changes in the protocol are an exception to the rule that forks should resolve themselves organically.

The Bitcoin network is composed of **nodes**. Nodes are computers connected to the internet, running the Bitcoin software. The Bitcoin network is a peer-to-peer network: all nodes are homogeneous. Nodes receive transactions and blocks from other nodes, and relay these transactions and blocks to other nodes. Each node keeps a full copy of the blockchain.

A newly created transaction that has not been included into any block is called an **unconfirmed transaction**. Once a transaction is included in a block it is said to be **confirmed**. Whether a transaction is confirmed is a matter of degree: the more blocks that have been added to the top of the blockchain, the harder it is to perform a double-spending attack against a transaction. Section 7.5 further explores the topic of transaction confirmation.

Nodes store the unconfirmed transactions they receive in an database called the **unconfirmed transactions' memory pool**, often referred to simply as **mempool**[17]. Not all received transactions are added to the mempool. If a transaction double-spends an input of another transaction already in the mempool, it is dropped. A transaction is also dropped if it is not a standard transaction (section 6.7). Once a node receives a new block, or mines a block itself, the unconfirmed transactions' memory pool is updated, removing all transactions included in the block.

Transactions are not deemed confirmed until they are included in a block. This usually takes several minutes, but it could take longer. If the network is under heavy usage and there are many unconfirmed transactions, it can take several blocks for a particular transaction to be included into a block. The question if a transaction can be considered valid before it is included in a block is explored in section 7.5.

When a transaction is created, it is relayed to the Bitcoin network through a small amount of nodes. The nodes that receive the new transaction check that it is valid (Chapter 6) and is not a double-spend of a transaction already in the mempool. If the transaction passes the check, it is relayed to other nodes in the network, and is otherwise dropped. This is the way unconfirmed transactions propagate through the network.

In summary, aside from a full copy of the blockchain, a node also keeps additional data structures, such as the unspent transaction outputs cache or the unconfirmed transactions' memory pool, so that it can quickly validate new received transactions and mined blocks. If the received transaction or block is valid, the node updates its data structures and relays it to the connected nodes. It is important to note that a node does not need to *trust* other nodes, because it validates independently all the information it receives from them.

When a miner finds a new block, it broadcasts it to the network. All receiving nodes first check the validity of the block, i.e. that it solves the partial hash inversion problem with the required difficulty. They then update their internal data structures to reflect the new information contained in the block:

  ▪ Update the unspent transaction outputs cache (UTXO)[18].

---

[17] The mempool is implemented in the class **CTxMemPool** found in `txmempool.h`.

[18] The code performing this update can be found in the function **ConnectTip** in `main.cpp`.

- Update the unconfirmed transactions' memory pool. This involves going through the list of transactions, and dropping those that are in conflict with (spend the same outputs) as a transaction in the new mined block[19].

Nodes maintain a number of connections to other nodes in the network. Some nodes will like to keep as many connections open to other nodes as the available resources (CPU, network bandwidth) allow, usually in the upper hundredths. For instance, a wallet node might want to keep connections to many other nodes, as geographically distributed as possible, to quickly detect and act upon double-spending attempts. Similarly, a mining node might want to have as many connections open as possible, so that it receives prompt notice of mined blocks. A faster reception of new mined blocks minimizes the time wasted trying to mine a block that will become orphan. For other nodes, having up-to-the second information is not so important, and so they usually connect to only a handful of nodes.

The propagation of a block in the network is delayed by the usual network delays, but also because each node checks the full validity of a block before relaying it. Researchers have found in Decker and Wattenhofer (2013) that new mined blocks take on average around 10 seconds to propagate through the network. Propagation delay is proportional to the size of the block, so large blocks can take considerable time to propagate. They also found that most of the forks in the blockchain could be attributed to the delay in block propagation. Finally, they propose several measures and changes in the protocol to reduce propagation delay.

There are two types of nodes, **mining nodes** and **passive nodes**. Mining nodes are nodes actively trying to solve blocks, in order to reap the rewards. They include transactions from their unconfirmed transactions' memory pool into the block they are mining[20]. Passive nodes are usually employed by services such as wallets, payment processors, market data providers and so on. All nodes keep an up-to-date snapshot of the state of the network, including a full copy of the blockchain, the UTXO cache and the unconfirmed transactions mempool.

As an example, nodes providing services to wallet clients perform these tasks on behalf of their clients:

- Relay to the network the transactions created by the clients.
- Keep track of the confirmation status of a transaction. That is, notify the client when a transaction has been included in a block, and when new blocks have been added on top of the block where the transaction was included.
- Send the client the unspent transaction outputs belonging to certain addresses. This allows the client to keep track of the funds available.

Mining nodes cannot change transactions. They can only decide whether to include them in the block they are currently mining or not, and whether to relay them to the rest of the network or not. The contents of the transactions are secured by public key cryptography

---

[19] The code performing this update can be found in the function **ConnectBlock**, which is called by **ConnectTip**. **ConnectTip** is in turn called by **ActivateBestChain**. All these functions can be found in `main.cpp`.

[20] Section 9.3 explores how transactions are selected into a block.

and cannot be changed by the node processing the transaction[21]. At the time of writing there are roughly 10,000 nodes connected to the network—that is, there are 10,000 copies of the Bitcoin transaction database online.

BOOTSTRAPPING THE BLOCKCHAIN

When a node connects to the network for the first time, it requests a copy of the whole blockchain since the beginning (January 3, 2009). As a node downloads the blocks, it checks their validity. First it checks that all transactions included in the block are valid:

- Their inputs must spend previously unspent outputs.
- The sum of the funds in their outputs must be equal to or lower than the sum of the funds in the inputs.
- The <*scriptPubKey*> must be a valid one, all the inputs must be correctly signed.

Next, the node checks that the hash of the block is well constructed (section 7.6) and that it satisfies the required proof-of-work. By making all these checks, a new node cannot be fooled by a malicious node sending it an invalid copy of the blockchain. The only way a malicious node can feed an incorrect copy of the blockchain would be to perform a 51% attack (see next section).

At the beginning of the bootstrapping procedure, the node creates the databases for the unspent transaction outputs cache (UTXO) and the unconfirmed transactions' memory pool. These are then updated with the information in each block as the block is processed.

Bootstrapping a node uses a lot of bandwidth and computational power. At the time of writing the size of the downloaded blockchain exceeds 17GB. On a modest laptop computer with 2 cores on a residential ADSL connection, downloading and verifying the blockchain can take several days.

It may seem that nodes have an incentive not to relay a transaction, especially if the transaction awards a considerable fee to the miner. There are, however, various factors against not relaying transactions:

- Clients usually connect to various nodes when relaying a new transaction, because it is in their interest that the transaction is relayed, so that it is included in the next block mined by the network. A client can monitor whether the nodes it is using are relaying its transactions, and punish the nodes not relaying them. This is an undesired outcome for a node, which will prefer to see transactions as soon as they are created.
- Nodes connect to each other, and can police whether a particular node is refraining from relaying transactions. If a "cheater" is caught, other nodes in the network can punish it, say in a tit-for-tat strategy that stops relaying transactions to that node.

---

[21] Transaction malleability is an exception to this rule (7.6.1).

- A node that does not relay transactions to other nodes can be enlisted by a malicious node to help perform a double-spending attack, by feeding it a transaction that is double-spent somewhere else in the network. This can be very detrimental for the node, because it could mean losing the block reward when the malicious node achieves its goal. Given that transaction fees represent a small percentage of the total compensation of a block, holding transactions is usually not worth this risk for a node.

On the other hand, mining nodes have an incentive to broadcast mined blocks as fast as possible in order to reduce the probability that another node might mine a different block.

7.5 DOUBLE-SPEND AND OTHER ATTACKS

A **double-spend attempt** occurs when two different transactions try to spend the same funds. The Bitcoin protocol defends against this attack by deciding that the valid transaction is the one that finds its way into the blockchain first. Thus Bitcoin solves the double-spending problem in a decentralized way, without the need for a central authority to decide which transaction is valid.

A transaction is further secured as more blocks pile on top of the block where it was originally included. This is illustrated in Figure 7.9. An attacker wishing to change the blockchain at a certain block would have to mine again all blocks from that block up to the blockchain head. Moreover, as the Bitcoin network keeps on adding blocks to the blockchain, the attacker would not only have to redo all the past work, but would have to keep up with the pace of new legitimate block creation and surpass it. The only way an attacker could perform such a feat is to command a hash rate as large as the hash rate of the rest of the network. Thus this attack is called a **51% attack**[22]. A "51%" attack is still possible for an attacker that controls less than half the network hash rate. But in this case the probability of success depends on what percentage of the network hash rate the attacker controls and the number of blocks she has to outpace. The probability of success decreases exponentially on both. Only when the attacker controls >50% of the network hash rate is the probability of success 100%.

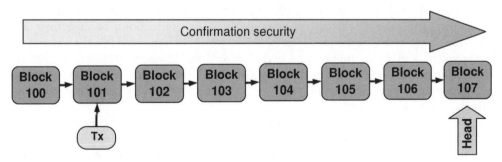

FIGURE 7.9 Security of a transaction inside the blockchain

---

[22] To be precise, it should be called a 50%+ attack.

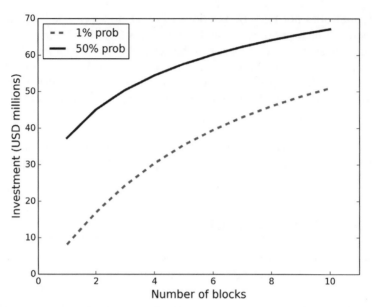

FIGURE 7.10 Investment required to pull off a 51% attack with 1% and 50% probability of success

Figure 7.10 shows an analysis of the investment an attacker should devote to be able to perform a double-spending attack. The analysis assumes that the network hash rate is 30,000 TH/s and that the cost of mining equipment is 3 USD per GH/s. An attacker needs to invest 90 USD million[23] to have as much hash rate as the rest of the network and to be able to perform a 51% attack. Figure 7.10 shows the amount an attacker should invest in new mining equipment to succeed with a probability of 1% and 50%. Note that with only 1 block confirming a transaction, an attacker should invest more than 8 USD million to have a 1% of success, or invest more than 37 USD million to succeed with a 50% probability. This analysis can be used to assess the risk a user is willing to accept when choosing the number of confirmations. For most purposes a few confirmations should be sufficient.

A 51% attacker can change transactions that she has control over, performing a double-spend on those funds. Although a 51% attacker could remove transactions from other users from the blockchain, she cannot alter the transactions, because these are protected by the ECC signature. That is, a 51% attacker cannot modify the amount or the recipient of arbitrary transactions in the blockchain. However, a 51% attacker can effectively prevent other miners from mining new blocks, by refusing to mine on top of the blocks produced by these other miners. Thus, a 51% attacker can successfully perform an attack *against other miners*.

Researchers have shown in Sompolinsky and Zohar (2013) that it is possible to pull off a successful 51% attack controlling significantly less than 50% of the network hash rate if there are delays in the propagation of mined blocks. They propose a modification

---

[23] The cumulative investment in mining equipment has been greater than this figure, because much of it was spent on less efficient technology (Chapter 9).

to the Bitcoin protocol, called GHOST, to make a 51% attack harder in the presence of block propagation delays. This proposal allows high block creation rates and large block sizes without increasing the risk of an attack.

The **GHOST (Greedy Heaviest-Observed Sub-Tree)** policy changes how the main chain is selected in the Bitcoin protocol. The GHOST policy takes into account the proof-of-work performed in orphaned blocks when selecting the longest chain. Starting from the genesis block, the main chain is selected by computing the total proof-of-work of every sub-tree in a fork (a sub-tree includes orphaned blocks). The sub-tree with the highest total proof-of-work is selected.

The 51% attack is the most cited attack on the blockchain. However, there are other types of attack, which are explored in the rest of this section.

7.5.1 Race Attack

When a node receives a new unconfirmed transaction that conflicts with a transaction in its unconfirmed transactions cache, i.e. it spends the same outputs, the new transaction is ignored. Thus nodes only keep in their cache a copy of the first transaction received[24]. A **race attack** occurs when a vendor accepts payment on an unconfirmed transaction by checking only a few nodes. The attacker could send a transaction to the nodes close to the vendor and a different transaction to many other nodes in the network. Thus only the nodes closer to the vendor show the transaction sending the funds to the vendor, while the rest of the network include in their mempool the double-spend. To defend against this attack a vendor should wait for the transaction to be included in at least one block.

A double-spend of a transaction is very unlikely if the majority of the mining nodes in the network already have a valid transaction in their unconfirmed transactions' memory pool. A payment processor or wallet service can take advantage of this fact by keeping connections open to a large portion of the mining nodes and checking that the correct transaction is in their unconfirmed transactions' memory pool. This allows the service operator to offer very fast transaction confirmation with limited risk.

In an ideal situation, all pending transactions in the network would be included in the next block mined. This assumes that all transactions propagate through the network with no delays, reach all miners and that miners include all pending transactions in their next block. In practice some transactions can suffer delays before being included in a block, and can even be dropped by the network and never make it to the blockchain[25]. It can even be possible for a transaction that was forgotten by the network to reappear after a node starts to broadcast it again. In cases where a transaction is not confirmed, a **double-spend** of that transaction to a different address should be forced. This has the advantage of preventing or at least making apparent problems with transaction malleability (7.6.1).

---

[24] Saving all unconfirmed transactions—even conflicting ones—carries several problems. First, a mining node would have to decide which of the conflicting transaction it should include in the block it is mining. Second, this could be easily abused in a DoS attack, where the attacker floods the network with double-spends of the same transaction.

[25] Nodes could drop transactions from the unconfirmed transactions' memory pool after a certain period, or after a restart of the node. However, most wallet implementations keep on resending a transaction periodically, i.e. after 1 hour, if it is not confirmed.

7.5.2   Finney Attack

This attack was discovered by Hal Finney (Bitcoin wiki, 2014h). The attacker (who is also a miner) secretly mines a block, including in it a transaction from one of her addresses to another of her addresses. This transaction has not been broadcast to the network, and is only included in the block that the attacker is secretly mining. Right before releasing the block, the attacker sends a double-spend of the TxOut included in her secret transaction. This attack would succeed in bypassing the protection of a user who just monitors that the transaction has propagated through the network. Once the victim has accepted the payment, the attacker would release the secretly mined block, thus performing a double-spend.

This attack has an associated opportunity cost because there is a delay from the time the block is mined to the time the block is released to the network. This delay is consumed in closing the deal with the victim and waiting for the double-spend transaction to propagate through the network. During this delay, there is the possibility that some other miner finds a block, and thus the double-spend attack fails and the attacker loses the block reward. This opportunity cost makes the attack impractical for low value transactions. For high value transactions, a defense against this attack is to require at least two confirmations.

In contrast to the 51% attack, an attacker does not have to control most of the hash rate in the network. A miner with a low hash rate could perform this attack, just waiting for the time when she mines the next block.

7.5.3   Transaction Spamming

An attacker could try to perform a denial of service on the Bitcoin network by creating many transactions where she sends the funds to herself. As space in the blocks is limited, this attack could prevent legitimate transactions to confirm. However, this attack is unlikely to work in practice because of the following factors:

- The number of "free" transactions an attacker can send to the network is limited. Blocks mined have a maximum block size of 50kB reserved for priority (free) transactions[26]. Transactions above this limit have to pay fees. So, at the end, an attacker would have to pay fees to perform this attack.
- The fees an attacker would have to pay would have to compete with the fees of legitimate transactions. As time passes the fees that legitimate transactions are willing to pay to be included in the blockchain will presumably rise, making this attack costlier to sustain over time.
- The transactions an attacker has to send have to be above a certain threshold, currently set at 0.0000054 bitcoins. Below this threshold a transaction is considered **dust** and dropped by the network. Therefore an attacker would have to possess some funds in Bitcoin to be able to perform the attack.

---

[26] More precisely, the limit for priority transactions in a block is defined in the static variable **DE-FAULT_BLOCK_PRIORITY_SIZE**, currently set to 50,000 bytes. This definition can be found in main.h. Furthermore, priority transactions are themselves ordered based on the age of their outputs and their size, see function CCoinsViewCache::GetPriority in coins.cpp.

A variant of this attack would be to send invalid transactions to some nodes. An invalid transaction is checked by the node that receives it and dropped. Checking the signature is a CPU-intensive operation (section 7.7) so this attack could succeed in slowing the nodes that are flooded with transactions. However, as the flooded nodes do not relay the invalid transaction to the network, this attack does not have an effect in the rest of the network. Nodes in the bitcoin network have to protect against this DoS attack in the same way regular internet servers have to protect against DoS attacks.

7.6   MERKLE TREES

Up to this point, block hashes have been assumed to be the hash of the whole block, which includes the hash of the previous block in the blockchain, and all the transactions in the block. But nothing has been said about how this hash is constructed. The naive solution, to concatenate the byte representation of the block header and all the transactions and then hash the whole byte string, has several disadvantages:

- If one transaction is changed, the byte string has to be updated, and the hash computed again. This forces nodes to keep the whole block byte string in memory. If a transaction in the middle of the byte string is substituted for a bigger transaction, memory has to be allocated in the middle of the byte string, a costly operation.
- To verify that a transaction belongs to a block, the whole block must be available. Only then can the hash be computed and verified.

A **Merkle tree**, or **hash tree**, is a data structure that addresses these issues. It was proposed by Ralph Merkle in 1982. According to Nakamoto (2008a), Satoshi took the idea of using Merkle trees to time-stamp a block of transactions from Massias et al. (1999). Merkle trees are also widely used in file sharing applications, to keep track of the blocks of a file that have been correctly downloaded.

Figure 7.11 shows how a Merkle tree is used to compute the hash of a block[27]. First, a **binary tree** is formed with the hashes of the individual transactions as their leaves. These are denoted by Hash0, … Hash3 in the figure. A binary tree is a directed graph, where each parent has two children. The hash of the parent node is the hash of its two children, themselves hashes[28]. This is shown in Figure 7.11, where Hash01 = Hash(Hash0 || Hash1) and Hash is the SHA256 hash function. Eventually the hash of the root node, the **root hash** or **Merkle root**, is computed. With this Merkle root, the block header can now be assembled.

The **block header** contains the hash of the previous block in the blockchain, the root of the Merkle tree of the transactions and the nonce included by the miner. The hash of

---

[27] The implementation of the Merkle tree in the Bitcoin source code can be found in function CBlock::BuildMerkleTree in `core.cpp`.

[28] If a node in the tree does not have a matching node, it is hashed with itself to arrive at the hash of its parent.

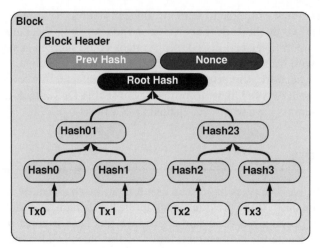

FIGURE 7.11   Merkle tree of the transactions in a block

the block is then the hash of the block header only: transactions are represented in this hash through the root of the Merkle tree[29].

One of the big advantages of using Merkle trees is transaction verification. Suppose a node wants to verify that a transaction, say Tx3, belongs to a block as in Figure 7.12. A node can perform this operation within a time that is related logarithmically to the number of nodes in the tree. Following Figure 7.12, the node only has to compute Hash3, Hash23 and the root hash, and check the result against the root hash stored in the block.

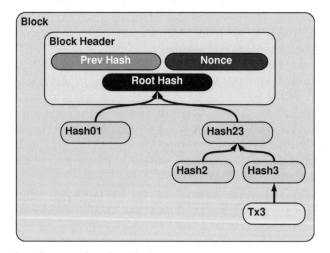

FIGURE 7.12   Pruning of transactions in a block

---

[29] The hash of a block is computed in the function **CBlockHeader::GetHash** in core.cpp. To be precise it includes: nVersion (version of the block; current version is 2), hashPrevBlock (hash of previous block), hashMerkleRoot (root hash of the Merkle root), nTime (time when the block is mined), nBits (block difficulty in compressed form; see box in section 7.4) and nNonce (nonce).

That is, the node only has to verify the **Merkle branch**, the part of the tree that allows to cryptographically prove that a transaction is included in the tree. The Simplified Payment Verification (SPV) protocol (section 8.8) makes extensive use of the fact that transactions are represented in Merkle trees.

7.6.1 Transaction Malleability

Transaction malleability is a "quirk" of the Bitcoin protocol, known since at least 2011 (Bitcoin wiki, 2014aa). Transactions in the blockchain are referred by their hash, whose value is included in the Merkle tree for the block. On the other hand, transactions are signed with the private key associated with the transaction inputs.

Transaction malleability refers to the fact that the subsets of transaction information that are used for the hash and for the digital signature are not equal. In other words, a transaction could be changed in such a way that its hash changes, but the digital signature is still valid.

The transaction is hashed before signing, as presented in section 6.5. Thus the transaction is hashed twice: once to sign it and another time to include it in the Merkle tree. The hash before signing does not include the *<scriptSig>* but in its place the *<scriptPubKey>* is copied. Thus a change in the *<scriptSig>* would not invalidate the digital signature, but would change the hash of the transaction that appears in the Merkle tree.

For a list of sources of malleability as well as proposed solutions, see Wuille (2014). The following is a non-exhaustive list of sources of malleability:

- Pushing extra data to the stack at the beginning of *<scriptSig>* that does not affect the evaluation of the script.
- Adding a sequence of non-push operations to *<scriptSig>* that do not yield any result, like appending an operation that pushes data to the stack followed by OP_DROP.
- Prepending one or more zeros to the ECC signature does not invalidate the signature[30].
- If *s* is the ECC signature to a message, then −*s* is also a valid signature (section 5.4). Thus changing the sign of the ECC signature in *<scriptSig>* does not invalidate the signature but changes the transaction hash.

The upshot of transaction malleability is that if a user is tracking transactions based exclusively on their hash, the transaction could be changed so that the hash changed, but the transaction was still valid and thus could be included in a block. The user would not notice that the transaction had been confirmed, and would not adequately update her records.

Transaction malleability climbed to fame in February 2014 when a large exchange discovered that this attack had been used against it[31]. Attacker(s) allegedly filled a Bitcoin

---

[30] Bitcoin uses OpenSSL for ECC signature verification. OpenSSL uses DER-encoded data, but it does not enforce it. So the ECC signature can be slightly changed, such as prepending zeros, and OpenSSL would still accept it. This was fixed in version 0.8 of Bitcoin Core, by rejecting transactions with invalid DER-encoded signatures.

[31] *The Economist* ran a piece in its print edition (*The Economist*, 2014a).

refund order with the exchange. As confirmation for the order, the exchange sent them the hash of the refund transaction after sending it to the network. The attacker(s) waited for this transaction to appear in the network, quickly changed it and flooded the network with the modified version. Once the modified transaction had been included in a block, the attacker(s) allegedly complained to the exchange that the order with the associated hash had not been confirmed, and the exchange would issue a new refund order. The second refund order would have to spend different funds than the first one, otherwise it would be an invalid transaction. This sequence was allegedly repeated many times. Basic accounting checks would have quickly spotted the leak of funds, thus raising the question of whether there were not such checks in place or whether the drain of funds was due to other factors (Decker and Wattenhofer, 2014).

Exchange software should force a double-spend on transactions sent to the network that have not been confirmed. This would have helped detect the double-spend problem after getting feedback that the forced double-spend transactions were not being confirmed.

7.7 SCALABILITY

With increased usage the size of the blockchain has been growing steadily. Figure 7.13 shows the size of the blockchain on a logarithmic scale. As of the time of writing the size stands at roughly 17 GB.

One of the criticisms often raised against Bitcoin is that it will not scale to handle a rate of transactions comparable to that of more mature payment processing networks. As of the time of writing, blocks include an average of 300 transactions. Thus the network currently handles on average 1 transaction every 2 seconds or 0.5 transactions/second (tps). This is two to three orders of magnitude lower than the average transaction rates of established online payment systems, which range from 50 tps to 2,000 tps (Bitcoin wiki,

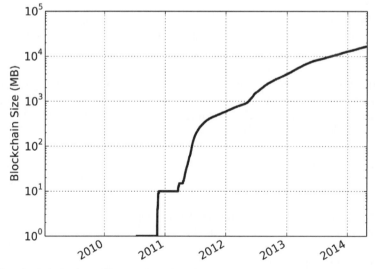

FIGURE 7.13 Blockchain size (MB) on a logarithmic scale. Data from blockchain.info

2014u). This section explores the bottlenecks that could prevent Bitcoin scaling to match the rates of established payment processing networks. This section is based on Bitcoin wiki (2014u).

There is a limit to the maximum block size hard-coded into Bitcoin Core. This limit is currently set at 1 MB[32]. This limit could be increased in future versions of Bitcoin Core if and when the tps of the Bitcoin network increases.

This section will present the limits imposed by current technology. The bottlenecks can be divided in three groups:

- **Computational power**. Nodes perform two main computing tasks: checking block hashes and checking transaction signatures[33]. Of these two tasks, signature checking consumes considerably more CPU. Transactions currently include an average of two inputs. This average is set to increase as multisignature and P2SH transactions increase in importance (Chapter 6). A current single core is able to process 8,000 ECDSA signatures/second[34]. Therefore a single core machine could process 4,000 tps. As signature checking is a highly parallelizable task, adding more cores can further increase the tps a machine could handle. Therefore CPU load does not seem to present a bottleneck on the increased utilization of Bitcoin.
- **Network**. Transactions currently average 0.5 kB in size. Again, this average will probably increase in the future with the increased importance of multisignature transactions. Residential ADSL connections have a bandwidth of 10 Mbits/s on the low end, and this bandwidth could accommodate a flow of 2,500 tps[35]. Higher bandwidths are readily available for network servers. Therefore network bandwidth does not seem to present a bottleneck on increase utilization either.
- **Storage**. As transactions take on average 0.5 kB of storage, storage utilization could quickly escalate for high transaction rates. For instance, a rate of 2,000 tps generates around 1 MB of data every second, or 30 TB of data every year. Furthermore, with the increased utilization comes an increase in the number of unspent transaction outputs, thus increasing the RAM memory requirements for the UTXO, probably making impossible for the UTXO to fit in RAM.

In summary, storage requirements are the biggest bottleneck for scalability. The problem of blockchain size has been amply debated in the community, and many ideas have been proposed, such as:

- **Ultimate blockchain compression**. For a going concern, the only information useful in the blockchain are the unspent transaction outputs. The rest of the data in the blockchain is useful for verification purposes, i.e. when a node bootstraps a new copy of the blockchain. It was proposed in Reiner (2012) to create an alternative

---

[32] More precisely 1,000,000 bytes, see static variable **MAX_BLOCK_SIZE** in `main.h`.

[33] Note that block mining difficulty is independent of the number of transactions: the difficulty of the partial hash inversion problem only depends on the total network hash rate.

[34] Optimizations have been proposed that increase the rate of ECDSA signature verification tenfold (Bitcoin wiki, 2014u).

[35] Denial of Service attacks have to be accounted for, which requires higher bandwidth requirements. In this respect, a Bitcoin node is not much different from a regular internet server.

blockchain to store a copy of the unspent transaction outputs cache (UTXO). The UTXO would be stored in a tree or similar data structure[36], sometimes called an **unused output tree** (UOT). This new blockchain would then be merge-mined with the regular Bitcoin blockchain. For details about how merged mining works see section 14.3, but the basic idea of merged mining is that the hash at the root of the UTXO tree is included in each regular block, thus securing the new blockchain using Bitcoin's computational power. Most of the nodes—even mining, wallet, or payment processing nodes—would only need to keep a copy of the UTXO blockchain. A full copy of the blockchain would then only need to be kept in **archival nodes**.

- **Finite blockchain**. A divide and conquer strategy was proposed in Bruce (2013). The blockchain would be divided into three pieces: an account tree, a mini-blockchain, and a proof chain. Although this proposal may be too radical to implement in Bitcoin in the short run, it could be picked up by other alternative cryptocurrencies.

For the time being, Bitcoin is not breaking at the seams. With the current value of the maximum block size set at roughly 1MB there is ample room to collect all the new transactions in the network: this block size could accommodate 3 to 4 tps. As the number of transactions increases, this value could be increased accordingly[37].

If space in the blockchain starts to become scarce transaction fees will increase. This would, on the one hand, increase investment in mining and, on the other hand, push the settlement of small transactions off the blockchain, thus decreasing the load of the system. Market forces, human ingenuity, and advances in technology will probably solve the scalability problems faced by Bitcoin.

---

[36] Different data structures were proposed: from Merkle trees, to binary-search trees, to a tree-like structure (Reiner, 2012).

[37] The maximum block size is represented by the **MAX_BLOCK_SIZE** variable. It was increased once from 250,000 bytes to the current 1,000,000 bytes. This required careful coordination of the miners to avoid a hard fork of the blockchain.

CHAPTER 8

Wallets

As explained in Chapters 6 and 7, bitcoins do not reside in a user's computers, rather bitcoins are an entry into a distributed ledger, the blockchain. This ledger holds the amount of funds available for each address. The private key associated with an address must be used to sign a transaction spending the funds from that address. A Bitcoin wallet is simply a collection of private keys. Although a Bitcoin wallet derives its name from an analogy with physical wallets, it is important to note the differences between the two:

- A physical wallet holds the physical money. Therefore it cannot be copied. In contrast, **a Bitcoin wallet can be copied**. Whoever controls a copy of the Bitcoin wallet can spend the funds. An attacker can "steal" a Bitcoin wallet by making a copy of it. In Bitcoin, ownership of funds is determined by spendability. Anyone in possession of the private key can spend the funds.
- **A Bitcoin wallet can be distributed across several devices**, in such a way that accessing the funds might require cooperation between the devices. This can be achieved with multisignature transaction outputs where the private keys of all the required signatures are distributed across several devices. The flexibility provided by the Bitcoin protocol allows for more types of wallets than physical wallets.
- **Receive-only Bitcoin wallets** are possible. These wallets only hold a copy of the public keys or the Bitcoin addresses. Receive-only wallets can receive funds but cannot spend funds from their addresses. Thus a compromised device that holds this wallet does not lead to a loss of the funds. Receive-only wallets (sometimes called watch-only wallets) are useful for situations where the user of the wallet is not trusted, or when she is at risk of theft. They can also be useful to monitor the funds and transactions in a wallet.

A **wallet software** is a piece of software that allows spending funds from the addresses in a wallet and to manage the wallet. It is very important for a Bitcoin user to have some knowledge of how a wallet software works, and so this is arguably the most important practical chapter in the book. The tasks performed by the wallet software usually include:

- Query the blockchain and present to the user a total of the funds available.
- Generate new addresses to receive new funds, or to receive the change coming from transactions performed by the wallet software.
- Interface with the user, for instance generating or reading QR codes representing addresses, transactions, etc.

- Allow the user to send funds to addresses of her choosing. To accomplish this, the wallet must gather addresses with enough funds under its control, assemble a transaction spending the funds from these addresses, create a new address or select an existing one to send back the change, sign the transaction with all the private keys, and publish the transaction to the blockchain.
- Track transactions' confirmation status.
- Make a backup of the wallet.
- Restore a backup of the wallet.

A Bitcoin address is like a bank account. The Bitcoin equivalent of opening an account is downloading wallet software (or signing up for a web wallet) and letting the software generate a private-public key pair. This key pair must be difficult to guess. For instance, if the wallet software were to choose $d = 1$ for the private key, then the public key would be just $B = d \cdot A = 1 \cdot A = A$ (section 5.4). This public key $B = A$ would then be converted to an address and used in the blockchain. Reversing this address to retrieve the private key is easy for an attacker. An attacker could brute-force "easy" private keys, such as 1, 2, 3, …, checking at every iteration whether the generated address matches an address in the unspent transaction outputs cache (UTXO cache). If a match is found, the attacker could use the private key to steal the funds from that address. There is evidence that there are attackers actively performing this attack on weak private keys (section 8.4).

To secure against this attack, the wallet software must generate private keys with a high degree of entropy. One way to achieve this is to use a good (pseudo)random number generator. This is the approach followed by many wallet software implementations, including the Bitcoin Core Wallet. The wallet software keeps a copy of the private keys, but only the addresses are usually shown to the user. Wallets generally allow the user to obtain a copy of the private keys, such as when the user requests a backup.

As new private keys are generated by the wallet software, the only place where this critical piece of information is saved is in the storage of the device running the wallet software. It is thus very important to **back up a wallet regularly and keep several copies of the backup in different safe locations**.

In an **address tampering** attack, a user is misled into sending funds to an incorrect address. An address tampering attack takes places when a user is about to send funds to an address and an attacker intercepts the legitimate address and substitutes it by an address under her control. An attacker that achieves man-in-the-middle status (section 5.1) could easily change the receiving address in a payment. Original wallets did not protect against the address tampering attack. This changed with the introduction of the "Payment Protocol" (BIP 70), that uses the established Public Key Infrastructure (PKI) to authenticate payment addresses (section 8.9). Aside from the man-in-the-middle technique, there are other ways to perform an address tampering attack, for instance superimposing a sticker with the QR code for the attacker's address in the menu of a restaurant that accepts Bitcoin payments. Bitcoin users should be aware of these types of attack and take the necessary steps to protect themselves.

This chapter will explain the technology behind wallet software, the different types of wallets and their security/usability trade-offs.

8.1 SYMMETRIC-KEY CRYPTOGRAPHY

To prevent unauthorized users from accessing the funds in a wallet, the private keys stored on the device are usually encrypted. When the user needs to access them, such as when signing a transaction, she provides the device with the password. The device temporarily decrypts the private keys, uses them to sign the transaction and wipes clean the memory where the unencrypted keys were stored. This process is shown in Figure 8.1.

Wallet encryption also works as a first line of defense in case the device is compromised and an attacker seizes a copy of the wallet. The strength of this protection is only as good as the chosen password. Given the weakness of most human-generated passwords and the recent advances in password cracking technology, a leaked password-protected wallet is at risk of being fleeced[1]. Thus it is advisable to keep a wallet only with limited funds online while storing most of the funds in offline wallets. Several technologies are available to keep funds offline (section 8.2).

To encrypt a wallet's private keys, symmetric-key cryptography is used. Symmetric-key cryptography was briefly introduced at the beginning of Chapter 5. The goal of a symmetric-key cipher is to "entangle" the original clear-text with the provided key in such a way that it is impossible to disentangle it without this key. Symmetric-key cryptography uses the same key for encryption and decryption. There are two types of symmetric ciphers:

- **Stream ciphers** which encrypt a stream of plain-text, one bit at a time.
- **Block ciphers** which encrypt blocks of plain-text, usually of 128 bits length.

Bitcoin Core Wallet, the reference implementation of the Bitcoin wallet, uses the AES-256 block cipher[2]. **AES** stands for Advanced Encryption Standard and was established

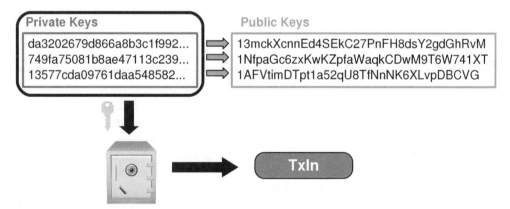

FIGURE 8.1 Encryption of wallet private keys

---

[1] To slow brute-forcing attempts, Bitcoin Core Wallet derives the symmetric-cipher key from the user password using a salt and 25,000 rounds of SHA512—see variable **nDeriveIterations** from class **CMasterKey** in `crypter.h` and function **CCrypter::SetKeyFromPassphrase** in `crypter.cpp`.

[2] Wallet encryption is implemented in the class **CCryptoKeyStore** in `crypter.h`.

by NIST in 2001, substituting DES (Wikipedia, 2014a). On a very high level, AES-256 performs 14 rounds of the following tasks:

- Key addition. This task mixes the symmetric key (actually a subkey derived from the symmetric key) with the message being encrypted.
- Byte substitution. Performs a non-linear transformation of the message being encrypted, which introduces *confusion* into the ciphertext.
- *Diffusion*. Shifts the bits of the ciphertext around, in order to spread the entropy added by the confusion task.

More details on AES can be found in any standard cryptography textbook, such as Paar and Pelzl (2010) and Wikipedia (2014a).

Bitcoin Core Wallet generates a new random change address for every transaction. This behavior is recommended to increase user privacy (Chapter 13). To guard against a loss of keys, a user should back up the wallet after every transaction. To make the backup process easier, Bitcoin Core Wallet generates a **key pool** of 100 new unused addresses in advance[3]. When the wallet software needs a new address, it taps the key pool following a first-in-first-out (FIFO) approach. The key pool is refilled every time a new key is used[4], so that the key pool always has 100 new addresses. Every time a backup is made, it includes not only the addresses holding funds, but also the 100 addresses from this keypool. Thus a backup is current for a while, until 100 new addresses are used. This does not remove the necessity to make frequent backups, but it alleviates it somewhat.

A Bitcoin Core wallet is not intended to be shared and used in several computers simultaneously. The fact that the Bitcoin Core wallet generates random addresses can lead to erratic behavior if the wallet is cloned and installed in another computer, because each computer will generate its own new addresses after a period of use.

Section 8.5 will introduce a technology that allows the generation of as many addresses as desired, only requires a single backup and can be shared among many devices.

8.2 OFFLINE WALLETS

Usually the device that holds a wallet is connected to the internet, in order to communicate with the Bitcoin network (receiving account status, sending transactions, observing confirmations, and so on). This is called an **online wallet** or a **hot wallet**. As every device connected to the internet is at risk of being compromised, it is good practice to only hold in online wallets the funds necessary for day-to-day operations. The rest of a user's funds should be kept in **offline wallets**, whose private keys are not accessible from the internet. Note that an offline wallet can sign transactions offline.

Cold storage refers to a place where the private keys are kept, that is not accessible from the internet. Private keys kept in cold storage have to be imported to a wallet (either an online or offline wallet) before spending the funds.

---

[3] This key pool default size of 100, can be changed with the command line argument -keypool=<n>.
[4] Every time a key from the key pool is used in **CWallet::ReserveKeyFromKeyPool**, it calls **CWallet::TopUpKeyPool** to fill up the key pool back to its original size (100 by default). Both functions can be found in `wallet.cpp`.

This section explores several options available to create an offline wallet and to handle cold storage.

8.2.1 External Storage Media

One way to create cold storage for the private keys is to save them in external storage media, such as USB flash drives or optical disks. Only when a private key it needed, such as when signing a transaction, is the private key retrieved from the external storage.

Note that storage media can degrade over time and the information contained is sometimes corrupted. Thus it is sensible to make several copies of the private keys.

If the private keys are retrieved by an online wallet, the device with the online wallet could be compromised and the file with the private keys stolen by an attacker. Therefore it is advisable to encrypt the file holding the private keys when saved in external media. Encrypting the files with the private keys would also protect the owner when the physical storage media is stolen.

Note that even if the file with the private keys is encrypted, an attacker that obtains a copy could attempt a brute-force attack. Moreover, if an attacker reaches root privileges on the device she could even get a copy of the encryption key or the clear-text of the private keys.

In summary, when using external storage, the weak link is the period where the private keys are imported to the online client to sign transactions. It is more secure to import the private keys from cold storage to an offline wallet.

8.2.2 Paper Wallets

Another way to create cold storage for the private keys is to print them on a piece of paper and to protect that piece of paper from physical theft. These are called **paper wallets**, although they are not technically a wallet.

In a paper wallet, public keys or Bitcoin addresses are usually printed alongside the private keys, so that the paper wallet can be easily identified without having to import the private key into a client. If the private keys are generated randomly, such as in the Bitcoin Core Wallet, a copy of each private key should be printed. Private keys are 256 bit (32 byte) integers, and can be represented in several ways:

- In **hexadecimal format**, for example "2cf24dba5fb0a30e26e83b2ac5b9e29e1b161e5c-1fa7425e73043362938b9824". This format does not have any error correction and is thus susceptible to transcription errors. Variants of this format include decimal representation, Base64 encoding, etc.
- Base58 **Wallet Import Format (WIF)**. This format uses the Base58 encoding of Bitcoin addresses with error correction. WIF keys start with a "5" and have 51 characters, for example "5Kb8kLf9zgWQnogidDA76MzPL6TsZZY36hWXMs-sSzNydYXYB9KF". This is the most widely used format to export private keys. For details on the encoding and decoding of WIF keys, see Bitcoin wiki (2014ab).
- **Mini private key format**, encodes a private key in 30 characters, including some address verification to guard against typos. Mini private keys start with the letter "S", such as in "S6c56bnXQiBjk9mqSYE7ykVQ7NzrRy". This format is used for

applications where space is critical, such as inside physical Bitcoin coins or in QR codes where low dot density is needed (Bitcoin wiki, 2014n).

- **Passphrase-protected private keys** were introduced in BIP38 (Caldwell, 2013). BIP38 keys are protected by a password, encrypted with AES-256, and the key derivation is performed using the scrypt hash function (Percival, 2012). They start with "6P", such as in "6PRVWUbkzzsbcVac2qwfssoUJAN1Xhrg6bNk8J7Nzm2ZoGg". As of the time of writing, this BIP is under discussion.

All these formats can be represented in QR codes, making the process of importing easier and less prone to typing errors. Figure 8.2 shows a paper wallet generated by bitaddress. org. The left of the image shows the address together with its QR code representation. The right side shows the private key (WIF encoded) and its associated QR code. Note the higher information density of the QR code of the private key—37 bytes—compared to that of the address—25 bytes—both including checksums.

Paper wallets can be a very secure way of storing Bitcoins if good security practices are followed when generating them. It is recommended that paper wallets are generated using offline devices, i.e. a computer connected to a printer, with both of them offline. The devices should be rebooted before and after generating the paper wallet to avoid leaving sensitive information in the devices' memory. It is advisable that the device generating the paper wallet is booted from a live CD (such as the Live CD provided by some Linux distributions) to avoid spyware stealing the private keys[5]. For a full list of these security practices, see Bitcoin wiki (2014o).

Once generated, the owner should avoid exposing the private keys, be it the WIF string or the QR code, to anyone[6].

FIGURE 8.2 Paper wallet generated using bitaddress.org

---

[5] This does not provide definitive security. An attacker could compromise the ISO of the Live CD on the distribution website, so that when the device is booted using the compromised Live CD, it could mount the bootable drive of the device and compromise it. Then it could capture the private keys that are being generated and save them in the device's main boot drive. Then when the user boots the device from the regular boot drive, the malware would be able to "phone home" with the private keys. Thus it is not totally impossible for malware to steal the private keys when booting from a Live CD, but it considerably raises the difficulty for the attacker.

[6] On December 2013 during a TV show, a host exposed the QR code of the private key of a paper wallet to the cameras. The funds were immediately taken and later returned to his owner.

As was the case for external storage, the private keys from the paper wallet must be imported into the wallet software to be able to sign transactions. If the paper wallet is imported to an online wallet, the keys are at risk of being seized by any malware that the device could be running. Thus paper wallets should only be imported moments before the funds will be used[7].

A **physical bitcoin** is a coin or piece of paper that hides a private key behind a tamper-proof mechanism. The address associated with the private keys holds certain amount of bitcoins. To spend the funds from the physical bitcoin, the private key must be recovered and imported to a wallet, much in the same way that a private key is imported from a paper wallet. The manufacturer of the physical bitcoins must be a trusted party, as the funds in a physical bitcoin are provided by the manufacturer.

8.2.3 Offline Devices

An offline wallet can be created using two devices, one connected to the internet and another offline. The connected device keeps a copy of the public keys or addresses only. When a user wants to create a transaction, the connected device assembles a transaction gathering the funds from the addresses in the wallet it sees fit, just like a regular wallet. However, this transaction cannot be signed yet, because the connected device does not have a copy of the private keys. The transaction must be sent to the offline device for signing, and the signed transaction transferred back to the connected device. Thus there must be communication between the two devices. This communication can take place, through external media, such as a USB flash drive. However, using storage media creates an indirect communication link between the two computers that can be exploited by an attacker[8].

A different approach would be to communicate the unsigned/signed transaction through out-of-band means, such as through scanned QR codes. In this configuration, the unsigned transaction could be encoded in a QR code. This QR code could be scanned by the offline device. Then, after signing, the signed transaction could be encoded in a new QR code and scanned by the online device.

In summary, the online device keeps a balance of the funds and initiates the transactions. Because the offline device is not connected to the internet it cannot know what funds are available in the addresses belonging to the wallet. The offline device is thus just a signing authority. If the online device is compromised, it constitutes a breach of the privacy of the wallet, but not of its security.

---

[7] There is the possibility that an attacker could have previously compromised the computer and tried to spend the funds in the wallet right before the legitimate owner. Both transactions would be competing to enter the blockchain first and spend the funds. An even safer practice would be to import the paper wallet to an offline device that would communicate with an online device via an out-of-band channel. This last procedure would probably leave the more paranoid security-minded users happier.

[8] This attack is not only theoretical: in 2010 a computer virus named **stuxnet** was discovered, that was allegedly used against Iranian nuclear facilities (Zetter, 2011). The malware spread through, among other means, USB flash drives, eventually reaching its target: an industrial control system computer not connected to the internet.

8.2.4 Hardware Wallets

Hardware wallets[9] are devices that both store private keys and sign transactions with these private keys. The private keys never leave the device, so they cannot be seized by malware installed on the computer of the user.

The hardware wallet communicates with a client wallet software in a computer. This client can be either a wallet program or a web wallet running inside a web browser. In any case, the client only acts as an intermediary between the hardware wallet and the blockchain, merely transmitting the transactions signed inside the hardware wallet. Some wallet software projects include support for hardware wallets.

Transactions are sent from the client wallet on the computer to the hardware wallet through some connection, usually USB. Signed transactions are returned from the hardware wallet through the same connection. Hardware wallets usually have a small screen to show the user information about the transaction, and some buttons to allow the user to decide whether to sign the transaction or decline it. If malware is installed in the user's computer, it could change the details of the transaction being sent over to the hardware wallet. The screen in the hardware wallet showing details of the transaction about to be signed is meant as a protection against this kind of attack. It is also common for the hardware wallet to require a PIN or a password to accept transactions coming through the connection.

Figure 8.3 shows a Trezor™ hardware wallet in operation, with an address and a bitcoin amount, prompting the user to either confirm or deny the transaction. The hardware wallet is connected to a computer through a USB port, and prompts the user for a PIN via the computer's wallet software.

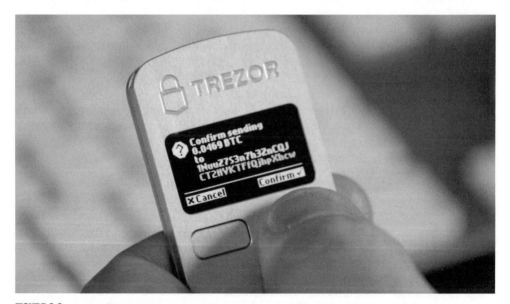

FIGURE 8.3   Trezor™ hardware wallet. Picture by SatoshiLabs (www.bitcointrezor.com)

---

[9] This discussion will be based on the Trezor™ hardware wallet, see www.bitcointrezor.com. For a list of other hardware wallets, see Bitcoin wiki (2014j).

To protect against loss, theft, or malfunction of the hardware wallet, the user must keep a copy of the private key on some other medium, such as paper or external storage. Hardware wallets usually allow the user to make a copy of the private key during initialization of the device. In particular, Trezor™ uses deterministic wallet technology (section 8.5) to generate many addresses from a single master private key, and therefore only a backup of this master key is necessary.

8.3   WEB WALLETS

Web wallets (also called **hosted wallets** or **cloud wallets**) are online accounts with an external provider, where a user can deposit her funds. The funds are controlled by the web wallet provider. By authenticating with the web wallet provider, the user can later access those funds, i.e. make transactions. The main advantage of web wallets are that they are easy to set up (just signing up to a web service) and that the management of the private keys is done by the web wallet provider, thus lowering the entry barrier for new users. There are additional advantages, such as low commissions[10] for transactions, or the possibility to settle transactions between users of the same service instantaneously and at zero fees. Many of the services offered by web wallet providers are also offered by online exchanges and so-called Bitcoin banks, so the considerations of this section also apply to these businesses.

Web wallets are similar to online banking, in the sense that funds are kept by the web wallet provider. However, in contrast to regular banks, where deposits are covered by deposit insurance, the user has no recourse against the web wallet provider absconding with the funds. Furthermore, web wallet providers are not as thoroughly regulated as banks are, which can increase doubts about their solvency (section 8.3).

Security practices for web wallet providers or exchanges are similar to the practices for individual users: users should store in online wallets only the funds necessary for day-to-day operations, and keep the rest in offline wallets/cold storage. Note that, in addition to the risk of the web wallet provider stealing their users' funds, there is the risk that the provider is hacked and loses the funds, thus making the service insolvent.

The use of web wallets has privacy implications too. On the one hand they can increase the anonymity of the user, because the addresses used in transactions are those of the web wallet with no direct relation to the user. On the other hand, anonymity is decreased because the web wallet provider usually keeps a record of the transactions, and also retains personal information about their users.

Hybrid web wallets are web wallets where the private keys are stored in the user's computer, but managed by software (usually written in Javascript) from the wallet service provider. Transactions initiated by the users are communicated first to the web wallet provider, who later publishes them on the blockchain. The advantage is a reduced exposure to the service provider, but at the cost of increasing the burden to the user of keeping a secure system.

---

[10] A web wallet service provider can pool many transactions before pushing them onto the blockchain, reducing transaction costs.

8.4   BRAIN WALLETS

Brain wallets generate a private key by hashing a long password or passphrase. Bitcoin private keys are 256 bits long, so a hashing function that yields a 256 bit hash, such as SHA256, can be used. A brain wallet's password does not need to be stored in a device; rather it should be stored in the brain of the user—hence the name. This has the advantage that no backups are needed, provided the user is able to remember the password. As was the case with paper wallets, they are called brain wallets although they do not constitute actual wallets: the password still needs to be imported to an actual wallet to access the funds.

Brain wallets have a big disadvantage that should dissuade anyone from using them: they are subject to brute-force attacks that could steal all the funds in the wallet if successful. A brute-force attack tries many passwords and checks if the address generated from the password exists and has funds. The chances of success of these attacks are very high. First, users are very bad at choosing passwords with a high degree of entropy. Second, password cracking technology has got much better in the last years, thanks to technologies such as dictionary attacks, rainbow tables, GPUs and the fact that several big password databases have been leaked[11]. An account of the recent advances in password cracking can be found in Goodin (2012).

Key stretching is a technique used to slow down password cracking. Key stretching uses a slow hash function, such as SHA256 applied 1,000 times in a row to derive the private keys from the password. There are also deliberate slow hash functions such as bcrypt or scrypt[12], that were specifically developed to curb password crackers—see "Password Hashing" in section 7.1.

Researchers tested sending small amounts to addresses generated using weak passwords: the funds have been quickly stolen. There are attackers actively searching the blockchain for addresses generated using weak passwords to steal the funds. As Bitcoin developers warn (Andresen, 2012): "Do not use a brainwallet! You are likely to lose your coins." In summary, **do not use brain wallets**.

8.5   DETERMINISTIC WALLETS

A **deterministic wallet** is a wallet that can generate many addresses (and their associated private keys) from a common private key. Deterministic wallets have several advantages over regular wallets:

- **Easier backups**. Regular wallets must be backed up every time a new (random) address is created. Some wallets generate addresses in advance, e.g. Bitcoin Core Wallet generates 100 addresses in advance by default. In contrast, a deterministic wallet requires only one backup when the wallet is set up.

---

[11] As a user posted in Reddit: "Just lost 4 BTC out of a hacked brain wallet. The pass phrase was a line from an obscure poem in Afrikaans. Somebody out there has a really comprehensive dictionary attack program running." (www.reddit.com/r/Bitcoin/comments/1ptuf3/).

[12] For instance some wallets use scrypt or 100,000 rounds of SHA256 for key stretching.

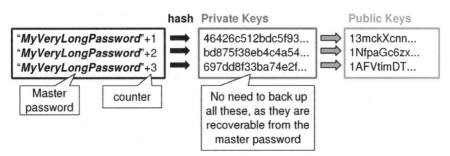

FIGURE 8.4 Type-1 deterministic wallet

- **Smaller backups**. The backup size of regular wallets grows over time, as more and more addresses are added to the wallet. This can be cumbersome when backing up a wallet on paper. The backup of a deterministic wallet has a small constant size, as only the master password needs to be backed up (see below).
- **Generation of new addresses without knowledge of the private key**. This is a feature of type-2 deterministic wallets, see below.

A deterministic wallet can be built from a brain wallet. Figure 8.4 shows how a sequence of addresses can be generated using a **master password** "MyVeryLongPassword" by appending a counter to the password before hashing it to yield the private keys:

$$priv = H(pw|n)$$
$$B = priv \cdot A \bmod p$$

Where pw is the master password, n is the counter, H is a secure hash function, $priv$ is the private key, A is the generator of the elliptic curve, B is the public key from which the address can be generated and p is the order of the prime field under which the elliptic curve operations are performed (section 5.4). This type of wallet is called **type-1 deterministic wallet** (Maxwell, 2011). The addresses generated by a type-1 deterministic wallet are impossible to relate to one another by anyone who does not know the master password.

As with brain wallets, type-1 deterministic wallets are susceptible to brute-force attacks and should not be used unless the master password has been generated with enough entropy.

Type-2 deterministic wallets (Maxwell, 2011) allow the separation of the roles of generating a private key and generating an address. These wallets use the properties of elliptic curves to calculate new public keys without revealing private keys (section 5.4). The main idea is to split the ECC private key into two parts:

$$priv = mpk + H(pw|n)$$
$$B = priv \cdot A \bmod p$$
$$= mpk \cdot A + H(pw|n) \cdot A \bmod p$$
$$= B_{mpk} + H(pw|n) \cdot A \bmod p$$

Where *mpk* is a **master *private* key** and B_{mpk} is the **master *public* key**. The private key *priv* is composed of two elements: *mpk*, which is kept secret, and $H(pw|n)$, which can be generated from a master password *pw*. Receive-only wallets are given only *pw* and B_{mpk}, so that they can compute addresses, such as *B*. However, only the owner of the master private key, *mpk*, can compute the final private key *priv* for the generated address.

Type-2 deterministic wallets increase security because of the separation of the roles of the master password *pw* and the master private key *mpk*. First, the *mpk* is a regular ECC private key which can be randomly generated and backed up following standard procedures. Second, although the master password *pw* is shared among many users, its compromise does not lead to a compromise of the funds (as with type-1 deterministic wallets), only to a loss of privacy.

An application of type-2 deterministic wallets is an online business with customer facing servers. The business administrator can give the servers a copy of the master public key B_{mpk} and the master password *pw*. Servers can then use them to generate new addresses used to receive payments from customers. As the servers do not have a copy of the private keys for those addresses, the funds cannot be stolen in case of a compromise. All an attacker can do is observe the funds stored in the addresses derived from the master public key.

Wallets that depend upon offline devices to sign transactions usually use the key-splitting feature of elliptic curves discussed. Only the offline device holds the master private key *mpk*, whereas the online wallet client is given only the master public key B_{mpk}. Thus the online client can generate new addresses and assemble transactions, but only the offline device can correctly sign them.

An undesirable property of type-2 deterministic wallets is that receive-only wallets can generate all addresses in the wallet, and can therefore observe all the funds available and all the transactions taking place. A useful property for a wallet would be that a receive-only wallet could only generate a subset of the addresses in the wallet. Hierarchical deterministic wallets, introduced later, have this property.

8.5.1 Message Authentication Code (MAC)

This section introduces Message Authentication Codes (MACs), a cryptographic primitive that will be used in Hierarchical Deterministic Wallets.

A **Message Authentication Code (MAC)** is a piece of data of fixed length that is appended to a message between two parties sharing a *symmetric key* known only to them. A **MAC function** takes two inputs, a message of arbitrary length and the symmetric key, and outputs a MAC. The sender generates a MAC using the symmetric key and appends the MAC to the message. The receiver can then verify that the message originated from the sender (*authenticity*) and that the message has not been tampered with (*integrity*). A MAC function can also be viewed as a hash function with the symmetric key as an extra input.

A MAC serves a similar purpose to a digital signature, but with an important difference: the key used to generate it is a symmetric key. Therefore, a MAC does not provide *non-repudiation*: as the receiver keeps a copy of the symmetric key, she can produce the MAC of any message of her choosing. Therefore, a MAC does not prove that the message was generated by the sender; it could have been generated by the receiver. The advantage of MACs over digital signatures is that they are much faster to compute.

MACs can be constructed from hash functions or from block ciphers. A **Hash-based Message Authentication Code (HMAC)** is a way to construct a MAC using a hash function as a building block. HMACs are provably secure under the assumption that the hash function is collision-resistant (Paar and Pelzl, 2010). Hierarchical deterministic wallets use an HMAC to derive the private keys, using the HMAC-SHA512 algorithm. For more details on HMACs, see Paar and Pelzl (2010), Ferguson et al. (2010), or Katz and Lindell (2007).

8.5.2 Hierarchical Deterministic Wallets

Hierarchical Deterministic wallets (HD wallets) are deterministic wallets whose derived addresses form a hierarchy. As with deterministic wallets, all their addresses can be derived from a starting secret. As was the case with type-2 deterministic wallets, public keys and private keys can be derived separately. The novelty introduced by HD wallets is that the addresses it generates are sorted in a tree structure such that a node has visibility of its descendants but not of its ascendants.

There are two types of nodes in the tree: **private nodes** that hold the private keys to the sub-tree originating from them, and **public nodes** that hold only the public keys to their sub-tree. Aside from the private and public keys, each node has an additional 32-byte field called the **chain code**. The goal of the chain code is to add additional entropy to each node. Thus revealing an address does not automatically reveal the tree derived from that node.

A node is represented by the key (either private or public) and the chain code. Figure 8.5 shows how nodes use an HMAC function to derive branches. There are two types of derivation: **private child derivation** that can be performed only by private nodes and **public child derivation** that can be performed by both private and public nodes. The figure shows how a private node (left) derives a private and a public node, and how a public node (right) derives a public node. The **child number** is a 4-byte integer that determines the branch that will be derived. Values over 0x80000000 denote private child derivation, and values below that number denote public derivation. Thus every private node in the tree can have 2^{31} private descendants and 2^{31} public descendants. Every public node can only

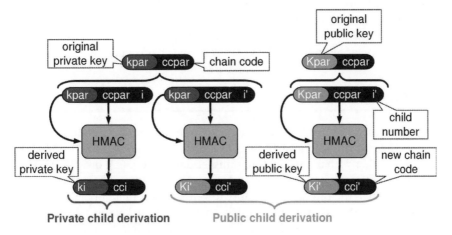

FIGURE 8.5 Hierarchical Deterministic Wallet (BIP 32)

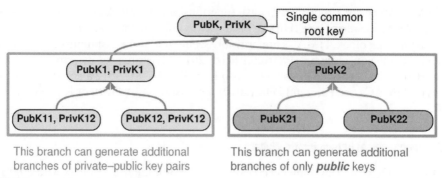

This branch can generate additional   This branch can generate additional
branches of private–public key pairs   branches of only *public* keys

FIGURE 8.6   Tree created by an HD wallet

have 2^{31} public descendants. Their descendants in turn can have their own descendants and so on. Nodes in the tree are represented by their path from the root (Wuille, 2012).

Hierarchical Deterministic wallets allow generating private and public tree branches from a single root key. Figure 8.6 represents two trees, one private and one public derived from a single common master private key. The owner of this master private key controls the funds in the whole tree. Additionally the holders of private nodes have control of the funds in those branches of the tree. Holders of public nodes can only generate public branches, but do not have control over the funds in those branches.

The often-cited application of HD wallets is a company where each business unit controls a private node, while the accountants and auditors receive the root public node. However, as explained in Buterin (2013i), this setup can be attacked if the holder of a branch private key and the holder of the root public key decide to cooperate, for instance if the department head and the auditor decide to run off with the money.

Historically, different wallet implementations have been incompatible: a wallet file generated with one wallet implementation is hard—if not impossible—to import to another wallet implementation. To help create compatibility between different wallets, hierarchical deterministic wallets have been standardized in BIP 32 (Wuille, 2012). This standardization will hopefully increase portability of wallet files. BIP 32 describes how nodes in an HD wallet can be represented by a 111 character Base58 encoded string that starts with "xprv" for private nodes and "xpub" for public nodes. This representation includes information about both the ECC keys and the chain code.

8.6   MULTISIGNATURE WALLETS

One way to increase the security of a wallet is to store the funds in multisignature outputs: outputs that require several signatures to unlock the funds. Multisignature outputs can be achieved either with multisignature transactions (section 6.3) or with P2SH transactions (section 6.6).

There is a push in the Bitcoin community towards wallets that handle multisignature transactions to avoid the single point of failure that the private keys in a wallet represent. A multisignature wallet presents the user the funds unlockable by multiple signatures and how many of the required private keys are part of the wallet. As of the time of writing, multisignature support in most wallets is a work in progress. **Second-generation web wallets** use multisignature transactions (section 8.3).

Multisignature wallets can be combined with hierarchical deterministic wallets in what are called **Hierarchical Deterministic Multisignature wallets (HDM wallets)** (Buterin, 2014d; CryptoCorp, 2014). HDM wallets use several HD wallets, each with its own independent seed, and combine the addresses generated by these independent HD wallets to form multisignature transactions. The advantage of HDM wallets is that many multisignature transactions can be generated from the private master keys, increasing convenience.

8.7 VANITY ADDRESSES

Most Bitcoin addresses are random in nature. But some users, like an online retailer, might wish to have a "personalized" address that starts with a message. For instance the author of this book might wish to have an address that starts with 1pfranco. This type of address is called a vanity address. Vanity addresses can be searched for by trial and error, using any Bitcoin wallet software. The user can ask the wallet to generate an address, inspect the address, i.e. to see if it starts with 1pfranco, and, if it doesn't, request a new address from the Bitcoin wallet software. Of course, this process can be automated. Originally users of Bitcoin who wanted to create a vanity address applied a patch to Bitcoin Core, called the vanity patch, that turned Bitcoin Core into a search engine for vanity addresses. Nowadays most users use a tool called vanitygen,[13] which, aside from being faster, offers several other advantages over Bitcoin Core with the vanity patch applied.

Vanitygen employs a brute-force algorithm. It works by generating a random 256-bit private key, computing the corresponding public key, i.e. the EC point, and then following the procedure of section 5.6 to arrive at the Bitcoin address. If there is a match with the desired prefix specified by the user, vanitygen presents the user with the private key and the address and exits. If there is no match, vanitygen generates a new random private key and follows the procedure again. The private key resulting from running vanitygen can then be imported to a wallet, and used regularly as with any other Bitcoin address.

Figure 8.7 shows vanitygen running in the author's laptop, trying to arrive at a Bitcoin address that starts with 1pfranco. The program shows the difficulty of the problem, i.e. the number of addresses that should be tested on average until the desired vanity address is found. It also shows the rate at which addresses are tested (317.16 Kkeys/s), the progress thus far (32141060 keys tested) and the estimated time to arrive at the desired vanity address with a 50% probability (3.6 years). Finding a vanity address is a computationally intensive problem. Furthermore, it increases exponentially with the number of characters to match. Figure 8.8 shows the output of vanitygen trying to find an address that starts with 1pfran. The estimated time with a 50% probability is 9.4 hours in this case. Being a brute-force algorithm, vanitygen can be used to find a match to a complete Bitcoin address. However, this operation would take an astronomical amount of time, as shown in Figure 8.9.

Vanitygen can run on a CPU or on a GPU. It is advisable to use it on a GPU to greatly speed up the task of finding a vanity address. Vanitygen also allows using regular

---

[13] Vanitygen can be found at github.com/samr7/vanitygen.

FIGURE 8.7   Vanitygen address generator

$ ./vanitygen **1pfran**
Difficulty: 15318045009
[308.65 Kkey/s][total 2300672][Prob 0.0%][50% in 9.6h]

FIGURE 8.8   Vanitygen address generator with a shorter prefix

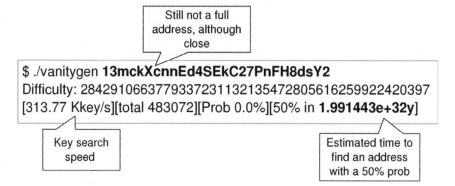

FIGURE 8.9   Vanitygen address generator with a string close to the size of an address

expressions, not just prefixes. It also allows the input of a file with the desired prefixes or regular expressions to search, which permits searching for several unrelated vanity addresses concurrently, thus achieving economies of scale. Someone with vast amounts of computing power could offer a service to search for vanity addresses, thus reaping the benefits of these economies of scale. The problem is, however, that the client of this service cannot be sure that the vanity generator she has hired would not keep a copy of the private key.

There is a workaround to this problem by using split-key elliptic curve math (section 8.5). The user generates a EC pair. She keeps the private key to herself and sends the public key to the vanity generator. The vanity generator *starts the search from the public key provided, instead of from the generator of the elliptic curve*. That is, the vanity generator searches for a partial private key. When found, the vanity generator sends this partial private key to the client. The client adds up the two partial parts of the private key to arrive at the final private key. The vanity generator never gets to know the full private key, and thus is not able to steal the funds in the address. There are services, called vanity pools, that allow users to post a partial public key and a desired vanity address. Then anybody with computational power can try to solve for those vanity addresses, getting a fee when a vanity address is found. The operator of the pool gets a cut of the fee.

Vanity addresses have their advantages, especially in terms of branding. However, using vanity addresses gives away with the (pseudo)anonymity of Bitcoin addresses, and makes it easier to data mine the transaction graph, facilitating the process of matching Bitcoin addresses with real world identities (Chapter 13). Also note that vanity addresses are usually reused, i.e. multiple transaction outputs are signed out of them. This could be a security problem if used with a wallet software that uses a weak random number generator (5.4.2).

Finally, a word of caution with vanity addresses: vanity addresses are subject to the address tampering attack introduced at the beginning of this chapter. A vanity address with a certain message in it does not necessarily belong to the company or institution on the address because anyone can generate it. For instance, a Bitcoin address that starts with 1pfranco does not necessarily belong to this author. Furthermore, there can be many addresses that start with 1pfranco, generated and controlled by different people. All that can be said about a vanity address is that someone has spent computational power to arrive at such an address.

8.8 SIMPLIFIED PAYMENT VERIFICATION (SPV)

Full Bitcoin nodes verify new blocks that are added to the blockchain, checking that all transactions included are properly signed and that the hash of the blocks satisfy the proof-of-work difficulty. During this process, full nodes maintain a cache of unspent transaction outputs, UTXO (Chapter 6). The UTXO can be queried by a wallet to determine the amount of funds available in the addresses controlled by that wallet. A wallet implementation following this approach has two disadvantages that make it unpractical for lightweight clients:

- It requires downloading and storing the full blockchain. The size of the full blockchain is already beyond the reach of smartphones both in terms of storage and network bandwidth.
- It requires a full node verifying all blocks and all transactions contained in those blocks. At the current level of network utilization of 0.5 tps (transactions per second) (section 7.7) validating all transactions in the block is within the reach of the average smartphone. The problem is, however, that this transaction verification would quickly drain the battery of the device.

One possible solution would be to run a wallet client that would connect to a trusted server. The wallet would use the trusted server as a proxy to connect to the Bitcoin network. It could query the server for new transactions to certain addresses periodically, and it could use the server to relay signed transactions to the network.

Another possible solution is to use a **Simplified Payment Verification (SPV)** wallet. SPV was introduced by Satoshi Nakamoto in the original Bitcoin paper (Nakamoto, 2008a), where Nakamoto proposed that an SPV client only keep a copy of the block headers. When an SPV client needs to verify a transaction it downloads the Merkle branch that binds the transaction to the block header (section 7.6). Note that SPV clients do not need to rely on trusted nodes. The SPV approach is followed by several open source Bitcoin wallets.

When there are conflicting branches, i.e. a fork in the blockchain, a regular node will assume the longest blockchain (in terms of difficulty) is the legitimate one. Thus a regular node determines the validity of transactions by their inclusion in a block that belongs to the longest chain. This is called the **block height** validity check. In contrast, an SPV client determines the validity of a transaction by how many blocks have been mined on top of the block where the transaction is included. This is called the **block depth** validity check.

The original Bitcoin paper did not address how an SPV client would receive information about the relevant transactions, i.e. transactions involving the addresses controlled by the wallet. A query mechanism between the SPV client and the node is needed. This need is filled by connection Bloom filtering, specified in BIP 37 (Hearn, 2012). **Connection Bloom filtering** allows nodes in the network to set up filters in their connection with other nodes.

A **Bloom filter** is a probabilistic data structure that represents a set. Testing if an element belongs to the set is an efficient operation. The idea behind bloom filters is to use an array of bits that are filled with the results of applying several hash functions to the elements[14]. That is, the hash functions perform a mapping from elements to the array of bits. To test if an element belongs to the filter, the result of its hashing is compared against the bits set in the filter. If all bits that are 1 in the hash are set in the filter the element belongs to the filter. Conversely if any bit that is 1 in the hash is not set in the filter the element does not belong to the filter (Bloom, 1970).

Bloom filters are probabilistic data structures because their results are not exact. False positives, where an element which does not belong to the set is flagged as part of the set, are possible. However, false negatives, where an element which does belong to the set is not flagged as part of the set, are not possible. This is not a limiting factor for SPV clients: false positives are just transactions that the client is not interested in and can be discarded.

A client can set up a filter with a node. The node will then serve filtered blocks, i.e. blocks that only include transactions (and their branch of the Merkle tree) captured by the filter[15]. To create a filtered block, the node parses all incoming transaction testing the hash of each transaction and every data element in the inputs and outputs of a transaction against the Bloom filter. If there is a match against the filter, the transaction is included in the filtered block. Because all data elements of a transaction are tested, addresses, public keys and even the hashes of P2SH transactions can all be added to a filter[16].

---

[14] Bloom filters proposed in BIP 37 use the Murmur algorithm to generate the hash functions used in the filter.

[15] Bloom filters are implemented in Bitcoin Core in the class **CBloomFilter** in `bloom.(h|cpp)`. The **CBloomFilter** class is then used by CMerkleBlock in `main.(h|cpp)`.

[16] Some meta-coins (section 12.7) use Bitcoin's blockchain to store their meta-coin transactions. Bloom filters can be set up to filter transactions belonging to these meta-coins.

The precision of a bloom filter is defined as the fraction of false positives. This precision depends on the percentage of set bits in the filter. A filter that includes many elements would have a large percentage of its bits set and would lead to many false positives. This behavior can be used by clients to increase the privacy of their queries to a node. Increasing the number of bits set in the filter would include more transactions than the desired ones, making it harder for the node to single out the addresses controlled by the client. However, this comes at the cost of an increased bandwidth. Thus Bloom filtering allows a trade-off between privacy and bandwidth.

Both lightweight clients that use trusted nodes and those that use SPV are called **thin clients**. A review of the security implications of thin clients can be found in Bitcoin wiki (2014y).

8.9   THE "PAYMENT PROTOCOL" (BIP 70)

The Payment Protocol is a communication protocol between a merchant and a client wishing to pay with bitcoins, specified in BIP 70 (Andresen, 2013c). Before the Payment Protocol, when a client paid a merchant with bitcoins, she had to copy and paste the merchant's Bitcoin address in her wallet client, select the amount and make the wallet send the payment[17]. This procedure is vulnerable to man-in-the-middle attacks (section 5.1): an attacker that controls the connection to the network can replace the Bitcoin address of the merchant with an address of her own.

The Payment Protocol extends Bitcoin addresses with a message that also contains the name of the merchant, the amount to pay, and an additional message from the merchant. The whole message is signed by the merchant with the private key of his X.509 certificate. **X.509** is one of the most widely used standards for public key infrastructure (PKI, see section 5.1) in the internet.

A transaction following the Payment Protocol takes these steps:

- The client decides to make a payment, i.e. clicks the "pay button."
- The merchant creates a payment request and signs it with its X.509 certificate. This payment request includes the address where the merchant wishes to receive the payment.
- The merchant sends the signed payment request along with the certificate to the client wallet.
- The wallet checks that the message is correctly signed with the X.509 certificate included in the payment request and that the X.509 certificate is signed by a Certificate Authority whose certificate is found in the device[18]. It then shows the user the name of the merchant and the solicited amount.

---

[17] This process had been somewhat streamlined with the introduction of the URI scheme in BIPs 20 and 21 (Dashjr, 2011; Schneider, 2012). Using the URI scheme, clicking on a payment link would open the wallet software with the address of the merchant and the correct amount already filled in. The URI scheme has been extended to support the Payment Protocol in BIP 72 (Andresen, 2013d).

[18] This procedure is standard and is followed by every browser when connecting to a website through https.

- If the user accepts the payment, the wallet creates and signs a transaction sending the funds to the requested address(es), and includes it in a message for the merchant. This message can contain additional information, such as a return Bitcoin address or a message to the merchant.
- The merchant receives the payment message, extracts the signed transaction and publishes it to the network[19]. It then returns a signed payment receipt to the client, who thus receives immediate confirmation of the payment.

Note how using X.509 certificates provides protection against man-in-the-middle attacks, as the merchant signs the payment address using her X.509 certificate's private key. Some additional features of the Payment Protocol include:

- The merchant and the client can use the Payment Protocol to send messages between them. In particular, messages sent by the merchant would be presented to the user by the wallet client.
- The merchant can split the funds to be received between many addresses. This could be used to implement merge avoidance (13.4.4).
- The client can include refund addresses to be used by the merchant in case the order cannot be fulfilled[20]. Return addresses can be generated automatically by the wallet software, for instance using BIP 32 (8.5.2), to automatically avoid address reuse.
- The payment receipt can include a proof of payment signed by the merchant that the client can later use in case of a dispute.

For a full specification of the protocol, consult BIP 70 in Andresen (2013c).

---

[19] The client could also publish the signed transaction to the network herself.

[20] Before this feature was introduced, the merchant would have to get in contact with the client—say by email—and request a refund address. Note that the merchant should not assume that the address it received funds from is a valid return address: the private keys for this address could have been deleted by the wallet after depleting the funds, the user could have been using a web wallet where the address belongs to the web wallet provider, or the user could have stopped using that wallet.

CHAPTER 9

Mining

Bitcoin mining was introduced in section 7.4, in the context of the blockchain. **Mining** is the process of adding blocks to the blockchain. Miners contribute their computational power to solve the blocks that are added to the blockchain, and the network remunerates them with the block reward and the fees collected from all the transactions included in the block.

Miners solve the partial hash inversion problem. To find a solution, mining software usually increments the block nonce and runs the proof-of-work algorithm to check if the chosen nonce generates a correct block hash (i.e. a block hash that meets the difficulty requirements)[1].

A typical optimization used by miners is to pre-compute the hash of the initial part of the block header that contains the previous block hash and the root of the Merkle transaction tree (section 7.6). This part of the block header is constant during the mining process and therefore can be stored in a buffer.

One of the advantages of the mining mechanism is that it rewards early adopters for supporting the network. This was very important in the beginning, when Bitcoin bootstrapped itself into relevance. Bitcoin does not have a corporation backing it, so marketing had to be done virally. This would have been impossible without the help of early adopters. Rewarding miners is a way to enlist them to create word of mouth.

Mining is similar to a market with perfect competition: as long as there is profit to be made, new entrants will enter the market until the profit opportunity is depleted. As described in 7.4, the mining difficulty increases as more miners enter the network, but the total block reward stays the same. At the creation of Bitcoin, the block reward was 50 bitcoins. This block reward is halved every 210,000 blocks[2], or roughly every 4 years, to comply with the pace of money creation set in the protocol. Figure 9.1 shows the amount of bitcoins issued. Note that the issuance of new bitcoins is not a smooth line, as the introduction of new mining capacity temporarily increases the rate of new block creation until the feedback mechanism catches on. Thus, under an increasing network hash rate, the issuance of new bitcoins accelerates somehow. On November 28, 2012—"halving day"—more than a month ahead of schedule, the block reward was halved to 25 bitcoins. As of the time of writing, the protocol awards a fixed reward of roughly $24 \cdot 6 \cdot 25 = 3,600$ bitcoins every day.

---

[1] Mining is implemented in Bitcoin Core in the function **BitcoinMiner**. The actual mining loop can be found in the function **ScanHash_CryptoPP**. Both functions are located in `miner.cpp`. The probabilities of finding a partial hash inversion are the same whether the block nonce is incremented or the nonce is generated randomly, so mining algorithms will implement whichever is faster. Mining was disabled by default in the Bitcoin client, as it became uneconomical to mine using CPUs.

[2] See variable **nSubsidyHalvingInterval** in `chainparams.cpp`.

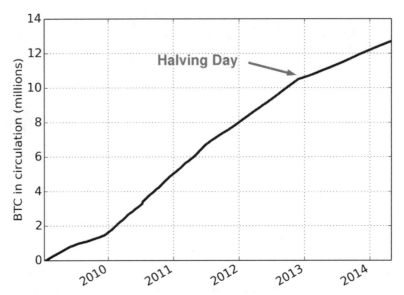

FIGURE 9.1 Bitcoins in circulation. Data from <u>blockchain.info</u>

Bitcoin is a peer-to-peer network; anyone can connect to it and start mining right away. New entrants do not have to ask for permission or adhere to a set of rules or regulations before they enter the mining market. Nor can incumbents collude to prevent new participants from entering. Thus new investment will enter the contest to capture the block reward, lowering the reward of all miners already in the network. Thus, in an scenario of increasing bitcoin price (or increasing technological advancement), miners have to keep increasing their hashing rate in order to obtain the same reward, in a process similar to the Red Queen Effect[3]. This process will continue until the marginal cost of the last miner to enter equals her expected reward. At this point the network has reached an equilibrium, which can only be perturbed by some external factor, such as a further increase in bitcoin prices.

There are, however, some factors that could confer a sustainable advantage to some participants, allowing them to enjoy higher profits:

- **Technological advantage**. This technological advantage could either stem from an innovation in the implementation of the proof-of-work algorithm (SHA256^2) in silicon hardware[4] or it could stem from a miner controlling a better chip manufacturing process, such as a big chip manufacturer entering the mining business.

---

[3] The Red Queen Effect refers to situations where competitors must constantly evolve, not to gain an advantage but merely to survive in a highly competitive environment. It gets its name from Lewis Carroll's Red Queen character when she explained to Alice that it took all the running she could do just to keep in the same place.

[4] At the time of writing, an SHA256 hash function takes approximately 20,000 gates to build. A technological breakthrough that reduces that number significantly could spark a new episode in the ASICs arms race.

- **Hedging Bitcoin volatility**. A miner could get an advantage if she were able to hedge the Bitcoin price volatility more effectively than her competitors. Any miner could in principle hedge the Bitcoin price volatility using Bitcoin futures[5] but, as of the time of writing, this market is almost non-existent. This advantage could be specially important during periods where the price of Bitcoin is depressed and competitors could be forced to shut down[6]. Furthermore, a miner who is able to hedge the volatility of her income would require a lower rate of return for her investment.
- **Lower electricity prices**. Miners who are able to secure low electricity prices have a cost advantage. Bitcoin mining would likely migrate to places with cheap and abundant electricity, such as Iceland. This might even decrease the environmental impact of Bitcoin mining, as places with cheap electricity are usually able to generate it from environmental-friendly sources, such as hydro-electrical plants.

In summary, barriers to entry to the mining business are generally low, as there is no way for the incumbents to collude and prevent new competition from entering the network. Therefore the network hash rate will probably stabilize at a rate where the mining reward just covers the marginal costs of running the mining equipment.

The marginal costs of running mining equipment include the cost of electricity, but also the renting costs of the datacenter, refrigeration costs, maintenance, and so on. Then there is the amortization cost of the equipment itself, or its opportunity cost. The only currently viable technology—ASIC—is highly optimized for Bitcoin mining, and does not have any other alternative use[7]. These factors, coupled with the lag in the production of mining equipment in response to Bitcoin's price increases, could create boom and bust cycles in the mining market.

It has been argued in Güring and Grigg (2011) that as botnet operators do not have to pay the operating costs of running the equipment (notably the electricity costs), mining botnets would displace legitimate mining, leading to the collapse of Bitcoin mining. However, with the current network hash rate (section 9.1), it is more economical for a bot-herder to use her botnet for other nefarious purposes (click fraud, email spam, or plain spyware) than to use it for Bitcoin mining.

---

[5] A short position in a bitcoin future would pay the difference between the price of bitcoin at the inception of the contract and the price of bitcoin at a predetermined date. For example, if the price of a bitcoin has dropped from 600 USD to 500 USD, the short future would pay 600 USD – 500 USD = 100 USD. A miner who holds a short position in this future contract would effectively lock a future bitcoin price of 600 USD: 500 USD coming from the market at the expiration of the contract and 100 USD coming from the payoff of the future contract.

[6] This might turn out not to be a significant advantage because, even though some miners would turn off the mining hardware during certain periods, the hardware is still there and could be turned on again if the price of bitcoin recovers.

[7] An alternative use to mining Bitcoin would be mining other cryptocurrency whose proof-of-work hash function is SHA256 or SHA256^2, such as Peercoin or Namecoin. As the prices of most cryptocurrencies are highly correlated, a drop in bitcoin prices would most likely lead to a switch-off of the uneconomical mining equipment.

9.1 MINING TECHNOLOGY

As of the time of writing, the network hash rate stands at around 30,000,000 GH/s (= 30,000 TH/s = 30 PH/s). Figure 9.2 presents the evolution of the network hash rate since Bitcoin's inception, on a logarithmic scale[8]. The figure shows the dates of introduction of new technologies and the corresponding "eras" in mining history. The exponential growth in the network hash rate has been due to two trends:

- Exponential growth in the price of Bitcoin itself, which has attracted a lot of mining investment.
- Advances in mining technology, as mining equipment manufacturers have caught up with state-of-the-art chip manufacturing.

Mining hardware has followed a trend toward more specialized hardware where a larger part of the circuitry of the chip is dedicated to the hashing function. There have been four phases in this transition:

- **CPUs**. CPU stands for Central Processing Unit: the main chip inside computers and other devices. It is general purpose hardware: its computational power can be applied to many tasks, including mining Bitcoin. The initial release of the Bitcoin Core implemented mining on the CPU. During the first phase of Bitcoin mining, running from 2009 to the summer of 2010, mining was performed only using CPUs. During this phase, the growth of the hash rate was due to new enthusiasts entering

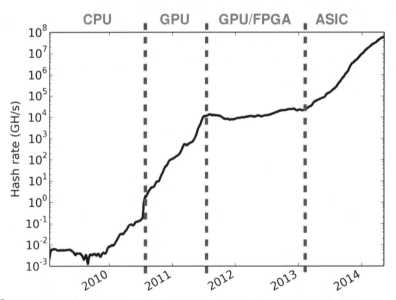

FIGURE 9.2   Hash rate of the Bitcoin network. Hash rate data from blockchain.info

---

[8] Linear growth on a logarithmic scale equals exponential growth on a linear scale. The growth of the network hash rate has been exponential so far.

the mining space. The latest retail processors offer a hash rate of approximately 20MH/s.

- **GPUs**. GPU stands for Graphics Processing Unit: the specialized computer chip originally used for graphic acceleration. There is a trend in computing of using the parallel power of GPUs to perform general computations, known as GPGPU or General-Purpose computing on GPU. Starting in mid-2010, GPUs were programmed to mine Bitcoins, quickly rendering CPU mining uneconomical[9]. GPUs offer an advantage over CPUs because they are composed of hundreds or even thousands of computational units, compared with the handful in a typical CPU. The computational units of a GPU are much more limited than those of a CPU, but enough to perform SHA256 hashes. For a more detailed explanation of why GPUs offer a greater hash rate than CPUs, see Bitcoin wiki (2014ac). The latest GPUs offer a hash rate ranging from 100MH/s to 500MH/s.

- **FPGAs**. FPGA stands for Field-Programmable Gate Array. FPGAs are chips built of logic blocks that can be programmed and interconnected to perform a particular task. As the name suggest, FPGAs are designed to be programmable "in the field," i.e. after shipping. FPGAs were introduced in Bitcoin mining in mid-2011 and for a time competed with GPUs. GPUs held the advantage on cost per GH/s and resale value, while FPGAs had an advantage in lower power consumption (Taylor, 2013). Typical FPGAs have a hash rate of approximately 1 GH/s.

- **ASICs**. ASIC stands for Application-Specific Integrated Circuit. ASICs are chips built for a specific application, in contrast to CPUs (or, to a lesser degree, GPUs) that accept software running many possible applications. ASIC parts have the logic of the SHA256 function copied as many times as the area of the chip allows, in order to run as many hash tries in parallel as possible. Early ASIC design reused the technology developed for FPGAs (Taylor, 2013). The hash power of an ASIC depends on its manufacturing process technology. At the time of writing, 28nm ASICs offer a hash rate of approximately 500 GH/s, with 20nm 3TH/s parts in sight.

Some of the periods of exponential increase (or even jumps) in the network hash rate have coincided with the introduction of new mining technologies (see Figure 9.2). The latest period—ASICs era—is still in progress at the time of writing. However, as the next ASIC iteration (20nm) catches up with the state-of-the-art in chip manufacturing process, the exponential trend in hash rate is set to level off. From that point on, economics suggest that increases in the network hash rate will follow advances in chip manufacturing process and bitcoin prices[10].

---

[9] Sathosi Nakamoto initially envisioned mining as computational democracy, saying "proof-of-work is essentially one-CPU-one-vote" in the original Bitcoin paper (Nakamoto, 2008a). He (she?) commented on the forums: "We should have a gentleman's agreement to postpone the GPU arms race as long as we can for the good of the network" (Marion, 2014). He felt the introduction of GPU mining would be detrimental to participation in Bitcoin mining, as GPU hardware is less widespread than CPUs.

[10] If, once the mining steady state is reached, the price of bitcoin falls, some mining equipment might be disconnected. This equipment will still be there, waiting for an increase in the price to make it viable. This would create a cap on the remaining miners' profit margin, as a subsequent increase in the bitcoin price would prompt the disconnected equipment to reconnect again.

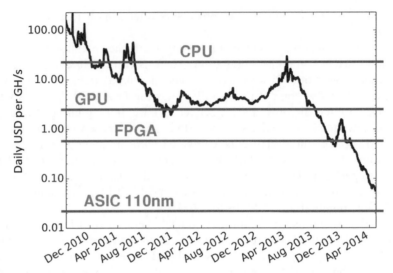

FIGURE 9.3 Mining revenue compared to electricity cost of different technologies. Price and hash rate data from blockchain.info

Figure 9.3 shows the daily revenue obtained from Bitcoin mining, in daily USD per GH/s. Superimposed in the figure are the levels showing the electricity cost of each technology that can be used for Bitcoin mining. The cost levels have been taken from Taylor (2013) with an estimated cost of electricity of 0.2 USD/kWh. As the expected revenue from mining has decreased and become lower than the electricity costs of running the hardware, mining technologies have become obsolete. As the figure shows, CPUs, GPUs and FPGAs are no longer profitable. The only viable technology to mine Bitcoin is ASICs. If the trend in Figure 9.3 is extrapolated, most ASICs based on old process technologies will progressively become obsolete, and the mining revenue will stabilize close to the electricity cost of the state-of-the-art ASIC technology[11]. As of the time of writing, the estimated electricity cost of 28nm ASIC technology stands at around 0.003 USD per GH/s.

With the increase in mining difficulty, miners holding hardware that is no longer competitive—like CPUs and GPUs—have migrated to mining other cryptocurrencies, notably Litecoin. Alternative cryptocurrencies will be covered in Chapter 11.

The current network hash rate is equivalent to approximately 1,250,000,000 latest-generation CPUs or 90,000,000 latest-generation GPUs, assuming that this hardware was put solely to the task of mining bitcoins. However, the comparison is not completely fair, because CPUs and GPUs are general-purpose hardware that can perform many more tasks than just mining Bitcoin. On the other hand, most Bitcoin mining is performed by ASICs that can only perform a very narrow computation (SHA256

---

[11] The mining revenue will likely be higher than just the electricity costs, to cover the rest of the costs associated with running a mining operation.

hashing)[12]. Following some of these measures, Bitcoin is claimed to be one of the biggest computational networks in the world.

The takeaway from these comparisons is that an attacker that wished to perform a 51% attack on Bitcoin would have to realize a large investment in mining equipment. Thus the network hash rate is an indication of the security underlying the blockchain. Increases in the hash rate raise the bar for an attacker wishing to perform a 51% attack. Conversely, a decrease in the hash rate would be detrimental to the security of the distributed database.

Some commentators have suggested a positive feedback loop between the price of bitcoin and the network hash rate. While it is true that mining investment follows the price of Bitcoin, the converse is not necessarily true. After a decrease in the price of Bitcoin, some mining power will be disconnected, and the security of the blockchain going forward will be lowered. But this mining dynamic should only affect the price indirectly, as the effect of a decrease in the network hash rate, if any, should be already incorporated in the new price where the market has found an equilibrium.

There has been some controversy regarding the environmental impact of Bitcoin mining. This controversy has been fuelled by incorrect estimates of the total **electricity consumption** of the network. Some journalists have quoted an estimate of the electricity consumption based on CPU technology. As mining technology has moved on, and the only current viable mining technology—ASIC—has a much lower energy consumption per GH/s, these figures overestimated the total energy consumption of the Bitcoin network.

As mining technology catches up with state-of-the-art process technology, mining cost will be driven primarily by electricity costs and mining power will then probably shift to locations where electricity is cheaper. The environmental impact of electricity in places with low electricity costs might be smaller, as these are usually places with large natural sources of energy. Besides, the energy consumed by Bitcoin mining is arguably not wasted: it is employed in securing the blockchain. A fairer comparison might be to the emissions produced by the current financial system in achieving a similar goal.

A compilation of the specifications of a long list of mining equipment spanning all four technologies can be found in Bitcoin wiki (2014m). A good account of the different steps in the evolution of the mining technology can be found in Taylor (2013).

9.2 POOLED MINING

Assuming the arrival of new blocks follows a Poisson process, the time between two arrivals (mining of a new block) should follow an exponential distribution. To test this hypothesis, a sample of times between blocks has been assembled. These times are computed as the difference between time-stamps of consecutive blocks in the blockchain,

---

[12] An even less meaningful comparison is sometimes made between mining FLOPs (floating point operations per second) and supercomputers' FLOPs. The problem with this comparison is that the SHA256 algorithm does not perform any floating point operation and mining ASICs do not have a floating point unit (FPU). Thus the conversion of the "computational power" of an ASIC to FLOPs is somewhat arbitrary.

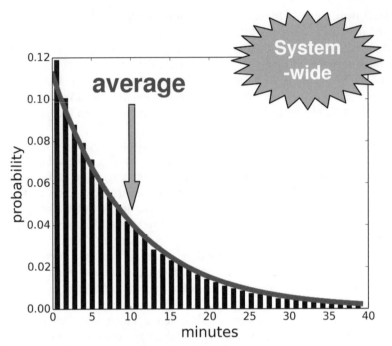

FIGURE 9.4 Probability of mining a block (network-wise)

using blocks between 200,000 and 250,000[13]. Figure 9.4 shows the empirical probability distribution of the sample, and Figure 9.5 shows an exponential distribution Q-Q plot of this sample. The fit is reasonably good, with a high $R^2 = 0.9993$, but there is some divergence from the exponential distribution in the right tail.

The sample average time between blocks is 553 seconds. The theoretical exponential probability distribution function, with a mean arrival time of 10 minutes (600 seconds), is superimposed in Figure 9.4.

Figure 9.4 shows the distribution of block arrivals for the network as a whole. An individual miner solving a block also follows a Poisson distribution, but with a larger time between arrivals. Individual miners are subject to a high degree of uncertainty as to when they will mine a new block. As an example, right before the introduction of ASIC mining when GPU mining was still profitable, the expected time between solved blocks for an individual miner with one GPU would have been in the order of 150 days.

To help miners manage this risk, mining pools started to appear at the end of 2010. A **mining pool** is an aggregation of miners, who contribute their hash power to the pool and share the mining rewards. Figure 9.6 shows an illustration of the expected time between mined blocks for several miners alone and for a pool that aggregates all their hash power. By forming a pool, miners can have a much more predictable income stream to

---

[13] Some differences between timestamps were negative, due to inaccuracies in the time settings of mining servers. These negative differences have been rounded to 0 in the analysis of figures 9.4 and 9.5. The sample average time during these periods was 544 seconds without adjusting for negative arrival times.

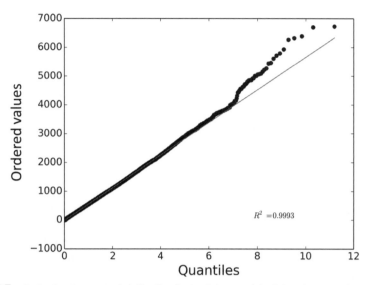

FIGURE 9.5 Q-Q plot (exponential distribution) of the empirical time between blocks

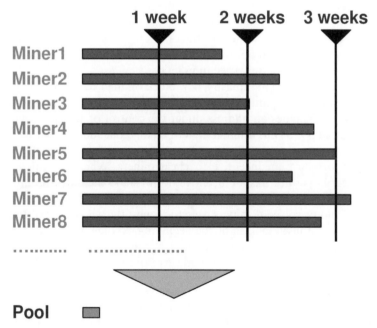

FIGURE 9.6 Expected time to mine a block

share among them. Revenue sharing in a mining pool is proportional to the hash rate contributed by each miner, minus a small fee charged by the pool operator, which is usually run for profit. An additional advantage is that miners participating in a pool do not have to keep a copy of the full blockchain or process all incoming transactions: it is enough for the pool operator to feed miners a copy of the block header[14].

After the introduction of ASICs, the need for mining pools may decrease, due to increased professionalization of the mining activity, such as the arrival of hosted mining services. Still, at the time of writing, most of the mining is done by a handful of pools, see Table 9.1.

A mining pool whose participants "promise" to share their computational work with the mining pool and whose operator "promises" to share the pool rewards honestly among its members, is fraught with conflicts of interest. Both miners and pool operators have an incentive to cheat:

- Miners have an incentive to overstate their hash rate, or contribute only a portion of their hash rate, while mining solo with the rest of the hash rate. A pool can control the work done by the miners by requiring them to present a valid proof-of-work of the block they are mining, but of a lower difficulty. These are called **shares**. The pool operator can measure shares received by its miners, and allocate the block reward proportionally to these number of shares. Another approach to control the work done by miners is for miners to submit **metahashes**. Metahashes are hashes of many hashes produced by the miner. The pool operator then checks the validity of the metahashes provided by its miners. Checking metahashes is computationally intensive: to check all the metahashes from all the miners, the pool operator would have to redo all the work of all miners, which defeats the purpose of a mining pool. Thus the pool operator checks the metahashes only periodically, usually in a round-robin fashion[15]. As the metahash approach is much more computationally intensive than the share approach, it is rarely used in practice.
- Miners have an incentive to publish a new block on their own when they find it. This can easily be avoided if miners are given the hash of the block header by the pool operator, which includes an address under the control of the pool operator in the coinbase transaction. Thus a miner cannot change the address that will be credited with the block reward.
- Block operators have an incentive to cheat miners. When presented with a new block, the pool operator has an incentive not to share the block reward, or share it only with the miner who presented the block, leaving the rest of the pool in the dark. This issue could be solved if miners were to request the whole block header from the pool operator, not just the hash of the beginning, so they would be able to monitor the blockchain themselves. Another approach to solve this problem is for the miners to receive a fixed payment for their work, irrespective of whether a block is mined

---

[14] There are several competing mining protocol standards. In some of them, pool operators only share the block header with the miners. But in others, such as the GetBlockTemplate (Bitcoin wiki, 2014i), operators share the whole block with miners. In these latter protocols, miners can choose which transactions to include or even include additional transactions of their own, that have not been broadcasted to the network.

[15] In a round-robin schedule, jobs are chosen from the available processes in a circular fashion. This scheduling assigns the same amount of work to each process. Applied in the context of metahash checking, it means that the pool operator checks the metahashes of each of its miners in circular order. Round-robin scheduling might be cheated if a miner is able to guess the frequency of metahash checking, thus some randomness is usually added to the process.

by the pool. This is the approach followed by pay-per-share (PPS) mining pools, see below.

Different pools follow different protocols to handle these conflicts of interest. Some examples of mining pools and the protocols they follow are:

- **Bitcoin Pooled Mining (BPM).** Miners submit shares, i.e. solved blocks with a lower difficulty. Older shares weigh less, to dissuade miners from switching pools in the middle of a round. A round finishes the moment a block is solved by the pool and the next round starts right away. Rewards are distributed to miners at the end of each round according to the number of shares submitted, but there is no mechanism to address the pool operator cheating.
- **Pay-per-share (PPS).** Miners submit shares and the pool operator pays an immediate flat fee for each share paid from the pool's existing balance, thus eliminating the risk that miners are cheated by the pool operator. The uncertainty of new block arrivals is transferred to the pool operator. The operator of a pay-per-share pool charges a small fee as compensation for this risk, making the payoff to miners lower than their expected payoff for solo mining.
- **Pay-per-last-N-shares (PPLNS).** This protocol is similar to pay-per-share, with the difference that the last N shares submitted by miners are taken into account to distribute the mining reward. The last-N-shares window can span several blocks: a share can be rewarded several times (if the pool gets lucky and it mines several blocks in quick succession) or not at all (if the pool gets unlucky and no block is mined during the window). In PPLNS, the uncertainty of mining a block is transferred from the pool operator to the participants in the pool, which usually translates into the pool operator collecting a smaller fee. Many of the largest mining pools at the time of writing use variants of this protocol.
- **P2Pool** is a peer-to-peer network of mining nodes that create a **share chain**. A share chain is a chain of shares, i.e. solved blocks with a difficulty lower than the network difficulty. Peers in the pool check that blocks in the share chain have a coinbase that distributes the reward proportionally to the *previous* shares in the share chain. When a block is solved, the miner who solves it publishes it in the blockchain, and the reward is automatically distributed among the peers through the coinbase. The chain of shares plays the same role as the pool operator in a pay-per-share protocol, but in a distributed way. As there is no pool operator, all mining rewards are distributed to the peers. The main disadvantage of P2Pool is that all miners have to operate a full node. This contrasts with the other protocols where miners are fed only the block header by the pool operator. Thus participating in P2Pool requires computing power and bandwidth to process the blockchain, increasing the cost to miners. Further details on P2Pool can be found in Bitcoin wiki (2014p).

Mining protocols based on miners creating shares of lower difficulty—such as PPS, PPLNS, or P2Pool—are subject to a block withholding attack. In a **block withholding attack** a malicious miner presents the pool operator with valid shares, but withholds solved blocks, depriving the pool from collecting the reward on these blocks. An attacker performing a block withholding attack suffers a small loss due to the pool's loss of revenue which will impact all users' payoff equally. The block withholding attack is akin to sabotaging a mining pool, and it is, in principle, uneconomical for an attacker as the attacker pays a small price. Nonetheless, this attack has been detected in the wild (wizkid057, 2014). A possible explanation is that the attacker could be a miner connected to a competing mining pool, with an incentive to harm the users of the pool under attack, pushing them to switch to the competing pool[16].

These are only some of the more direct mining protocols, but many other protocols have been proposed. More details on the approaches followed by different mining pools can be found in Bitcoin wiki (2014e, 2014q) and Rosenfeld (2011).

Concentration of mining in a few pools is generally viewed as problematic by the Bitcoin community. The problem is that concentration makes it easier, and more profitable, to attempt attacks against other miners, such as the selfish mining attack (section 9.4). Another potential problem stemming from mining concentration is that, as miners choose which transactions to include in a block (see next section), pools have the power to censor particular transactions, for instance the transactions using funds from certain addresses, which would break the fungibility of bitcoins.

9.3 TRANSACTION FEES

As seen in section 7.7, blocks have a limitation of roughly 1MB total size. The size of a transaction depends on the number of addresses that the transaction draws funds from and on the number of addresses that the funds are sent to. The size of a transaction with only one input and one output is in the order of 157 bytes[17]. Each additional input to a transaction adds 113 bytes to its size, while an additional output adds 34 bytes. Note that 157 bytes is the size of a very compact transaction, but most transactions use several inputs and outputs.

Miners have to choose which transactions to include in the block they are mining from their unconfirmed transactions' memory pool. This is an optimization problem over the block size. Miners generally use a greedy algorithm to solve this problem, as shown in Figure 9.7. Candidate transactions are ordered by their fee-per-kilobyte ratio in descending order and chosen from this list. This is the current implementation in Bitcoin Core[18], but of course miners are free to tweak this implementation or to use other mining software with a different transaction selection algorithm.

There might be scenarios under which miners would refuse to include transactions in the blocks they mine because of the "bigger blocks take longer to broadcast" problem (Andresen, 2014): including more transactions in a block makes the block bigger, which takes the block longer to broadcast through the network, increasing the risk that another miner might simultaneously find and broadcast a competing block. If the total

---

[16] In June 2014, following concerns that a mining pool had amassed over 51% of the mining power, some miners allegedly performed a block withholding attack against this pool with the intention of punishing it and driving its users to other pools (Buterin, 2014g).

[17] This comprises 10 bytes of headers, 40 bytes for the reference to the previous output, 73 bytes for the <scriptSig> that signs the previous output (ECDSA signature in compressed form) and 34 bytes from the output (including 25 bytes from the <scriptPubKey>). See Shirriff (2014a), although the example uses an uncompressed form for the ECDSA signature that doubles the size of the <scriptSig>.

[18] This logic is performed in the class **TxPriorityCompare** in `miner.cpp`.

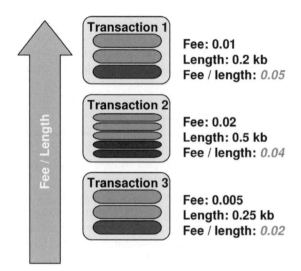

FIGURE 9.7 Prioritization of transactions by miners

transaction fees are low compared to the block reward, the revenue lost by not including a transaction might be more than compensated by the reduced risk of a competing block.

There is a minimum transaction fee in the protocol[19]. The goal of this fee is to prevent denial-of-service attacks that could flood the network with transactions that pay no fee. The minimum transaction fee is currently set to 1,000 satoshis or 0.00001 bitcoins, as of version 0.9.1 of Bitcoin Core.

The priority of a transaction is computed as the sum of its input's value (in satoshis) multiplied by the input's age (in number of blocks) divided by the size of the transaction (in bytes):

$$Priority = \frac{\Sigma Input\,Value \cdot Input\,Age}{TxSize}$$

Every block reserves certain space, called the **priority block**, for priority transactions[20]. Transactions with a priority higher than a certain cut-off[21] are considered priority transactions, and are eligible to be included in the priority block. Priority transactions are also allowed not to include any fee, while non-priority transactions must have a minimum fee to be relayed by the network[22]. For further information on transactions fees, see Bitcoin wiki (2014z).

---

[19] This fee can be found in the variable **CTransaction::nMinRelayTxFee** in `main.cpp`.

[20] The size of the space reserved for priority transactions is controlled by the variable **DEFAULT_BLOCK_PRIORITY_SIZE** in `main.cpp` and is set to 50,000 bytes as of this writing.

[21] This cut-off is set to **COIN * 144 / 250** in `main.h`, where COIN is the value of a bitcoin expressed in satoshis, that is 100,000,000. Thus a transaction whose inputs sum 1 bitcoin and are 144 blocks old and whose size is 250 bytes is considered the priority threshold.

[22] The minimum fee for a transaction to be relayed and eligible to be included in blocks is of 0.01 mBTC per kB (as of version 0.9 of Bitcoin Core). However, this fee does not guarantee that the

Traditionally, minimum transaction fees have been fixed in the Bitcoin Core Wallet implementation (and most other wallets), with a user option to change their value. Ideally transaction fees would be determined by a market mechanism. Miners already behave like rational participants in this market, choosing the transactions that maximize their profits. Wallets with a fixed transaction fee miss the mark either overpaying to be included in the block, or underpaying, being excluded from blocks and taking a long time to confirm. Bitcoin developers (Andresen, 2013e) have been working around the concept of **smart fees** or **floating fees**, i.e. an algorithm that estimates the fee so that the transaction has a high probability to be accepted in the next mined block. As of the time of writing floating fees have been implemented and are ready to make their way into the next version of Bitcoin Core (Andresen, 2014).

Transactions that are not included in a block are kept in the unconfirmed transactions' memory pool and are considered for inclusion in the next blocks. A transaction with a low fee could remain unconfirmed for some time, especially during periods of heavy volume. Miners can have an incentive to eventually include transactions, even those with very low fees, in order to free memory in their unconfirmed transaction memory pool. On the other hand, including many transactions in a block makes the block bigger, leading to higher block propagation delays. For this reason, miners have sometimes chosen to limit the amount of transactions included in their blocks.

Finally, note that transactions are not only competing with other transactions for space in the blockchain: they are also competing with other applications wishing to insert data into the blockchain (section 12.6).

9.4 SELFISH MINING

An attack called **selfish mining**[23] was proposed in Eyal and Gun Sirer (2013). In this attack, a miner works on a private branch, without disclosing it to the public network. As long as her private branch is longer that the public branch, she keeps mining on this branch. Eventually when the public branch is about to catch up, she makes her private branch public. This renders the public branch invalid, because all miners that follow the protocol will discard the public branch and will switch to the newly released private branch. The result is that all the work employed by miners working in the public branch is wasted. This yields an advantage to the selfish miner, because her effort on the private branch is not wasted. The selfish miner that follows this strategy is able to collect bigger rewards than those proportional to her share of the network hash rate. The strategy gives an advantage to the selfish miner by fooling the rest of the miners and making them waste their time. Unlike previous attacks introduced in section 7.5, this attack is not directed against recipients of funds; it is directed against other miners.

It is shown in Eyal and Gun Sirer (2013) that it is advantageous for the selfish miner to invite other miners to her pool (creating one if necessary). It is also profitable for other miners to join this pool. This shift will continue until the selfish mining pool has a

---

transaction will be mined, especially during periods of heavy usage. Thus Bitcoin Core Wallet sets a default fee of 0.1 mBTC per kB for low-priority transactions.

[23] This attack was previously proposed in the bitcointalk forums by RHorning (Heilman, 2014), but was formalized in Eyal and Gun Sirer (2013).

majority of the network hash rate. At this moment it is "game over" for the rest of the miners. The selfish mining pool does not release the blocks it mines, it only periodically releases a whole branch. Thus other miners will not be able to mine new blocks and would presumably exit the network. A negative consequence of the growth of a selfish mining pool is that it concentrates the control of mining. A group controlling the network can censor transactions, or factor out transactions already included in the blockchain. This is counter to the philosophy of openness and non-censorship that underpins Bitcoin. Another negative consequence of selfish mining is an increase in the uncertainty of confirmed transactions, which could lead to much longer confirmation times.

Selfish mining is profitable even for relatively small miners, according to Eyal and Gun Sirer (2013). A change in the Bitcoin protocol has been proposed to raise the size a miner must have for selfish mining to be profitable. When confronted with a fork in the blockchain, currently miners arbitrarily choose the first branch (of equal length) to come to continue mining. They also only rebroadcast the first branch to come, while keeping the other in their memory. Under the proposed change in the protocol, nodes would rebroadcast all competing branches and miners would choose randomly which branch to mine on top of. This change is argued to raise the threshold of hash rate for selfish mining to be profitable from 0% to 25% of the total network hash rate.

A selfish mining attack might be difficult to pull off in practice. First, the selfish mining strategy is easy to detect. A selfish miner releases blocks in bursts. The bigger the selfish miner is, the longer the private chains that are released. Other miners can monitor for this behavior and take action. Moreover, if a selfish miner is successful other miners have an incentive to stop following the protocol, i.e. releasing all mined blocks immediately, and form their own selfish mining cartels. A war of selfish mining cartels could then ensue, and the outcome of this war may not be profitable for the original selfish miner. Or the rest of the "honest" miners could decide to band together and follow a **tit-for-tat strategy** against the selfish miner. The game-theoretical implications of these strategies have not been fully explored.

Another solution to selfish mining, proposed in Heilman (2014), is to discriminate the acceptance of blocks based on verified time-stamps, which would make it more difficult for a selfish miner to release a long branch all at once.

Table 9.1 shows the distribution of mining power among the different mining pools. Although this distribution seems relatively balanced, there have been several episodes of a mining pool accumulating close to—and even surpassing—50% of the total hash rate: once in 2011 and twice in 2014. These episodes have prompted calls for miners to abandon these mining pools, often resulting in the offending mining pools taking steps themselves to decrease their size (Hajdarbegovic, 2014). Table 9.1 shows the distribution of mining power a few days after one of these episodes. Several proposals have been put forward (Buterin, 2014g) to deter the concentration of mining power:

- Modify the mining algorithm in a way that forces miners to store a copy of the full blockchain and process it. Then, as miners have to store and process the blockchain anyway, there will be no advantage of centralized mining pools over P2Pool, pushing miners to switch to P2Pool.
- **Non-outsourceable Puzzles** (Miller et al., 2014). This proposal modifies the mining algorithm allowing miners to "steal" the block reward from the pool operator in a way that is not detectable by the pool operator. As miners could divert the block

TABLE 9.1 Distribution of hash rate among mining pools. Data retrieved from <u>blockchain. info/pools</u> on June 17, 2014. Average of 4 days

Pool	Percentage
GHash.IO	32%
Discus Fish	14%
BTC Guild	12%
Eligius	8%
Slush	4%
Polmine	2%
BitMinter	1%
EclipseMC	1%
Unknown	26%

reward to themselves *a posteriori*, this modification would render pooled mining impractical. The proposal extends blocks with the inclusion of a zero-knowledge proof[24], and it would require a hard fork.

- **Multi-PPS** (Rosenfeld, 2013). In multi-PPS, miners assign the block reward to different pools, allocating to each mining pool a different percentage of the total block reward. Miners then present shares to all these mining pools, and mining pools compensate them accordingly. It is shown in Rosenfeld (2013) that under this arrangement it is optimal for miners to distribute their processing power proportionally to the pools' sizes. If all miners followed this protocol, big pools would cease to grow their market share and small pools would be able to survive.

---

[24] Miners prove in zero-knowledge that they know a nonce and a Merkle-tree root that meet the required mining difficulty. The zero-knowledge proof construction is similar to that used in Zerocash (13.5.7).

The Cryptocurrencies
Landscape

The Origins Of Bitcoin

This chapter is an overview of the main ideas in cryptographic money over the last three decades, culminating in the development of Bitcoin. There are two difficult features for electronic money to achieve: anonymity and decentralization.

Anonymity is usually understood as both lack of knowledge of the users and impossibility to link operations performed by the same user, such as withdrawal and spend operations. Anonymity is also deemed important because it generates fungibility. Fungibility is the property of money that makes different units mutually substitutable. The lack of anonymity breaks fungibility because it makes possible to trace the origin of the funds.

Most proposals, including Bitcoin, lean towards achieving either anonymity or decentralization. Early proposals focused on preserving user privacy, while later developments shifted the focus more towards decentralization. It has been notoriously difficult to merge the two requirements into a coherent system. One notable early exception is the proposal of Sander and Ta-Shma (section 10.4).

Bitcoin leans towards achieving robust decentralization, while leaving the users pseudonymous. However, there has been renewed interest in increasing the anonymity of Bitcoin, or creating decentralized cryptocurrencies that are fully anonymous. This topic is explored in Chapter 13.

Many of the ideas used to create digital currencies were generated inside the cypherpunk movement, and some proponents of cryptocurrencies were members of this movement.

THE CYPHERPUNK MOVEMENT

The cypherpunk movement was born in the 1990s from a series of meetings of cryptographers with liberal views that opposed the actions of the US government against the research and publication of cryptographic ideas. Cypherpunks advocate the use of cryptography as a means to change society.

The term cypherpunk was coined by a technology writer, who was attending one of the first meetings and, after listening to the discussions, said "you guys are cypherpunks." Attendants liked the name and used it subsequently (Levy, 2001).

The cypherpunks movement has its roots in early cryptographic developments, such as public key cryptography (section 5.1) or blind signatures (5.5.1).

For the first meeting, a document titled the *Crypto Anarchist Manifesto* was created (May, 1992) and later a second document titled *A Cypherpunk's Manifesto*

(Hughes, 1992). These documents urged the creation and use of encryption tools to achieve the goals of privacy and anonymity: "cypherpunks write code." They also advocated the use of decentralized systems: "software can't be destroyed and [that] a widely dispersed system can't be shut down." And also from the manifestos: "We the Cypherpunks are dedicated to building anonymous systems. We are defending our privacy with cryptography, with anonymous mail forwarding systems, with digital signatures, and with electronic money."

Shortly after, the group discussions migrated to a mailing list where members covered topics ranging from mathematics, cryptography, or computer science to politics. An account of the creation of the cypherpunk movement can be found in Levy (2001).

A few years after its creation, the cypherpunk movement lost momentum, probably due to low consumer uptake of cryptographic technologies (Green, 2012b). Some people whose discoveries have been instrumental in the creation of Bitcoin are well regarded cypherpunks.

10.1   DAVID CHAUM'S ECASH

David Chaum is a cryptographer who did ground-breaking work in the field of anonymous communication, voting systems, and digital currencies. He introduced several new cryptographic primitives, such as blind signatures and group signatures. He proposed a system for anonymous electronic payments called **ecash** and founded a company to commercialize the technology.

In Chaum (1982), Chaum proposed an untraceable payment system based on blind signatures (5.5.1). This payment system allows users to obtain anonymous tokens from a bank, each token representing a fixed amount of money. First, a user would present the bank with a blinded serial number. The bank would then sign the blinded serial number and deduct the corresponding amount from the user's account. The serial number is chosen at random by the user and is not communicated to the bank. Thus at the time of signing the bank does not know this serial number.

The user could then strip the token of the blinding factor, leaving the original serial number signed by the bank. This signed serial number is a token that can be redeemed by anyone at the signing bank. The user can buy products from a merchant and give the merchant this token in return. The merchant would then present the token to the bank, who first verifies that it is correctly signed, then checks that the serial number has not been spent yet (the bank keeps a database with the number of spent serial numbers) and finally credits the account of the merchant with the amount (or signs a brand new token for the merchant). Withdrawals and spends are unlinkable: the bank does not know who the original owner of the serial number was, because it signed the serial number blindly. All the bank knows is whether a particular serial number has been used before[1].

---

[1] Ecash is anonymous by design, while Bitcoin is only pseudonymous. Chapter 13 presents ways in which users of Bitcoin could be identified as well as extensions to Bitcoin's technology that provide anonymity.

The original implementation of Chaum's untraceable payment systems could be attacked by a double-spend: the owner of the token could give the same token to two different merchants. Thus this system could only be used as an online payment system: the merchant would have to redeem the token with the bank before accepting the payment.

Ecash, proposed in Chaum et al. (1990), is a refinement of this system that was proposed for offline transactions. The ecash scheme is also based on blind signatures. However, the user has to send the bank not just a random serial number but a carefully crafted piece of data that includes this random serial number and also some hidden information about the user. A merchant that receives the token as payment cannot access the identity information about the user. But if two merchants receive the same token as payment, these tokens can be combined to recover the hidden identity of the spender. Therefore the anonymity of a user that only spends the tokens once is protected, but her anonymity is revealed if she spends the tokens more than once. Note that before signing the token, the bank has to check that the identity information is correct, i.e. that the hidden information correctly reveals the true identity of the user. Ecash design allows the bank to check the identity information while not revealing the serial number, thus preserving untraceability for the honest user. A summary of how ecash works can be found in Finney (1993).

Identifying cheaters was hoped to deter users from double-spending. However, discovering the identity of a cheater might not be enough deterrent if the cheater is able to successfully double-spend large amounts of funds. Or some attacker might compromise the wallet of a legitimate user and repeatedly spend the funds in the wallet as much as she can. The blame of the double-spend would lie in this case with the unsuspecting user.

Another drawback of ecash is that each token represents a fixed amount of money. Tokens of different denominations could be created (for instance, the bank could use different public keys for different denominations), but this would entail a partial loss of anonymity for the users. There have been no clones of the ecash system until very recently as the technology was covered by several patents issued throughout the 1990s.

Some refinements of Chaum's ecash system to make it more efficient have been proposed. For example Brands (1993) introduces an extension that supports multiple denominations and makes the identification of double-spenders much more efficient, as well as some other features such as protection against framing (i.e. the user being framed as a double-spender by the bank), anonymous accounts, and multi-spendable coins. Another example is Camenisch et al. (2006), which proposes a system that is very efficient storing multiple coins, and where the whole spending history of a double-spender is revealed, not just her identity. An overview of Chaum's ecash as well as some of these extensions can be found in Green (2012a).

Chaum's ecash and all its extensions require a central server (a bank) in contrast with Bitcoin's decentralized nature. Trust in the central server is required in all systems based on Chaum's ecash. This could be problematic as the central server could decide to issue more tokens or it could have its private key stolen and an attacker could issue as many tokens as she wanted.

10.2 ADAM BACK'S HASHCASH

Adam Back introduced Hashcash in 1997 (Back, 2002) as a method to limit email spam. Hashcash proposes adding a token, called a hashcash, to the header of email messages.

This token requires some computational cost to create but a negligible cost to verify. Adding a hashcash to emails would change the economics of spammers by forcing them to spend a considerable amount of computational cost to operate. Hashcash is not a digital payment system; however, it is included in this chapter since it fills an important place in the creation of Bitcoin.

To create a hashcash, a user has to solve the following cryptographic puzzle: find the value of a counter that when appended to a header[2] results in a hash that starts with a given number of zero bits. The number of starting zeros in the hash value controls the difficulty of finding the counter, and can be adjusted to a sweet-spot where the hashcash computation is not noticeable for the user, but deters spammers—say half a second per email on a regular computer. To find the value of the counter that creates the hashcash, the sender of the email starts with a value for the counter and successively increments it, computing at each iteration the result of the hash function, until it solves the required difficulty. More details about the Hashcash protocol and an example of the construction of a hashcash can be found in section 7.3.

Every hashcash is specific to a recipient, so the recipient can verify its validity without a trusted third party, making Hashcash decentralized. It is also anonymous, as anybody can create a valid hashcash, and therefore fungible. In principle, hashcash could be traded: somebody with dedicated computational power could generate hashcash tokens on demand, thus freeing the users of the need to spend the computational power themselves.

The main innovation introduced by Hashcash is the proof-of-work function: an elegant and easily adjustable proof-of-work function which underpins Bitcoin's distributed transaction ledger.

10.3 NICK SZABO'S BIT GOLD AND WEI DAI'S B-MONEY

In 1998 both Nick Szabo and Wei Dai independently proposed similar distributed digital money schemes called **bit gold** (Szabo, 1998a) and **b-money** (Dai, 1998). Neither of these need a central server to function: the main idea behind these proposals was that balances were stored in a distributed database.

In b-money, money is created by submitting a solution to a computationally difficult problem, whose solution is easy to verify, i.e. a proof-of-work. The amount of money created is proportional to the difficulty of the problem. How to set the difficulty of the proof-of-work is decided by the network through voting. This system is vulnerable to a single entity with large computational resources swamping the network with a large amount of newly created money before the network has the opportunity to update the difficulty.

In bit gold, money is also created by solving a proof-of-work problem, with the difference that the proof-of-work of each problem is linked to the previous solution, making money creation sequential. This allows the network to have the opportunity to adjust the difficulty of the proof-of-work problem in an episode of rapidly increasing money creation. However, neither scheme completely addresses how the participants can agree on the growth of the money supply.

Users are represented by public keys in both proposals. A user can transfer funds to another user by signing a message with the public key announcing the transfer of

---

[2] This header includes the recipient email and the date, so that it cannot be easily reused.

funds and broadcasting this message to the network, in much the same way that Bitcoin transactions work.

Dai proposed enforceable contracts for b-money, where the parties sent funds to be put in escrow by the network with a deterrent purpose. If the contract was successfully filled or the parties reached an agreement, the escrow funds were liberated. If the parties did not reach an agreement, both parties sent their proposal for the use of the escrow funds and the nodes on the network decided how to apportion the escrow funds. It was not detailed in the proposal how would the nodes reach a consensus, or how to cope with Sybil attacks on the network[3].

Szabo was an early proponent of smart contracts and many of his ideas are currently being implemented[4] (Chapter 12).

Both schemes are pseudonym-based, where the pseudonym is the user's public key. As transactions are publicly broadcast to the network, they are linkable using network analysis (section 13.1). Thus these schemes do not provide full anonymity, similarly to Bitcoin (Chapter 13).

In both systems, servers communicate with each other to maintain a common database, and therefore the Byzantine Generals' problem arises. The **Byzantine Generals' problem** (Lamport et al., 1982) refers to the problem where several generals have to agree on the strategy for a battle and, due to their physical separation, they must communicate using messages. However, messages can be corrupted and there can be traitors among the generals. The (loyal) generals must solve the problem of how to arrive at a common strategy in the face of faulty messages and traitors. In the context of b-money and bit gold, the problem is how the network can agree on the state of the distributed database when both messages between the nodes can be corrupted and there might be attackers trying to subvert the distributed database. B-money does not address the Byzantine Generals' problem. Szabo proposes in a subsequent paper (Szabo 1998b) a "Byzantine Quorum System" which relies on a quorum of network addresses that can be used by bit gold as a protocol to accept changes to the distributed database[5].

Both b-money and bit gold were theoretical proposals and neither of them was implemented in practice. However, Bitcoin is a realization of many of the ideas present in these designs, solving several important details these proposals glossed over[6].

10.4 SANDER AND TA-SHMA'S AUDITABLE, ANONYMOUS ELECTRONIC CASH

In 1999 Tomas Sander and Amnon Ta-Shma proposed an anonymous electronic cash system that did not require a central server issuing blinded signatures (Sander and Ta-Shma, 1999). In Sander and Ta-Shma's system, a coin is represented by the hash of its

---

[3] In a **Sybil attack**, the attacker creates many identities in a peer-to-peer network to exert a disproportionately large influence. In the case of b-money's contracts an attacker could create many nodes to be able to sway the opinion of the network in its favour when resolving a dispute about some escrow funds.

[4] See szabo.best.vwh.net/ for a collection of his essays.

[5] Bit gold also proposes time-stamping the solutions to the proof-of-work chain that creates new tokens.

[6] It is possible that Satoshi Nakamoto was not aware of either b-money or bit gold, and could have arrived at the same ideas independently.

serial number. A list of the valid coins is kept by the bank. The list of valid coins is represented by a Merkle tree (section 7.6), so that it is efficient to store and transmit. The root of the Merkle tree is made public: the bank sends it to the participants in the system. To prove that a coin belongs to the tree, only the hash chain from the leaf of the tree, where the hash of the coin is, to the root of the tree is needed. As new coins are added to the tree, the root is updated and sent again to the participants. In the proposal, the tree is composed of several live trees, say one for the last minute, one for the last hour, one for the last day, and so on. After an hour, the hour tree is merged into the day tree, and a new hour live tree is created. In reality powers of two are used for the live trees instead of minutes, hours or days. Each live tree has a live root, and the root information is in practice a list of all the live roots. This list is updated periodically as the more frequent live roots are merged into less frequent trees and new trees are created.

To withdraw a coin, the user creates a random serial number s for the coin, and uses a trapdoor function to compute a coin number z from the serial number. For a description of trapdoor functions see section 13.5. The trapdoor includes information that can be used to de-anonymize the user in case of double-spending[7]. The user then sends the coin number z to the bank, which then publishes it in the tree[8]. The bank then sends the user the hash chain from her coin to the live tree root. Every time the root of the live tree is changed (because it is merged with a live tree of lower frequency), the bank sends the user a new hash chain to the root of the new live tree. The frequency of these updates decreases exponentially with time[9].

To make a payment, the merchant sends the user a list of all the live roots kept by the merchant. The user then proves that she knows a hash chain from her coin to one of the members in the root list. This proof is a zero-knowledge proof of set membership (see section 13.5 for an introduction to zero-knowledge proofs). A proof in zero knowledge does not leak any additional information, so the merchant does not know which coin belongs to the user, or even which of the live roots the coin is attached to. The merchant only learns that the coin is a valid coin, thus preserving the user's anonymity. The zero-knowledge proof includes the original serial number of the coin[10]. Finally, the merchant presents the bank with the zero-knowledge proof. The bank checks the validity of the zero-knowledge proof and whether the serial number of the coin has not been used before, and credits the merchant with the funds. The serial number is then added to the list of used serial numbers.

The system is auditable because all updates to the Merkle tree are broadcast. Thus all coins added to the tree are observed by the participants: the increase in the money

---

[7] The trapdoor function used in Sander and Ta-Shma is roughly $g(s',r) = g_1^{s'} \cdot g_2^r$ where $s' = u1\|u2\|s$ is the concatenation of some user information $u1\|u2$ with the serial number of the coin s. r is a pseudo-random number.

[8] The user also sends the bank a zero-knowledge proof that the coin is well formed and that the correct de-anonymizing information is included in the trapdoor function. This zero-knowledge proof does not reveal the serial number.

[9] A user will only receive a number of updates proportional to $log N$ with N the total number of coins.

[10] An extra parameter is included in the zero-knowledge proof. If a coin is double-spent, the two instances of this extra parameter can be combined with the information sent to the bank in the withdrawal operation to de-anonymize the user.

supply is public. Also, the lack of a private key used for signing new coins makes the system secure against a malicious bank or the theft of the private key.

The original proposal assumed the existence of a bank whose task is to update the Merkle tree with the new issued coins and to keep a list of the used serial numbers. However, these tasks could be performed in a decentralized fashion, taking away the need for a trusted third party, much like the role of the Bitcoin network.

This scheme achieves full anonymity, as transactions are not linkable: withdrawal operations cannot be linked to spend operations. In contrast to previous anonymous payments systems it uses zero-knowledge proof of set membership instead of blinding signatures (section 10.1). This makes the scheme somewhat inefficient both in terms of the computational power and the size of the data required to create and verify operations. The more recent proposals of Zerocoin and Zerocash share some similarities to this approach (section 13.5).

Satoshi could have integrated some anonymity insights of this approach into Bitcoin, but it is unclear whether he was not aware of this work when he released Bitcoin, whether he was familiar with it but decided not to use these features because of their high computational cost, or whether he consciously decided to leave Bitcoin pseudonymous.

10.5   HAL FINNEY'S RPOW

Hal Finney introduced RPOW in 2004. **RPOW** stands for **Reusable Proof-Of-Work**. It is a generalization of Hashcash (section 7.3), where instead of creating a hashcash tied to a particular email address, a POW (Proof-Of-Work) token is not tied to any particular application and can be spent freely. Clients can create POW tokens by performing a proof-of-work computation. RPOW uses Hashcash as its proof-of-work system. Thus the value of the POW tokens is underpinned by the computational resources spent in their creation.

The main innovation introduced by Finney was to allow the exchange of POW tokens without the need to regenerate them again. A token is first generated by a user performing the Hashcash proof-of-work. When the user decides to spend it, she sends it to another user, who redeems it in the RPOW server for a brand new POW token. Note that when a user receives a POW token, she must quickly turn it over to the RPOW server and exchange it for a new POW token to avoid double-spending by the original owner. Thus the RPOW system is an online system.

The RPOW server allows sequential reuse of the tokens, reissuing a new POW token when one is presented to it. The RPOW system depends on a central server that keeps a database with all spent POW tokens. This server is not able to create new tokens, only to reissue tokens when presented with previously unspent tokens. Finney created an implementation of an RPOW server and released it under an open source license. RPOW was set up in a server that included a cryptographic coprocessor[11] that allowed remote attestation to be done using "trusted computing" techniques. The cryptographic coprocessor kept a copy of a private key that never left the coprocessor and could use this private key to sign the hash of the code running in the server. Users could verify that the code running in the server was exactly the published code and it had not been

---

[11] The RPOW server used the IBM 4758 PCI Cryptographic Coprocessor, which has been since been discontinued.

tampered with. However, if an attacker was able to get a copy of the private key from the cryptographic coprocessor manufacturer, she could potentially replace the RPOW server with a server running a malicious version of the code—say one that minted new tokens for the attacker—but that produced a correctly signed certificate when inquired through remote attestation.

The RPOW server was eventually taken offline and the service discontinued. Details of the RPOW protocol can be found in Finney (2004). For an account of Finney's early involvement with Bitcoin, see Greenberg (2014).

10.6   SATOSHI NAKAMOTO

Satoshi Nakamoto is the creator or creators of Bitcoin. It is not clear whether the name is his real name or a pseudonym. He (or she or they) published the Bitcoin paper (Nakamoto, 2008a) in 2008, writing to the metzdowd cryptography mailing list in November 2008 (Nakamoto, 2008b). At the beginning of 2009 Satoshi released the Bitcoin source code and compiled binaries on Sourceforge (2014), schematically shown in Figure 10.1. Satoshi initiated the Bitcoin peer-to-peer network and started mining on January 3, 2009.

During the early days of Bitcoin there were very few people mining and the mining difficulty was low. These few miners were able to amass many bitcoins. An analysis of the blockchain seems to indicate (Demian Lerner, 2013) that Satoshi mined roughly 1 million bitcoins[12], which amount to around 10% of the money supply as of the time of writing.

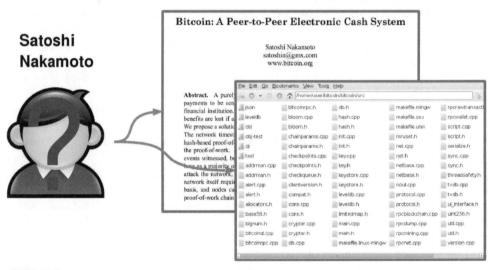

FIGURE 10.1   Satoshi Nakamoto

---

[12] This analysis is based on observing the field ExtraNonce in the coinbase (section 7.4). This field was incremented sequentially instead of initialized randomly in the server run by one of the very first miners believed to be Satoshi. Thus the blocks mined by this miner can be observed in a graph plotting this ExtraNonce field (Demian Lerner, 2013).

Surprisingly, none of those bitcoins have been spent. The reason is not clear. However, when Satoshi starts spending all those bitcoins, he will open the trail that could eventually lead to him. As transactions in the blockchain are public, spending the bitcoins would create a link between the accounts Satoshi controls and a real world person.

Satoshi created a decentralized system on purpose, as some comments (Nakamoto, 2009) made by Satoshi make clear: "I think there were a lot more people interested in the 90s, but after more than a decade of failed Trusted Third Party based systems, they see it as a lost cause. I hope they can make the distinction that this is the first time I know of that we're trying a non-trust-based system." And then: "I would be surprised if 10 years from now we're not using electronic currency in some way, now that we know a way to do it that won't inevitably get dumbed down when the trusted third party gets cold feet."

It is not clear whether Satoshi is a member of the cypherpunk movement. What seems clear, though, is that he is familiar with the movement's ideas.

CHAPTER 11

Alt(ernative) Coins

Alternative coins or **alt-coins** are cryptocurrencies that copy many of the features of Bitcoin. Most of the alt-coins are based on Bitcoin's source code with some changes. As Bitcoin's code is released under an open source license (section 1.2) it is acceptable to take a copy of the code, modify it, and release a new cryptocurrency. Many developers have done exactly that, creating many alt-coins.

Development in Bitcoin has been conservative and value-preserving, focusing on avoiding the introduction of errors. On the other hand, alt-coins often do not have the restrictions of a production system like Bitcoin, or the requirement of backward compatibility, allowing them to test new tweaks and features. However, Bitcoin can opt-in some of these features if the developers consider them worthy.

One controversial feature of some alt-coins has been pre-mining. **Pre-mining** refers to the fact that the developers of some alt-coins kept a large portion of the coins prior to the launch. The often-cited rationale for pre-mining is to create a reserve to pay developers to maintain and extend the alt-coin. However, a large percentage of pre-mined tokens is often counterproductive as it deters potential users, thus thwarting adoption.

Alt-coins can suffer from a multipool entering their network. **Multipools** are mining pools that switch from one alt-coin to another opportunistically, always mining the most profitable alt-coin at the time. Mining profitability depends on the alt-coin's mining difficulty and its exchange rate. A multipool can create wild fluctuations in the mining difficulty of an alt-coin, because when a multipool enters an alt-coin it drives the mining difficulty higher. Once this multipool leaves the alt-coin, it can take a long time to revert back to the original mining difficulty.

Note that alt-coins are often distinguished from meta-coins such as Counterparty, Ethereum, or Ripple that will be introduced in section 12.7. Alt-coins commonly refer to currencies whose implementation is a fork of the Bitcoin source code with some tweaks, while meta-coins refer to new implementations from scratch (or layers on top of Bitcoin such as Counterparty or Mastercoin) that add features, such as support for digital assets, not available in Bitcoin currently. This distinction is somewhat tenuous, and the terms alt-coin and meta-coin are sometimes used interchangeably.

This chapter will only cover some alt-coins that have proposed interesting changes, either technical or to the economics of Bitcoin. The focus of the chapter is to highlight these changes with respect to Bitcoin.

11.1 LITECOIN

Litecoin (LTC) is arguably the most successful alt-coin. It was released in 2011 and as of the time of writing had a market capitalization of roughly 5% of that of Bitcoin (see Table 11.1). It is sometimes referred to as "silver to Bitcoin's gold."

The differences introduced in Litecoin compared to Bitcoin are:

- It uses **scrypt** as its proof-of-work algorithm. Scrypt is a memory hard key-derivation function introduced by Colin Percival (Percival, 2012). A memory-hard function requires a reasonably large amount of Random Access Memory (RAM) to be evaluated. This makes implementation in special purpose hardware, i.e. ASICs, less efficient because it requires some die area to be reserved for memory. In the words of Colin Percival, the creator of scrypt, "the point of scrypt is to limit how many hashes you can compute per second per mm^2 of ASIC" (Percival, 2013)
- Block generation time is targeted at 2.5 minutes, which makes for faster inclusion of transactions in a block. Note that faster inclusion time should not be interpreted as faster confirmations. The security of a transaction in the blockchain depends on the computational effort spent in mining the blocks which are on top of the block that includes the transaction (section 7.5). Assuming the network hash rate stays constant, a lower block generation time makes the mining difficulty of each block lower, and thus does not have any effect on the security of a transaction over time. There is, however, an advantage to lower block generation times because inclusion in a first block is usually enough security for low-value transactions (7.10).

The main idea behind scrypt is that it generates a large amount of pseudorandom numbers that it stores in RAM so they can be accessed on demand. The algorithm then accesses this memory in a pseudo-random fashion a number of times before returning the result. An implementation where no RAM is used is possible. In this case the pseudo-random numbers would be generated as needed. However, as the generation of these pseudo-random numbers is computationally intensive and the numbers are accessed several times, it is computationally very costly to compute scrypt this way. Thus scrypt follows a marked time-memory trade-off. The parameters of the scrypt algorithm can be tweaked to require more or less RAM and computing power. However, the implementation of scrypt used in Litecoin is somewhat watered down, requiring only 128kB of memory, allegedly not to stress too much the computers of users running non-mining nodes. This parameterization of scrypt makes it possible to implement Litecoin mining in ASICs, although still less efficiently than Bitcoin in ASICs: it is estimated that the ASIC advantage in Litecoin is reduced by a factor of 10 compared to Bitcoin (Litecoin wiki, 2014).

Scrypt is a recent cryptographic algorithm that has received much less scrutiny by cryptographers than the SHA256 hash function This makes it in some ways a riskier choice as the chances that a vulnerability is found are higher. See Percival (2012) for details of the algorithm.

The main advantages of a memory-hard proof-of-work function (Ethereum wiki, 2014) are:

- It can increase the number of miners as everybody with a computer has an equal chance of mining, in contrast with Bitcoin mining, which requires specialized equipment. Having many small miners, proponents argue, provides greater network resilience.
- It can lead to lower resource waste compared to regular proof-of-work. In particular a lot of resources were invested in early mining equipment for Bitcoin that were later put to rest because the mining technology made them obsolete.

The main arguments against memory-hard functions are that all functions will eventually be implemented in ASICs, and that if mining is generally done using PCs, then a large portion of mining will be done by botnets, i.e. armies of compromised computers.

The mining reward in Litecoin is kept the same as Bitcoin's, i.e. 50 coins per block, halving roughly every 4 years and leading to a maximum supply of 84 million litecoins, or 4 times the money supply of Bitcoin.

As the mining algorithm is different, the hash rate of Litecoin is not directly comparable to that of Bitcoin, i.e. Litecoin's GH/s are not comparable to Bitcoin's GH/s. Comparisons of the relative security of both networks have to take into account the relative cost of the hardware required to pull off double-spending attacks, such as in Figure 7.10.

Litecoin has benefited from the migration of Bitcoin mining to ASICs, as many early Bitcoin miners have re-purposed their hardware, CPUs first and then GPUs, to mine Litecoin. The fact that Litecoin uses scrypt, which is more ASIC-resistant than $SHA256^2$, is perceived as an advantage by enthusiast miners.

11.2 PEERCOIN

Peercoin (PPC) was introduced in 2012. Its main innovation is that it uses a hybrid proof-of-stake/proof-of-work system. In a proof-of-stake system new blocks are minted—analogous to mining—by holders of coins in proportion to how many coins they control. Proof-of-stake does not involve solving a partial hash inversion problem and thus requires minimal electricity consumption. For this reason it is argued that Peercoin is a green alternative to Bitcoin. The differences between proof-of-stake and proof-of-work are explored in more detail in 14.2.1.

In Peercoin there are two types of blocks, those generated with proof-of-stake and those generated with proof-of-work. Blocks generated under proof-of-work follow similar rules to Bitcoin's block generation. However, the block reward for proof-of-work halves every time the difficulty increases 16 times (King and Nadal, 2012).

Blocks generated under proof-of-stake are awarded to *transaction outputs* in a manner that is proportional to their coin age. Coin age is the product of the number of coins in the transaction output multiplied by the time since those funds were last spent. The protocol that awards a new block to a particular transaction outputs proceeds as follows:

- First a transaction called coinstake (similar to Bitcoin's coinbase) is created. This transaction spends the funds in the transaction output, destroying its coin age.
- Then a hash of a header that includes this transaction and the time (in seconds since 1970) is computed.

- This hash is then checked against a proof-of-work requirement, whose difficulty is inverse to the coin age. Note that only one hash per second per transaction output is computed, a very low computational load.
- If the hash matches the proof-of-work requirement, the user in control of the transaction output can mint a new proof-of-stake block and receive the block reward.

The proof-of-work system also uses coin age to determine the security of the blockchain: in case of a fork, the branch that consumes more coin age is the correct one. Initially proof-of-work is used in Peercoin, but over time proof-of-stake becomes the primary source of coin generation, as the block reward for proof-of-work blocks diminishes.

Transaction fees are fixed at 0.01 PPC, but unlike Bitcoin, these fees are destroyed. Users minting blocks are solely compensated through the block reward. The proof-of-stake block reward is set at a 1% annual rate (Wikipedia, 2014j). Thus, in the long run, the inflation will be 1% minus the fees destroyed.

Initial versions of Peercoin included checkpointing, i.e. the inclusion of hash values of certain blocks in the software releases, as a protection against attacks. It is planned that this practice will be phased out in the short future.

Further details on Peercoin can be found in King and Nadal (2012).

11.3 NAMECOIN

Namecoin (NMC) is both a crypto-currency and a decentralized key/value store. This decentralized key/value store is used to implement an alternative **Domain Name System (DNS)**. The DNS is the piece of the internet infrastructure that enable human-readable addresses to be resolved to IP addresses[1]. The internet DNS is under the control of ICANN. Namecoin implements an alternative DNS using the .bit top-level domain[2].

The Namecoin protocol adds new transactions to interact with the key/value store:

- name_new and name_firstupdate[3]. These transactions create a new key/value. Any piece of data can be registered in Namecoin's key/value store. If the key happens to start with "d/", it is considered a .bit domain. For instance, registering "d/understandingbitcoin" would register the domain understandingbitcoin.bit.
- name_update. This transaction allows a user to renew a name, paying a (small) fee. An update transaction can also be used to change the value of the key/value

---

[1] When a web browser connects to a website, such as understandingbitcoin.blogspot.com, the browser makes a DNS query to a layer of DNS servers, asking for the IP address that resolves to the domain understandingbitcoin.blogspot.com. Once it gets a response—say 173.194.67.191—it connects to this IP address. This procedure is all done under the hood by the web browser.

[2] The .bit top-level domain is not assigned by ICANN, and therefore users with Namecoin name resolution enabled in their computers can browse .bit domains as if they were regular domains. To enable .bit domains, a user must be running a copy of the Namecoin server in her computer or must connect to a DNS server which can resolve .bit domains.

[3] There are two separate transactions to prevent nodes in the network from registering names ahead of new transactions they receive. Thus a new name is first reserved with the name_new transaction that includes an encrypted copy of the name to register. A few blocks later the user sends a follow up name_firstupdate transaction with the unencrypted name, which registers the name properly.

pair, such as changing the IP address associated with a domain name. An update transactions also allows transferring a name from one Namecoin address to another. Names registered in Namecoin expire after 36,000 blocks, approximately 250 days if no update is sent (Wikipedia, 2014j).

Users running a Namecoin node have a full copy of the key/value store and can access it at any time. Or some users might prefer to connect to a Name-coin node and query the node for specific information, much in the same way that an SPV wallet queries a full Bitcoin node (section 8.8).

Other Namecoin settings are kept at their default Bitcoin values: proof-of-work function is $SHA256^2$, block generation targets 10 minutes, block reward starts at 50 namecoins and halves every 4 years, final monetary base will be 21 million namecoins, and so on. Namecoin allows merge-mining with Bitcoin after a change in the protocol in 2011 (section 14.3).

A traditional DNS domain registration is associated with a name and a physical address. In contrast, a Namecoin .bit domain registration is only linked to a Namecoin address, whose private key has control over the domain. Thus changes to a domain or transfers of domains between two addresses can be done pseudonymously. Advocates of Namecoin also argue that its decentralized nature makes censorship of domain names much more difficult. Other advantages over traditional DNS is that it is cheaper, faster, and more secure[4]. Other applications of Namecoin are an ID name-space (for storing contact information), a messaging system, a web of trust, or a notary.

11.4 AURORACOIN

Auroracoin (AUR) was launched in February 2014. It is a straightforward fork of Litecoin, so it uses scrypt as its proof-of-work. Its main innovation is not technical, but instead is in the distribution of the currency. Auroracoin was 50% pre-mined, that is, 50% of its total monetary supply was already created at its inception. The remaining 50% of the monetary supply will be awarded to regular miners. The purpose of the 50% pre-mine was to distribute it to the population of Iceland, using the national identification system. This distribution began on the "airdrop" date, March 25, 2013 (Wikipedia, 2014b). Each citizen of Iceland could claim, during the first stage of the "airdrop," 31.8 auroracoins, which amounted to roughly 385 USD around the date of the "airdrop" (Cawrey, 2014). Distributing the cryptocurrency among the population could help create a community around it.

11.5 PRIMECOIN

Primecoin (XMP) was launched in 2013. The main innovation introduced by Primecoin is that its proof-of-work function produces somewhat useful scientific results (Buterin, 2013f). This contrasts with most proof-of-work functions, such as SHA256 or scrypt, whose results do not have any value except to secure the blockchain. Primecoin's

---

[4] Having the DNS database in the local machine prevents **DNS hijacking** attacks, where the responses to DNS queries are subverted to point to malicious IP addresses.

proof-of-work function searches for chains of prime numbers, known as Cunningham chains. The chains of primes found through the proof-of-work could help researchers understand the distribution of prime numbers, which in turn could lead to advances in other scientific disciplines such as physics, or could have useful applications still unknown.

Practical proof-of-work functions must have two properties:

- They must be efficiently verifiable. Verification must be computationally fast. Many scientific computations are not easily verifiable. One example is folding@home, whose goal is to solve the problem of protein folding. The problem with using protein folding as a proof-of-work is that there is no fast way to verify that a given result (the shape of the folded protein) is correct. Thus miners would have an incentive to present fake results to collect the mining reward. The only way to check the solution would be to run the whole folding algorithm again, which defeats the purpose of a proof-of-work function.
- The difficulty must be easily adjustable. The proof-of-work difficulty should be easy to adjust gradually in reaction to new miners entering or exiting the network.

The SHA256 hash function meets both properties, but it has been notoriously difficult to find scientific problems which can be adapted to these properties. Primecoin is the first proposal of a scientific problem that meets both requirements. Verification of a (relatively small) prime number is efficient on current hardware. Verification of chains of primes is similarly efficient. The length of the prime chains is used to adjust the difficulty. The only problem is that the length of a prime chain is a discrete value whose difficulty increases exponentially. Primecoin developers solved this problem, using a fractional chain length (King, 2013).

Primecoin targets a block generation period of one minute, with a difficulty adjustment after every block. The block reward is not a fixed number of coins, as in Bitcoin, but it is a function of the difficulty: $blockreward = 999/difficulty^2$. It can be shown that this self-adjusting block reward will lead to a fixed monetary supply (Buterin, 2013f).

Primecoin could be a first step towards creating proof-of-work functions that would solve useful problems. See King (2013) for the specification of Primecoin's proof-of-work function and Buterin (2013f) for an overview of the project.

11.6 DOGECOIN

Dogecoin (DOGE) was introduced in 2013. Dogecoin is a straightforward fork of Litecoin. Its main innovation lies in its marketing strategy. It associates with the famous internet doge meme, transmitting a message of light-headedness and fun that will hopefully cater to a wider demographic than other cryptocurrencies.

On the technical side, Dogecoin targets a block generation time of 1 minute. The supply of dogecoins is frontloaded with 98 billion dogecoins entering circulation during its first year, and a fixed 5.2 billion in subsequent years (Wikipedia, 2014f). Thus Dogecoin is inflationary (5% increase in the supply during its second year), but its rate of inflation decreases over time[5]. According to its supporters this large supply of dogecoins

---

[5] There was some discussion within the Dogecoin community whether it was better to have an inflationary or deflationary money supply profile. It was finally decided to keep an inflationary one.

breaks the psychological barrier of spending or giving them away, with the result that Dogecoin is widely used as a tipping system.

11.7 FREICOIN

Freicoin (FRC), launched in 2012, is an alt-coin based on Bitcoin with the main differentiator that it has demurrage. **Demurrage** is implemented as a tax on transactions that levies a certain fraction of the freicoins. This fraction increases with the time lapsed since the freicoins were last transacted. Thus demurrage acts as a negative interest rate on currency holders. Freicoin applies an annual demurrage fee of approximately 5%, depending on certain operations in the network (Freicoin, 2014). The name Freicoin is a tribute to the monetary system Freigeld proposed by Silvio Gesell.

According to its proponents, demurrage serves two purposes:

- It creates an economic incentive to investment. In this sense demurrage is similar to expansionary monetary policies that increase the money supply and thus create inflation. The advantage of demurrage over inflation is that the demurrage effect is constant and thus it is easier to account for[6].
- It allows miners to be compensated indefinitely through block rewards without creating an inflationary monetary base, because the block reward will be paid with the demurrage fee. This might be an advantage over cryptocurrencies that rely on transaction fees substituting block rewards on the medium term.

Demurrage disincentives hoarding of freicoins, as the coins will lose value quickly. This contrasts with the estimations that a large percentage of bitcoins have never been involved in any transaction, presumably because they are being hoarded. On the other hand, critics argue that this could limit its growth (Krawisz, 2013). Later versions of Freicoin plan to implement digital assets and contracts (Friedenbach and Timón, 2013).

11.8 OTHER ALT-COINS

This section presents a quick assortment of other alt-coins in no particular order, stressing the singular features of each:

- **SolarCoin** aims to incentivize solar energy. SolarCoin uses two mining algorithms: a regular proof-of-work algorithm, and a second one that relies on a verified energy meter reading. Producers of solar energy can submit their proof-of-generation and be granted SolarCoins (SolarCoin, 2014).
- **Aphroditecoin** replicates the concept of Auroracoin in Cyprus. Similarly, **SpainCoin** replicates the concept in Spain.
- **Splash** is a fork of Ripple (12.7.6) where the native currency is mined (Bitcoin wiki, 2014x).

---

[6] Though critics argue that it is not clear how the demurrage feature would affect a cryptocurrency competing with many other cryptocurrencies as well as fiat currencies.

- **Anoncoin** is a fork of Bitcoin that works over the Invisible Internet Project (I2P), an anonymizing network (AnonCoin, 2014).
- **DarkCoin** is a fork of Bitcoin that incorporates technology for sending transactions with increased privacy for its users (Wikipedia, 2014e).
- **CryptoNote** is an open source project that allows the creation of cryptocurrencies. Its innovation is that it uses ring signatures[7], instead of ECDSA signatures, for increased untraceability (CryptoNote, 2014).
- **TAGCoin** is positioned as a reward system for merchants. Merchants can buy tagcoins and give them to their customers, who can then use the tagcoins with other merchants or cash them in (TAGCoin, 2014).
- **Devcoin**, whose purpose is to support open source developers (Devcoin, 2014).
- **Safecoin**, whose purpose is to fund the SAFE network, proposed by Maidsafe. SAFE is a peer-to-peer network where users contribute computational power and storage to a public cloud, where data can be stored securely in a decentralized way (Maidsafe, 2014).
- **CureCoin** whose goal is to reward scientific/medicinal research, such as protein folding computations (CureCoin, 2014).
- **Qixcoin** (QixCoin, 2014) is a cryptocurrency whose purpose is to support peer-to-peer gaming, both strategy and chance games. It has a built-in engine to verify card games.

11.9   THE CASE FOR/AGAINST ALT-COINS

The cost of launching an alt-coin is very low: just forking the Bitcoin Core source code and changing the logo is enough to create an alt-coin. For this reason the number of alt-coins launched is very large[8]. Many of the first alt-coins introduced few changes to Bitcoin's implementation, and critics argue that their main goal was to replicate the scarcity race of Bitcoin.

Critics of alt-coins argue that only alt-coins that have some feature impossible to add to Bitcoin and that fulfills some unmet need will survive. Otherwise Bitcoin will capture a dominant market share because of the network effect. The **network effect**, or **network externalities**, refers to the property of a product or a technology whose demand increases with the number of users (Varian, 2003). The classic example of a product with network effect is the telephone, which is more useful the more people are connected to the network. These are *direct network effects*. Another classical example is the DVD standard, where the more users that have a DVD player, the more attractive it is for content producers to support the platform. These are *indirect network effects*. Bitcoin advocates argue that Bitcoin exhibits both direct network effects (the more people use Bitcoin as a store of value, the more value it has) and indirect network effects (the more people would like to spend Bitcoin, the greater the incentive of merchants to support it).

---

[7] **Ring signatures** are a type of digital signatures where any member of a set of possible signers can sign a message. The verifier of a ring signature does not get to know who, among the members of the set, has signed the message, only that one member has signed it. Ring signatures where introduced in Rivest et al. (2001).

[8] There are even websites that enable users to create their own alt-coins with a few mouse clicks.

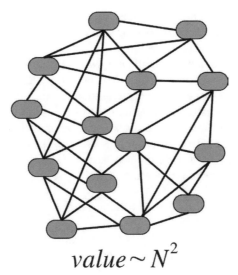

$$value \sim N^2$$

FIGURE 11.1 Network effect

Suppose a network has N users. Each user can make a total of $N-1$ connections, one to each of the other users. As there are N users, the total number of connections across the network is $(N \cdot (N-1))/2 \sim N^2$. Assuming that the value of a network is proportional to the possible number of connections, the value of a network is proportional to the number of users squared. This is known as **Metcalfe's law** and is a way to measure network externalities[9]. Figure 11.1 shows a illustration of the network effect and Metcalfe's law. Note that the number of connections is much larger than the number of nodes in the network: this non-linear effect is captured by Metcalfe's law.

Liquidity is the economic manifestation of the network effect. The **liquidity** of an asset is the degree to which it can be sold quickly without affecting its price. Liquidity is a measure of the trade-off between the speed of the sale and the price drop. The liquidity of a currency depends on the size of the network of users of that currency. Critics of alt-coins argue that liquidity is self-reinforcing, and thus users will gravitate towards the most liquid cryptocurrency, making it even more liquid. This process, they argue, will drive alt-coins to extinction (Krawisz, 2014).

On the other hand, proponents of alt-coins (Buterin, 2013h) argue that the network effect does not necessarily happen on a global scale, and there can be room for network effects to kick in along, say, national borders or language divides. Furthermore, there might be room for complementary technologies to Bitcoin, even with the network effect taking place.

Aside from network effects, other economical arguments criticizing alt-coins (Krawisz, 2013) are:

---

[9] Metcalfe's law assumes that every potential connection has the same value. This might not be true if there are barriers, such as different languages, to create useful connections between nodes.

- Competing standards do not make sense for currencies. A single standard increases the value to all users. Thus competing standards serve no purpose, and currency competition can lead to fragmentation.
- Switching costs. There can be significant switching costs from Bitcoin to alt-coin once much of the payment infrastructure is laid out. Defendants of alt-coins argue that switching can be done via a software upgrade in most cases, and that several cryptocurrencies can easily co-exist thanks to tools such as multi-currency wallets and exchanges that automatically integrate with such wallets.
- Coordination problems. Even if most users would like to substitute Bitcoin for an alt-coin—say because of a technological advantage—they suffer from a coordination problem that makes the transition difficult.

Arguments often put forward in favor of alt-coins are:

- Competition is good because it leads to innovation. However, critics of alt-coins respond that there is already a lot of innovation inside the Bitcoin community, and this internal innovation is more important that innovating the basic technology. Furthermore technical innovation is already happening using Bitcoin as a layer, such as in several meta-coins projects (section 12.7). Proponents of alt-coins argue back that it is very risky to include new technology into Bitcoin (or in some cases it cannot be technically included) and that innovating by creating a new alt-coin is a much safer option. Moreover, alt-coins enable permissionless innovation, that is, they allow trying ideas that would be vetted by Bitcoin developers. Critics reply that innovation on the features of digital currencies can be achieved without diluting the monetary base of Bitcoin using side-chains (section 14.4).
- Multiple blockchains can help reduce the load on the network. If at some point Bitcoin encounters dis-economies of scale, such as blockchain scalability troubles (section 7.7), alt-coins could be of an advantage as they would allow reducing the load on the Bitcoin network. Critics of alt-coins reply that if another blockchain is needed for some functionality, then nodes will have to support the new alt-coin blockchain and the original Bitcoin blockchain. Moreover, as there might be transactions between the two, the overall burden on the nodes will be greater.
- Some alt-coins can help achieve a public function. One example are alt-coins whose proof-of-work achieves a useful scientific goal such as Primecoin. Another example are alt-coins created to fund public goods, such as Devcoin, CureCoin, or Safecoin (section 11.8). Similarly, branded alt-coins can be created to fund artists or other projects.
- Alt-coins can help lower Bitcoin's volatility, by putting a cap on its market capitalization (Buterin, 2013h).
- Some alt-coins do not need to compete directly with Bitcoin, but might cooperate in a mutually beneficial relationship. One example could be an alt-coin that allows for very low transaction costs—say to use in micropayments—and could reduce Bitcoin's scalability pressures.

Critics of alt-currencies also cite practical disadvantages to the development of alt-coins:

TABLE 11.1 Market capitalization of some alt-coins. Data retrieved from coinmarketcap.com on April 19, 2014

Cryptocurrency	Market capitalization (USD millions)
Bitcoin	6,037
Litecoin	325
Peercoin	52
Dogecoin	44
Namecoin	21
Primecoin	5
Auroracoin	1
Freicoin	0.5

- Alt-coins are a way to get around Bitcoin's fixed money supply (Andresen, 2013a). Critics argue that the main objective of most alt-coins is to create a scarcity race that tries to mimic the scarcity race carried out by Bitcoin, with the objective of enriching their creators. The end result is that with many alt-coins the money supply just becomes infinite[10].
- Alt-coins divert talent. Time and effort spent developing and promoting alt-coins could be used instead to advance Bitcoin's technology and marketing message.
- They confuse potential users, who would have to learn the differences between many cryptocurrencies before deciding to use any of them.
- If an alt-coin were to supersede Bitcoin, this would open the door for yet another alt-coin to supersede it and so on. Eventually users would hesitate to give significant value to any cryptocurrency because of fear that it would get supplanted by the next one.

A tally on the rivalry between different cryptocurrencies can be taken by comparing their market capitalizations. Table 11.1 shows the market capitalization of some alt-coins introduced in this chapter compared to the market capitalization of Bitcoin.

Bitcoin and several alt-coins have been competing for some years now. As of the time of writing, it seems Bitcoin has been able to benefit from the first-mover advantage, enabled by network effects and liquidity, and capture a significant portion of the cryptocurrencies' market. Time will tell whether this current advantage will extend over time or whether some alt-coin or meta-coin (section 12.7) could challenge Bitcoin.

---

[10] Note that this argument is not consistent with the network effect argument that states that Bitcoin will drive out other alt-coins. If the network effect takes place, there will not be an increase in the monetary base of cryptocurrencies.

CHAPTER 12

Contracts (the Internet of Money or Cryptocurrencies 2.0)

A wide range of applications are possible using Bitcoin, besides the storage and transfer of funds, thanks to the transaction scripting language (section 6.1), multisignature transactions (section 6.3), transaction signature options (section 6.5), and pay-to-script-hash (P2SH) transactions (section 6.6).

This chapter will present some applications that the community has come up with. Although there has not been wide deployment of any of these applications yet, it is interesting to understand them, as some of them might become important in the future.

The blockchain technology and cryptography allow users to enter into contracts with no central entity to enforce their clauses. Digital contracts could in some cases substitute the legal system: interactions that today are governed by law could be governed in the future by digital contracts and cryptoledgers[1].

Many of the applications of this chapter could be achieved using Bitcoin's blockchain as it is today or with minor modifications. But some examples require more profound extensions to the current Bitcoin protocol. The technologies that aim to extend or supersede Bitcoin are usually called meta-coins, and will be introduced in section 12.7.

An extensive catalogue of contract applications can be found in Bitcoin wiki (2014f) and Swanson (2014).

12.1 DIGITAL ASSETS

A **digital asset** is an asset whose ownership is recorded digitally and which is directly controlled by its owner. Bitcoins are an example of digital assets, as their ownership is recorded in the blockchain and their owners directly control them, through the private key.

The blockchain was originally used to register the ownership and transfer of bitcoins. But the blockchain is a **decentralized asset register** and it could potentially be used to register ownership and transfer of any digital asset besides bitcoins. Digital assets could be stored in the blockchain, or more precisely in an unspent transaction output in the blockchain. The blockchain could then enforce property of the asset through the private key associated with the address where the digital asset is stored. In the same way

---

[1] A **cryptoledger** is a generalization of the Bitcoin blockchain, including the blockchain of any alternative coins (Chapter 11) or any other decentralized digital ledger that is secured using cryptography.

that bitcoins can only be spent by someone in possession of the private key, digital assets could only be transferred or used by someone in possession of the private key.

If the digital asset is a financial asset, it could use bitcoins for its financial settlements. For instance, a digital bond could pay coupons and redeem the principal to the address holding the digital bond. Thus digital assets could disintermediate the role of custodians (Brown, 2014b). Digital assets stored in the blockchain are pseudonymous, that is, the identity of their owner would not be known, only the address associated with the private key, as is the case for bitcoins. For many applications, such as a digital bonds or digital shares, the identity of the owner is irrelevant for their settlement. And for some applications pseudonimity might possess certain advantages.

Figure 12.1 presents a straightforward way in which digital assets could be created. An issuer publicly declares that the funds in a certain Bitcoin address represent ownership of an asset. The issuer could be a custodian in possession of the asset or it could be the issuer of a financial obligation directly, like a company issuing its own shares. The issuer must be trusted, otherwise the digital asset would not be recognized to have any value. The issuer could sell the asset to several buyers, transferring ownership through regular Bitcoin transactions. As Figure 12.1 shows, the ownership is transferred using a transaction with two inputs and two outputs. The transaction must be signed by both buyer and seller of the digital asset, so there is no risk that one of the two parties cheats: unless the transaction is correctly signed by both, it is invalid and no transfer would take place[2].

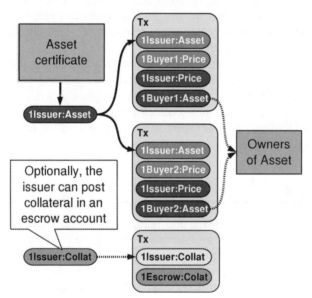

FIGURE 12.1   Digital assets

---

[2] The transaction has to be signed by the two parties before it is published in the blockchain. Thus the two parties need a communication channel aside from the Bitcoin network to send back and forth the partially signed transaction. Previously the communication of unfinalized transactions could be performed through Bitcoin network's unconfirmed transactions' mempool. But this "mempool transaction replacement mechanism" was removed in 2010 to prevent denial of service attacks (section 6.5 and Bitcoin wiki (2014f)).

The issuer of the digital asset can track ownership of the asset through the blockchain. Thus the issuer can keep a record of which addresses own the digital asset at every moment, and could use this record to make payments to these addresses, say dividends or coupons. Note that in this case it is the issuer who pays the cost of tracking the owners of the digital assets, and not the custodian. However, the costs of tracking the owners of a digital asset are reduced considerably.

Digital assets stored in the blockchain allow services such as voting. Say a company issues shares through the blockchain. Voting could be exercised via a message signed with the private key associated with the address holding the shares. Digital assets have the feature that owners of the shares do not have to identify themselves to exercise their right to vote.

Issuers that face difficulty publishing digital assets in the blockchain because of their credibility could create an escrow account, managed by a third party, that could act as guarantee (see Figure 12.1).

Digital assets could open the door to new entrants into the securities issuing business, opening the capital markets to projects that could not access it before. Some projects have started to fund themselves in this way (*The Economist*, 2014b).

Up to this point it has been assumed that digital assets can be represented in the blockchain. Meta-coins address the problem of representing digital assets in a blockchain (Bitcoin or others). A review of these technologies can be found in section 12.7.

12.2 SMART PROPERTY

Smart property is property that has access to the blockchain, and can take actions based on the information published there. Another way to look at it is that smart property can be controlled via the blockchain. A common example of smart property (Bitcoin wiki, 2014w) is a car whose ownership is represented by a digital asset in the blockchain. The physical car is connected to the internet and can read the blockchain, and thus can keep track of the status of the digital asset representing it. In case the digital asset is transferred from one address to another, the physical car can see this status update in the blockchain and take necessary actions, i.e. change its owner.

Figure 12.2 presents the steps required to transfer ownership of a smart asset, the car in the example. First, seller and buyer agree on the price and assemble a transaction with two inputs and two outputs. One of the inputs references the address that holds the digital asset associated with the car and the other the funds to buy it. The transaction achieves simultaneously the transfer of funds from the buyer to the seller and the transfer of the property from the seller to the buyer. Both buyer and seller sign the transaction. As the transaction is not finalized unless both buyer and seller have signed it, there is no counterparty risk for either of them.

Once the transaction is correctly signed, one of them—say the seller—publishes it in the blockchain. As the car can read the blockchain, it sees that a change of ownership has occurred and updates the public key of its owner accordingly. The new owner of the car could then access it, signing a message with the private key associated with her Bitcoin address.

Smart property is usually assumed to have access to the blockchain. However, many of the features of smart property can be achieved even if the asset does not have access

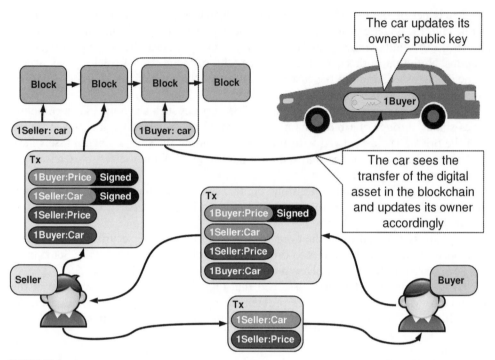

FIGURE 12.2 Smart property

to the blockchain. In this case, the buyer of the car can take a copy of the confirmed transaction, together with the Merkle branch linking it to the block header. She may also take a copy of several block headers on top of the block where the transaction was confirmed, to prove to the car that the transaction has been confirmed by several blocks. She could then present the car with this information, say through some wireless protocol such as Bluetooth. The car checks that all the information is correct and then updates the public key of its owner. Once this process is finished, the new owner can open the car and start the engine by signing a message with her private key and sending it to the car, via a wallet application in her smartphone.

More complex applications are possible. For instance, the car could grant an address access for a limited period, say for a rent contract. Or a car could be bought with a loan, and the car could monitor the timely payment of the bills in the blockchain. In case a payment is missed, the car could revert to its previous owner. Details of how to set a car loan contract without the need for the car itself to monitor and interpret the blockchain can be found in Bitcoin wiki (2014w).

Smart property applications could increase privacy. A user does not need to prove identity to prove ownership of a smart asset: possession of the right token (private key) is enough.

12.3 MICROPAYMENTS

Micropayments or **microtransactions** are transactions of very small amounts that are not viable using existing payment methods, such as credit cards, because the transaction fees would represent a large portion of the value transferred. It is often said that Bitcoin makes micropayments viable, given Bitcoin's low fees. Although low transaction fees are important for micropayments, the flexibility of Bitcoin transactions offer additional advantages for microtransactions.

An **off-chain transaction** is a transaction that is valid, but has not been published in the blockchain yet. The transaction is correctly signed and in the hands of the recipient of the funds. But the recipient of the funds in the off-chain transaction usually holds the publication of the transaction under the expectation that the transaction will be modified, i.e. the funds transferred increased by a small amount.

Off-chain transactions can be used for frequent micropayments in the following way. First, a user and a service provider—say a newspaper—enter into a relationship. The newspaper wishes to charge the user a small fee for every article read. The first time the user reads an article, the newspaper provides the client with its address and the client creates a master transaction with the small price of the article read, signs the transaction and sends it to the newspaper. But the newspaper does not publish it because it is expecting the user to read more articles and thus increase the amount in the transaction. When the user reads another article, the newspaper sends the client the master transaction with an updated amount which the client signs and sends back to the newspaper. If the user refuses to sign the transaction, the newspaper can publish the latest signed transaction and break the relation with the user. Note that this set-up for micropayments is subject to double-spending attacks on the part of the user. See 14.1.1 (micropayment channels) for a slightly more complicated protocol that is not subject to double-spending attacks.

The advantage of using off-line transactions for micropayments is that the funds in the transaction can be rapidly adjusted, to the tune of 1,000 times per second[3]. Furthermore, each micropayment could be of a tiny amount, below the dust threshold level (Chapter 6), assuming that the total amount is greater than this threshold level.

One often-cited application of micropayments are WiFi hotspots (Bitcoin wiki, 2014f) where users pay exactly their data consumption. A user could preallocate a budget for connectivity and a micropayment software could take care of paying for the data connection with no user intervention.

12.4 AUTONOMOUS AGENTS

Autonomous agents are agents that are run without human assistance. They follow a computer program and have an existence of their own. These agents can enter into contracts, receive and spend funds, or even enlist the help of humans to perform certain tasks for them. As these agents can presumably perform all the functions of a corporation, they are sometimes called **Decentralized Autonomous Corporations**, **Decentralized Autonomous Organizations**, or **Distributed Autonomous Corporations** (DACs or DAOs for short). They are sometimes simply referred to as **decentralized** applications.

Autonomous computer programs running on the internet are not new. However, one hurdle for autonomous agents was how to fund themselves and enter into contracts

---

[3] This rate of adjustment depends on the bandwidth and the processing power available to the parties in the transaction. 1,000 adjustments per second is a rough estimate based on the current bandwidth and computing power of consumer devices.

without human intervention. The introduction of the blockchain technology and the digital contract platform that it enables, allows this hurdle to be efficiently overcome.

Bitcoin is arguably an example of a Decentralized Autonomous Corporation (Larimer, 2013). It is an algorithm that has taken a life of its own, enlisting the help of humans to perform certain tasks for it, such as software development, mining, promotion, and so on. It rewards the humans working on its behalf by awarding them tokens, bitcoins, that increase in value with the growth of the network. Thus humans working for it are aligned with it in their objectives.

Some of the most common proposed applications of autonomous agents are:

- Distributed file hosting, i.e. distributed Dropbox. A file storage agent could rent storage space and offer file hosting services. See Garzik (2013a) for more details of such an application.
- Cloud computing or server brokers. An autonomous agent could buy bulk server capacity and then resell it.
- Decentralized exchange. An autonomous agent could operate an exchange between different cryptocurrencies, or between cryptocurrencies and other digital assets.
- News aggregator. Writers contribute their articles and are paid based on the fees generated by the advertisements displayed by their articles. A news aggregator autonomous agent could run code that filtered the writers' contributions.

An autonomous agent could be funded at its creation. It then could find hosting for itself, paying for it with its own funds, and could start operating and offering its services. Successful (profitable) autonomous agents could replicate themselves, spawning children and funding them in turn. This would increase the offer for their services. On the other hand, if an autonomous agent were not profitable it would liquidate its assets and shut itself down. The code running the autonomous agent could be open sourced to ensure that the autonomous agent follows business practices that are beneficial to society, say spawning more children when demand for its services increases instead of raising the price. Visibility of the code could also increase confidence in users of the autonomous agent's services, for instance users of an autonomous agent offering banking services could check that it follows sound financial practices.

There are some technical challenges to the deployment of autonomous agents. The code running an autonomous agent could be subverted by an attacker and deviated from its initial goal to the attacker's benefit. Therefore the autonomous agent must assume that it will run inside a hostile environment, say a malicious operating system. Assuring an autonomous agent is running its legitimate code could be done using **trusted computing** technology, such as Trusted Platform Modules (TPM) (Garzik, 2013b). More recent advances in cryptographic obfuscation techniques could improve the feasibility of autonomous agents (14.7.2).

Furthermore, secrets stored inside the autonomous agent's code, notably the private key that controls its funds, could be stolen. It is notoriously difficult to obfuscate secrets inside code. Testament to this is the difficulty faced by DRM schemes. However, recent advances in **homomorphic encryption** (14.7.1) could provide a solution.

The spread of autonomous agents also faces legal challenges, as the legal framework for these "corporations" is not well developed.

12.5 OTHER APPLICATIONS

The potential applications for digital contracts are numerous. This section will explore only a handful of other applications. Some applications such as multisignature escrow have already been covered in section 4.5. Also, several known applications such as decentralized lotteries, prediction markets, online auctions, and even the creation of new currencies on top of the existing infrastructure have been left out. No doubt new applications to digital contracts will surface that might grow to be more important than those covered in this chapter.

12.5.1 Crowd-funding

An **assurance contract** is a contract where users pledge to contribute funds but only if a funding goal is reached. This can easily be implemented by assembling a transaction with many inputs and only one output. Using the hash types SIGHASH_ALL and SIGHASH_ANYONECANPAY (section 6.5) every participant signs her input and the output. New inputs can be added to the transaction, but the output cannot be changed because changing it would render all the signatures invalid. If enough inputs are added to the transaction to reach the amount in the output (the goal), then the transaction is valid and can be published in the blockchain. If not enough inputs are added, i.e. the goal is not reached, then the transaction is invalid and the participants are free to spend the pledged funds elsewhere. Assurance contracts can thus be created in Bitcoin without the need for a central agency.

An entrepreneur launching a crowd-funding campaign could create an assurance contract: a transaction with a single output representing the crowd-funding goal. Users can pledge funds to the project by sending the entrepreneur their signed inputs to the transaction. The entrepreneur collects all the inputs into a single transaction that she can publish in the blockchain to collect the funds if the goal is met[4].

The provision of public goods is often cited as one of the arguments for the collection of taxes. Assurance contracts could facilitate the creation of some public goods, providing an alternative way to fund public goods: a road could be funded with the pledges of its potential users.

Dominant assurance contracts are assurance contracts where an entrepreneur promises to pay the participants a kickback if the target funding is not reached. They were introduced by the economist Alexander Tabarrok (Tabarrok, 1998). As participants have an extra incentive to participate in the contract, namely the kickback they receive if the project does not reach its funding goal[5], the chances of successful funding increase compared to a regular assurance contract. Dominant assurance contracts can also be implemented in Bitcoin (Bitcoin wiki, 2014g).

---

[4] If any of the originally pledged inputs has already been spent, the entrepreneur should remove it from the transaction before publishing it to the blockchain. Otherwise, the whole crowd-funding transaction would be flagged as a double-spend and discarded by the nodes.

[5] In game-theoretic terms, the Nash equilibrium for the participants is to pledge funds to the project because they benefit both if the funding goal is reached as well as if it is not.

12.5.2 External State Contract

Some applications may require the transmission of funds if certain conditions are met. For example, a bet on the result of a match would require sending the proceeds of the bet to the winner according to the result of the match. This rule cannot be encoded into a transaction, because Bitcoin is a self-contained system which does not reference outside data. However, the release of the funds can be made conditional on the signature of an oracle server. An **oracle server** accepts requests, evaluates them, and produces an output. One of the outputs provided could be a signature to unlock the funds in a transaction. In the bet example, the oracle server could sign a transaction to send the funds to the winner of the bet.

An **external state contract** or **oracle contract** is a contract where an oracle server decides the recipient of the funds based on some previously defined rules. To create a bet, two users might decide to put funds into a 2-of-3 multisignature transaction output, where the three keys that can unlock these funds are the two users' keys and the oracle server key. Once the event for the bet is decided, the winner creates a transaction sending the funds to herself, signs this transaction, and sends it over to the oracle server. The oracle runs the rule script and if it resolves favorably, signs the transaction and publishes it in the blockchain.

In a external state contract, the two parties and the oracle server have to agree on a rule script to be run by the oracle server and how to link that rule script with a particular transaction. The transaction could include a hash of the rule script such as:

```
<rule script hash> OP_DROP 2 <oracleAddress>
<party1Address> <party2Address> 3 OP_CHECKMULTISIG
```

However, the inclusion of OP_DROP makes the transaction non-standard. Non-standard transactions can be included in the blockchain but they are not relayed by nodes in the network running Bitcoin Core Server (section 6.7).

External state contracts can be extended to more than two participants, using a general m-of-n multisignature transaction. Note, however, than m-of-n multisignature transactions, where $n > 3$, are not standard transactions.

As external state contracts depend on an external server, there is risk that this external server could cooperate with an attacker or be compromised. For more details on external state contracts, see Bitcoin wiki (2014f) and alp (2013).

12.5.3 Contract for Differences

Contract for Differences or **CFDs** are financial contracts between two parties, where one of the parties pays (or receives) from the other the difference between the price of an asset—say a particular stock or commodity price—and a reference price set in the contract. It is a financial instrument similar to forwards or futures but without a defined expiry date. CFDs can be used to bet that the price of an asset will increase or decrease without having to actually purchase the asset or sell it short[6].

---

[6] Short-selling involves borrowing an asset to then sell it in the market. Before returning the asset to its original owner, the short-seller has to buy it back in the market. If the asset price has decreased

CFDs are usually over-the-counter instruments, i.e. private contracts between two parties. Therefore both parties bear the risk that the other party might default on its promise. Future contracts are a similar instrument where this counterparty risk is mitigated by introducing an exchange: both parties trade the future against the exchange. Furthermore, the exchange requires both parties to post a margin and keep topping it up when the position moves against them. Thus the parties to a future contract hold counterparty risk against the exchange, which is considered to have a high credit quality, instead of against each other. CFDs settled in the blockchain can work similarly to futures, but without the need for a central counterparty: all the margining rules can be fulfilled by the contract rules. A feature of CFDs settled over the blockchain is that parties to the CFD do not have to present their identities.

CFD contracts cannot be created using the current Bitcoin infrastructure. First, there must be a reliable data stream of asset prices. There are several ways to embed external data into the blockchain (section 12.6). Second, there must be an infrastructure to use this data stream to settle the CFD contract. This infrastructure does not exist in Bitcoin as of the time of writing, but most meta-coins address this issue (section 12.7).

12.5.4 Distributed Exchange

In a centralized exchange, the exchange receives market orders from its participants and runs an auction algorithm to match those orders. In contrast, in a **distributed exchange** participants publish their offers (or bids) in a distributed ledger, i.e. a blockchain, and these orders are matched by the protocol running the blockchain. The instruments traded in a distributed exchange are typically CFDs or digital assets, both of which are settled in the distributed ledger. There is no need for a central clearing house to either run the auction algorithm or settle the trades.

Market participants also retain their privacy: other participants scouring the blockchain only observe the bids and offers and the addresses behind them, but may not readily obtain information about the parties behind those addresses.

The infrastructure to create distributed exchanges is not available in the Bitcoin protocol as of the time of writing, but most meta-coins do have this functionality built in (section 12.7).

12.5.5 Deposits

Some service providers request a deposit from their users. The downside for the users of these services is that the service provider could unilaterally decide to confiscate the funds. This might be legitimate when the service provider suffers losses as a consequence of the user actions. But in other cases, a deposit is required merely as a proof of commitment on the part of the user. One example of the latter could be a website that requires a proof that there is a real person behind a user registration.

Digital contracts allow the creation of a deposit that neither party can spend, and in such a way that the funds are returned to the depositor unless the deposit is renewed. One way to accomplish this is as follows (Bitcoin wiki, 2014f):

---

in the interval, then the short-seller makes a profit. Conversely, if the asset price has increased, the short-seller makes a loss. Thus short-selling is a way to bet that an asset price will decrease.

- The service provider and the user interchange their addresses.
- The user creates a transaction sending funds to a 2-of-2 multisignature address (section 6.3). She does not send the service provider the transaction, just the hash of it.
- The service provider creates a transaction sending the funds in the multisignature address back to the user and signs it, but with a lock time (section 6.5) set some time in the future. The service provider then forwards this transaction to the user. The user is certain she will be able to retrieve the funds when the time comes, because she has a valid transaction spending the funds in the multisignature address.
- The user then broadcasts both transactions. The service provider can monitor the blockchain for proof that the first transaction has been confirmed and then grant access to the user.

At this point neither the user nor the service provider can spend the funds. If the user decides to close the relationship before the original date, she can ask the service provider to sign a transaction returning the funds. In case the service provider refuses, she has to wait until the lock time is reached.

12.5.6 Saving Addresses

Savings addresses are addresses designed to hold saving funds. These addresses must prevent the funds from being spent quickly, or they must provide a mechanism to claw back the funds during a certain period, in case they are stolen.

This functionality is not available in the Bitcoin protocol, but it is offered by several meta-coin implementations. For instance, Mastercoin allows marking an address as a "savings" address, and to reverse transactions from this address during a certain period. Other meta-coins, such as Ethereum, allow setting up saving addresses by creating contracts where the user can only spend a fraction of the funds daily—say 1%—by herself but can spend larger sums with the additional signature of an escrow service (Buterin, 2014b).

12.6 INSERTING DATA INTO THE BLOCKCHAIN

There is an increasing demand to embed arbitrary data into the blockchain. Meta-coins built on top of Bitcoin's blockchain are one example of services using this feature[7]. There are several ways to insert data into the blockchain, the most common are[8]:

- **In the coinbase**. The coinbase is the first transaction in a block. Miners specify the addresses where the mining reward should be sent in the output of the coinbase. The input of the coinbase transaction is discarded by the protocol, thus any arbitrary data can be included in this input. Note that only miners have access to this field, and

---

[7] There are some interesting uses of the blockchain to secure data, such as a Bitcoin aficionado who stored a hash of his DNA to prove his "existence."

[8] There are other ways, such as using the OP_PUSHDATA2 command, but these usually result in non-standard transactions.

so anybody who wants to include data in this field must convince, or pay, miners to include the data there.

- **Fake Bitcoin address**. Arbitrary data can be encoded into fake Bitcoin addresses. Then a transaction can be assembled to send funds to this address. The funds sent to this address are lost, as the private key that controls this address is unknown. Funds sent to fake addresses are usually very small quantities. To avoid a denial of service attack against Bitcoin, the protocol sets a minimum amount of funds that can be sent to an address (Chapter 6). Transactions with outputs below this limit are called dust transactions and are discarded. As the funds sent are lost, there is a cost associated with this method. Furthermore, this method bloats the unconfirmed transactions' memory pool (UTXO) with undesired data (section 7.4) and so it is discouraged.
- **Multisignature transaction**. Data can be encoded in fake addresses and these addresses included in a 1-of-n multisignature transaction. The first address of this multisignature transaction is a valid address under the control of the sender. Thus the sender can later recover the funds. This also avoids bloating the UTXO as these transactions are removed from it after they are spent. A total of $n - 1$ fake addresses can be included in one of these transactions. The current limit for a standard multisignature transaction is $n = 3$, so a total of two fake addresses can be encoded.
- **OP_RETURN**. The command OP_RETURN was introduced in version 0.9 of Bitcoin Core as a means to insert arbitrary data into the blockchain, and is the preferred method to do so (section 6.4). The contents of this transaction output can be safely pruned, i.e. forgotten by all nodes except those nodes that want to keep a record of the complete blockchain, called **archival nodes**.

THE OP_RETURN CONTROVERSY

OP_RETURN is the preferred way to insert data into the blockchain. When OP_RETURN was announced, it was set to allow 80 bytes of data per transaction. When it was finally incorporated to the Bitcoin Core in version 0.9 it allowed only 40 bytes of data. Controversy ensued, with some meta-coin developers arguing 40 bytes was not enough, while Bitcoin developers argued it was designed to accommodate enough space for a hash (Bradbury, 2014a). Bitcoin developers argued that additional data could be stored in a Distributed Hash Table and only the root hash of this table needed to be stored in an OP_RETURN transaction. A **Distributed Hash Table (DHT)** is a data structure similar to a hash table, with the peculiarity that it is decentralized and therefore maintained by a cluster of nodes in a network. This makes it resilient to the failure of some of its nodes. This proposal would force meta-coins to create a separate DHT infrastructure, instead of relying on the Bitcoin blockchain to store all of their data.

Part of the controversy is about fees. Any piece of data could be stored in the blockchain if divided into the necessary amount of pieces, but a higher number of transactions will translate into larger fees. Thus data storage in the blockchain and fees are interconnected, and both Bitcoin developers and meta-coin developers must strike a balance.

An additional application of the ability to embed arbitrary data into the blockchain are digital notaries. **Digital notaries** are services that allow users to secure the existence of data into Bitcoin's blockchain, backed by the computational power of the network[9]. These services are similar to the time-stamping services introduced in section 7.2 but considerably cheaper, as they do not have to pay for advertisements in published media. Proof of existence—say of a contract—can be published on the blockchain, without revealing its contents. There are currently several enterprises that offer this service commercially. The author has used one of these services to register (the hash of) an early version of this book in the blockchain.

12.7 META-COINS

Meta-coins are networks that use Bitcoin's blockchain (or a new blockchain) to store metadata allowing new applications, such as digital assets, autonomous agents, external state contracts, CFDs, distributed exchanges, saving addresses, and so on[10]. Not every meta-coin supports all the features presented, but most meta-coins support a considerable subset of these features. All meta-coin implementations can handle digital assets, thus new digital currencies can be issued using the infrastructure provided by any meta-coin.

This section is a short overview of the competing networks being built for this purpose. Meta-coins are a work in progress and innovation is proceeding at a brisk pace. As of the time of writing there are several competing technologies in this space. Network effects and economies of scale will probably accelerate consolidation in just a few of these meta-coins in the medium term. Figure 12.3 shows the market capitalization of several meta-coins[11].

Some meta-coins are built on top of Bitcoin's blockchain (**on-blockchain**)[12], while others roll out their own ledger (**off-blockchain**).

The advantages of using on-blockchain to build meta-coins are:

- They benefit from the high degree of security of Bitcoin.
- Protocols could be easily built for on-blockchain meta-coins to interact with one another.
- There is a reduction in the fragmentation of the digital currencies' ecosystem.

The disadvantages of on-blockchain meta-coins are:

- Meta-coins take space from Bitcoin's blockchain to store their metadata.

---

[9] Data could also be secured into other alt-coins blockchains (Chapter 11) but Bitcoin's blockchain is usually preferred because the block difficulty is highest, increasing the security of the embedded data.

[10] This classification might not suit all tastes. Some people prefer to save the term "meta-coin" for those networks built on top of Bitcoin, and call the other networks "next generation cryptocurrencies".

[11] Ethereum is not included as it had not been launched before the date the data was captured.

[12] No changes in Bitcoin's protocol are required to build these meta-coins. Thus anybody could release a meta-coin protocol on top of Bitcoin or other alt-coin, with no prior authorization.

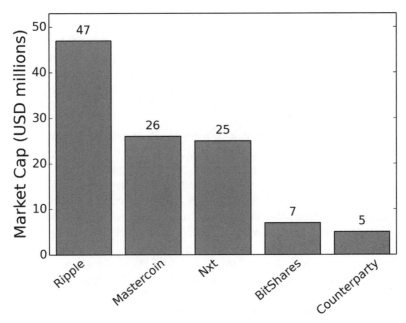

FIGURE 12.3   Market capitalization of some meta-coins. Data from coinmarketcap.com on April 19, 2014

- Meta-coins are harder to secure than Bitcoin as they have to handle conflicting me-ta-coin transactions that are valid regular Bitcoin transactions, and thus make their way to the blockchain.
- The SPV features of Bitcoin (section 8.8) are lost for meta-coins. Therefore meta-coin wallets have to download and store a large portion of the blockchain. Lightweight wallets for these meta-coins would have to build their own SPV features separately from Bitcoin or rely on a trusted server.

Supporters of on-blockchain technology argue that Bitcoin is similar to TCP/IP[13]—a set of communication protocols used by the internet—on top of which other applications can be built. Critics argue that Bitcoin is more similar to SMTP, the protocol underlying email, good for one particular application but lacking flexibility. The jury is still out on which approach (on-blockchain, off-blockchain) will succeed.

All meta-coins have open-sourced their code, presumably because a close sourced implementation is deemed to present a competitive disadvantage as it can generate dis-trust among its users.

This review of the different meta-coins is necessarily short and shallow. All me-ta-coins are complete ecosystems unto themselves and the reader is encouraged to fur-ther delve into the workings of the meta-coins found most promising.

---

[13] See any standard computer networks textbook, such as Tanenbaum and Wetherall (2013) or Kurose and Ross (2012) for a review of the basic internet protocols.

12.7.1 Colored Coins

Colored Coins are probably the simplest implementation of a meta-coin protocol. The main idea of Colored Coins is that a Bitcoin transaction output can be used to represent a digital asset, aside from the bitcoins it holds. To create a digital asset, the issuer of the digital asset only has to declare that those bitcoins hold the digital asset. Colored Coin protocols create an infrastructure around this idea that allows the creation of digital assets on top of the Bitcoin framework.

An overview of Colored Coins can be found in Rosenfeld (2012). An early Colored Coins specification can be found in Assia et al. (2014). The following explanation of a Colored Coins protocol is based on this specification. Although there are newer protocol specifications, this protocol will serve as an illustration of the technology.

Figure 12.4 presents how Colored Coins can be issued inside a regular Bitcoin transaction. The transaction can have several inputs, but only the first one is considered to hold Colored Coins. The first outputs receive the Colored Coins. They are followed by an OP_RETURN transaction that holds metadata that marks the transaction as a Colored Coin transaction, as well as additional data about the Colored Coin. The last outputs in the transaction are additional addresses where the remaining uncolored funds should be sent. Note that change Colored Coins can be returned to the address of the issuer, mirroring how Bitcoin change addresses work. Colored Coins in the blockchain are distinguished by their **issuing address**.

Colored Coins are initially issued through a **genesis transaction**. There are two types of genesis transactions: non-reissuable and reissuable. The type of transaction is marked in the OP_RETURN metadata field, see Figure 12.4. An issuer can reissue new assets as she sees fit. This might be useful, say, for a company issuing stock.

Once a Colored Coin is in circulation, it can be passed along through a **transfer transaction**. Transfer transactions are more complex than genesis transactions, as they follow somewhat more involved rules on how to distribute the Colored Coins held by the inputs—which can include several types of Colored Coins—to the outputs (Assia et al., 2014). If a transfer transaction does not follow the Colored Coin protocol, it is flagged as

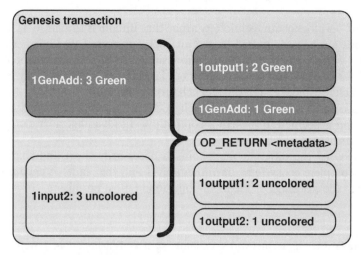

FIGURE 12.4 A Colored Coin genesis transaction

an invalid color transaction, even though it could be a valid Bitcoin transaction, and the Colored Coins will be destroyed.

Colored Coin wallets would need to traverse the blockchain to create an index of where the Colored Coins are[14]. An issuer of Colored Coins can keep track of which addresses own the Colored Coins it has issued. This can be useful for applications such as issuing a stock as Colored Coins and then paying dividends to the stockholders.

Asset swaps are possible using **multi-colored transactions**, where different Colored Coins are exchanged one for another. This opens the door to decentralized settlement of digital assets. However, there is still the need for a way to post enforceable bids and offers to create a decentralized exchange. The solution followed by ChromaWallet is to create a peer-to-peer decentralized exchange (called "P2P Trade") alongside the Bitcoin network.

More recent Colored Coins protocol specifications are those followed by the ChromaWallet (Mizrahi, 2013) and CoinPrism (Charlon, 2013) projects. As of the time of writing these protocols are not compatible, although integration between the two could be possible.

The ChromaWallet implementation is closer to the description of the original Colored Coins protocol: the Colored Coin values are taken from the amount of bitcoins in the transaction. The ChromaWallet implementation uses padding to solve the issue of small value outputs dropping below the dust threshold. Information about the Colored Coins is stored in the transaction input's *nSequence* field.

CoinPrism for its part uses the Open Assets protocol, where Colored Coins are associated with the issuing address, and further details of the Colored Coin transaction (quantities and the distribution of inputs to outputs) are encoded into an OP_RETURN transaction. In CoinPrism all assets are reissuable, and issuing and transfer transactions can be mixed in a single Bitcoin transaction.

Further information about ChromaWallet can be found at chromawallet.com. Further information about CoinPrism can be found in www.coinprism.com.

12.7.2 Counterparty

Counterparty is a meta-coin that uses Bitcoin's blockchain to secure its data. Counterparty allows the creation of digital assets and the publication of data feeds. It creates a distributed exchange infrastructure that allows trading of these digital assets and making bets and CFDs based on the prices published by data feeds.

The native currency of the Counterparty network is the **XCP**. XCPs were created during the period spanning Bitcoin blocks 278310 to 283810 (PhantomPhreak, 2014). XCPs were created through proof-of-burn where bitcoins were burnt, that is spent to an address that is verifiably unspendable[15]. The advantage of proof-of-burn is that the XCP are distributed in a fair and transparent manner. The disadvantage is that the bitcoins

---

[14] Colored Coins do not work with current SPV wallets (section 8.8). Bitcoin nodes would have to be retooled, or special Colored Coins SPV nodes created, to allow SPV wallets to operate with Colored Coins.

[15] In the case of Counterparty proof-of-burn, bitcoins were sent to the address 1CounterpartyXXXXXXXXXXXXXXXXXUWLpVr. This address is made up, ensuring that no one possess the private key to unlock the funds. Note that the last six characters of the address ensure that the checksum is correct, and therefore that the address is valid (section 5.6).

burned are spent[16] (14.2.2). Bitcoins burned at the beginning of this period were awarded a larger sum of XCP than bitcoins burned at the end of the period.

Counterparty transactions include an input address, an output address and a **transaction data output**, i.e. an OP_RETURN transaction embedding Counterparty data into the blockchain. This OP_RETURN transaction is called a **message**. Counterparty messages are read from the blockchain and parsed in chronological order[17]. There are several message types including:

- **Issue**. Used to issue a digital asset. The original issuing address can later reissue more digital assets, or it can transfer the ability to reissue the digital asset to another address. Digital assets can also be marked as *locked*, so that no further reissue is possible. Assets can be either divisible or indivisible. Assets can be called by the issuer, returning a pre-specified amount of XCPs—the call price—in return.
- **Send**. Used to send digital assets. Sends, as well as orders, can be filled partially.
- **Order**. Used to place orders to exchange one digital asset for another. When a new order is issued, the protocol automatically checks if there are open orders against which the new order could be filled. Filling of orders is automatic. If the order cannot be filled, it is kept as a pending order for a user-specified number of blocks. Funds, i.e. digital assets, for the order are automatically held in escrow, thus preventing fake order spamming. These funds are returned after the order expires. Settlement of the orders is automatic except if one of the assets exchanged are bitcoins, in which case settlement must be done in a subsequent transaction with a message to pay bitcoins (BTCPay message).
- **Broadcast**. Used to publish an entry from a data feed. A data feed is associated with the address that publishes it, i.e. it can only be published from this original address. Bets can be made on the numerical values of a feed. A feed can be terminated by publishing a broadcast marking the feed as *locked*. If a feed is finished while there are still bets pending on it, those bets expire.
- **Bet**. Used to place bets and CFDs on the outcome of a feed. There are two types of bets: *wagers* that bet that the value of a data feed will be equal (or not equal) to a certain value, and *CFDs* with a settlement date (12.5.3). Bets are matched and settled similarly to orders.
- **Dividend**. Used to pay dividends to the holders of a digital asset. Dividends are paid in the form of a digital asset or XCP. Dividends paid in bitcoin can be carried out in a regular Bitcoin transaction to the addresses holding the asset.
- **Burn**. This message type was used during the initial issuance of XCPs in the proof-of-burn process.

A Counterparty transaction can have output change addresses, but these do not play any role in the protocol. Bitcoin addresses and the associated Public Key Infrastructure are used to issue digital assets, hold digital assets and to settle CFDs and bets.

---

[16] It can be argued that the bitcoins burned are a gift to other bitcoin holders, as it decreases Bitcoin's money supply.

[17] A Counterparty server requires a Bitcoin Core Server running.

Details of the Counterparty protocol can be found in the white paper (Phantom-Phreak, 2014). More information, including wallets and other tools can be found at www.counterparty.co.

12.7.3 Ethereum

Ethereum is an open source second-generation distributed ledger with an associated Turing-complete platform, that can be used to build and distribute decentralized applications. Ethereum will create its own blockchain. As of the time of writing, the project is still being built, although the test network is up and running.

The Turing-complete nature of Ethereum allows users to code applications through a mechanism called contracts. Contracts in Ethereum are pieces of code that are executed by nodes on the blockchain every time a transaction is sent to the account holding the contract[18]. The account holding the contract can keep an internal memory state that can be used by the contract. A contract also has access to several arguments from the transaction that activates it, such as the amount, sending address, and other auxiliary fields. The execution of a contract can result in the creation of new transactions, which in turn can activate other contracts. Transactions sent by contracts can return a value to its original issuer. In this respect contracts behave much like program functions.

Contracts are written in a low level language and executed by the **Ethereum Virtual Machine (EVM)**, similar in spirit to the Java Virtual Machine. To support the development of contracts, several high level languages are available at the time of writing: Serpent based on Python, Mutan based on Go, and LLL based on Lisp.

Contracts have three types of memory at their disposal:

- A last-in-first-out stack. This memory is erased after the contract code is executed.
- A heap where as much memory as desired can be allocated, although at a cost. This memory is erased after the contract code is executed.
- A long-term key-value store, called storage. This is the only type of memory that persists once a contract script is executed following a transaction, so it can be used to save the state of a contract. This feature is very useful for the deployment of autonomous agents (section 12.4).

Contracts in Ethereum resemble autonomous agents that are executed in the blockchain. Ethereum supporters believe that a Turing-complete language would lead to the development of many innovative applications (financial and otherwise), much in the same way that the introduction of Javascript led to the development of innovative web applications (Buterin, 2014b).

Ethereum blocks include the state of the system. This is not strictly necessary, as the state could in principle be reconstructed from the initial block. In Bitcoin the state of the system is captured by the UTXO (Chapter 6), which can be reconstructed by parsing the blockchain (see Figure 6.2). In principle, the same procedure could be followed in Ethereum. However, this would require running all contract code again, which can be

---

[18] Some accounts do not have associated contracts. These are called externally owned accounts. Accounts with associated contracts are called contract accounts, as the contract has access to the funds in the account.

inefficient. For this reason, the state of the system is stored at each block. This has the advantage that nodes do not need to store the whole blockchain[19].

Some proposed applications (Buterin, 2014b) of the contract mechanism in Ethereum are:

- Digital assets, such as other virtual currencies, application coins, metacoins[20], and so on. These assets would delegate their security and bookkeeping to the Ethereum network.
- Derivatives, such as contract for differences. In fact, any derivative payoff function could be programmed into a contract. Derivatives whose payoff depends on external prices require an external data feed.
- Multisignature escrows. These are possible with Bitcoin (section 4.5), but the flexibility of Ethereum contracts allows more complex rules.
- Saving accounts, where the funds can only be spend at a slow pace. This can be combined with multisignature escrow for some interesting applications.
- Peer-to-peer gambling.
- Digital assets and applications that can take advantage of Ethereum memory store.
- Decentralized exchanges.
- Decentralized data storage. This would require a separate network specialized in data storage. Ethereum could handle the contractual and financial aspects of the service.
- Decentralized identity and reputation server. Users can register their pseudonyms in an Ethereum contract that could then be queried by other applications, offering functionality similar to that of Namecoin (section 11.3).
- Offering bounties for solutions to computational problems.
- Autonomous agents. The code defining the autonomous agent could be distributed among several contracts that could call one another. Autonomous agents could then be built using different pieces—contracts—that coordinate to perform a complex task.
- Asynchronous multisignature escrow. Users send their partially signed transactions to the blockchain, instead of having to communicate offline as in Bitcoin. More advanced features are possible. For example, a 3-of-5 multisignature escrow, where two signatures can spend only 10% of the funds but three signatures can spend 100%.

In Bitcoin, transaction fees are not set by the protocol: it is left to the miners to decide whether to accept a transaction given its fees (section 9.3). Also Bitcoin transactions are deliberately limited on their size and the contents of their scripts, see standard transactions in section 6.7.

The fee structure in Ethereum is more elaborate. Transactions that are sent to a contract have to include the fees necessary to pay for the cost of executing the contract code unlocked by the transaction. When a transaction is sent, it includes a total number of fees it is ready to spend and at which price. Miners choose transactions based on these prices. When a transaction is chosen, the contract code is executed, and miners subtract fees from this execution. If the fees included in the transaction are enough to pay for the

---

[19] The state is saved as a Patricia tree to make it more efficient (Ethereum, 2014).
[20] Any meta-coin could in principle be replicated in Ethereum due to its Turing-complete nature.

execution of the contract, the transaction is committed to the blockchain. If there are not enough fees in the transaction, all effects of the contract execution are reverted and the fees are kept the miner. In this latter case, the contract did not execute due to insufficient fees. If after executing the contract there are still some fees left, these are returned to the sender of the transaction.

Execution fees are levied for things like creating a new contract, storing data, or performing cryptographic computations. These fees deter users from creating abusive contracts, such as entering into infinite loops[21] or requiring large amounts of memory. They also give an incentive to the contract creators to make sparse use of resources and keep memory usage to a minimum.

Senders of a transaction have to indicate the maximum number of steps that a contract can run, and nodes in the network will stop the execution when that maximum is reached. This solves denial-of-service attacks based on the halting problem. The **halting problem** in computer science states that given an arbitrary algorithm it is not possible to construct another algorithm that can decide a priori whether the original algorithm will finish or run forever. An attacker could use this result to create a contract with an infinite loop that included a very large amount of fees. The contract would run until it runs out of fees, and its state would be reverted. However, as the contract included a large amount of fees, the miner executing it would probably have skipped several blocks in the blockchain and thus cannot include the transaction to claim the fees. Forcing transactions to declare the maximum allowed execution steps allows miners to prevent this kind of attack.

The native currency in Ethereum is the **ether (ETH)** that serves as the basic transactional token as well as to pay fees. Once the network is operative, ether will be issued to reward miners permanently at a constant rate (Lubin, 2014). Therefore the supply of ether is not fixed as in Bitcoin, but instead will grow linearly. The supply growth rate, i.e. the increased supply over the total supply, will tend to zero over time. On the other hand, ether will be lost due to loss of private keys. Therefore, when the loss rate is greater than the supply rate, ether will be actually deflationary. This way, supporters argue, will make ether not too inflationary or deflationary, will prevent the speculative action seen in Bitcoin due to its fixed total supply, and will reduce wealth concentration compared to Bitcoin.

As of the time of writing, Ethereum mining is still not completely fleshed out. The goal is to make mining decentralized and ASIC-resistant (Buterin, 2014f). The current mining proposal follows these steps:

- Take one pseudo-random transaction from each of the last 16 blocks.
- Modify each of these transactions pseudo-randomly.
- Apply these modified transactions to the state of the system, resulting in a new state.
- Hash[22] the resulting state of the system together with a nonce.
- This hash is compared with the mining difficulty, and if the proof-of-work requirement is met, a valid block has been found.

---

[21] Loops in Ethereum could be created in two ways. First, the instruction set includes jump instructions. Second, an attacker could create an infinite recursion using contracts that call themselves recursively or two contracts that call one another.

[22] The hash function to apply is still undecided as of the time of writing.

The key of this mining procedure is that a miner has to repeat this process for every nonce that she tries. As the scripting language is Turing-complete, the mining equipment would have to include Turing-complete processors. To create ASICs that can mine ether, these ASICs would have to equip Turing-complete cores, making them much more costly than Bitcoin ASICs, which only have to implement the SHA256 hashing algorithm.

Another consequence of this design is that miners would have to keep a complete copy of the blockchain, thus somehow reducing the advantage of pooled mining (section 9.2). Ethereum supporters hope this would help democratize mining, with a majority of miners participating in peer-to-peer mining pools instead of centralized pools.

The specification of Ethereum can be found in Ethereum (2014) and Wood (2014). More information, including the client and other tools, can be found at www.ethereum.org.

12.7.4 Mastercoin

Mastercoin is a meta-coin that uses Bitcoin's blockchain to store its metadata. The protocol is called the Master protocol: Master stands for Metadata Archival of Standard Transaction Embedding Records. As Mastercoin supporters put it: Mastercoin is to Bitcoin as HTTP is to TCP/IP (MasterCoin wiki, 2014). Mastercoin features include creation of digital assets (or user-currencies), publication of data feeds, decentralized exchanges, CFDs, and bets.

The native currency of the Mastercoin network is mastercoin or **MSC**. MSC was initially created during a fund-raising in August 2013. MSCs were credited to the Bitcoin addresses that sent bitcoins to the **Exodus address**, 1EXoDusjGwvnjZUyK-kxZ4UHEf77z6A5S4P. The total number of MSC available is fixed at 619,478.6 MSC (MasterCoin wiki, 2014).

Mastercoins and other digital assets are held in regular Bitcoin addresses. These digital assets can be transferred using Mastercoin transactions. Mastercoin transactions are regular Bitcoin transactions where the first output address is the Exodus address. This serves the double purpose of flagging the transaction as a Mastercoin transaction as well as sending a small Bitcoin fee to the Exodus address. The second output of a Mastercoin transaction is the recipient address. This output is followed by an OP_RETURN output that inserts the Mastercoin metadata into the blockchain. This metadata gets parsed by Mastercoin nodes and wallets. Some features introduced by Mastercoin transactions are[23]:

- **Purchasing mastercoins.** This type of transaction was only allowed during the fund-raising period in August 2013, and at present bitcoins sent using this transaction will be returned to the sender.
- **Sending mastercoins and other digital assets.** Uses Bitcoin addresses and their corresponding signatures, but encodes the digital asset information and the quantity to send in the Mastercoin data field.
- **Creating digital assets.** Digital assets can be either discrete or divisible. This allows the creation of user-backed currencies. The Mastercoin specification (Willett et al., 2014) introduces a protocol to create **self-stabilizing currencies**. These currencies are

---

[23] As of the time of writing some of these features are not yet available, as the Master protocol is still under development.

endowed with a fund and a strategy to issue more currency when the price overcomes an upper barrier, and to buy the currency when the price hits a lower barrier. There is some controversy over whether self-stabilizing currencies can work in practice (Buterin, 2013k), or whether they would susceptible to trading strategies that short-sell them with the aim of depleting their funds.

- **Creating "savings" addresses.** Addresses can be marked as "saving," which makes transactions from these addresses reversible. The reversibility period—up to one year to avoid accidents—can be chosen by the user. The savings rule applies to all digital assets stored in a savings address. Saving addresses have an associated **guardian address**, which is usually kept in cold storage. Only the guardian address can reverse the payments, in which case the reversed payments, as well as all the funds left in the saving address, are transferred to the guardian address.
- **Creating "rate-limited" addresses.** The rate of depletion of an address can be limited, say to 1% of the funds per day. Rate-limits are applied to each of the digital assets in an address individually. Rate-limited addresses have a guardian address associated, which can be used to remove the rate limitation. Rate-limited addresses could be useful for pay-as-you-go services, such as internet access, where the owner of an address could allow rate-limited access to the funds in the account to the service provider.
- **Paying dividends to digital assets.** Dividends on a digital asset can be sent from the issuing address with a single transaction. The protocol automatically credits the current holders of the asset, thus freeing the issuer from the task of keeping track of the owners.
- **Submitting and executing buy/sell orders.** The Master protocol runs a decentralized exchange that automatically finds matching orders and performs settlement of the trades. Orders can be partially filled. Funds for an order are automatically deducted upon publication of the order and returned if the order is not executed. The price of an order can be changed by simply resubmitting the order with the new price, and counter-offers can also be made. Orders involving bitcoin funds have a time limit to settle. Bitcoin funds must be sent before this time limit for the correct settlement of the order. There is a reputation system built in, where buyers of digital assets can leave feedback and rate transactions.
- **Registering data streams.** Data streams can be registered from an issuing address. The owner of this issuer address can then publish ticker data on that stream. Mastercoin's data streams follow a category tree to assist with stream discovery.
- **Submitting and executing bets and CFDs.** Bets and CFDs on the outcomes of data streams are supported. Bets and CFDs can be settled using any digital asset. Trade closing and settlement is automatically performed by the protocol.

A good overview of Mastercoin can be found in Buterin (2013k). The specification of the Master protocol can be found in Willett et al. (2014). More information, including wallets and other tools, can be found at www.mastercoin.org.

12.7.5 Nxt

Nxt uses a different code base than Bitcoin, written from scratch. Nxt also creates its own blockchain, secured using a 100% proof-of-stake system. The main applications of Nxt are a decentralized exchange, voting system, messaging, and DNS.

Addresses use elliptic curve public key cryptography[24]. Transactions, and other messages, are registered in the blockchain. Nxt blockchain uses a proof-of-stake algorithm (14.2.1). Nxt assumes that all clients in the network run a full node. Addresses where at least one incoming transaction has been confirmed by 1440 blocks are called **unlocked addresses** or **active accounts**. These addresses are eligible to generate the next proof-of-stake block (Nxt wiki, 2014b).

The native currency of Nxt is **NXT**, with an initial supply of 1 billion NXTs (Nxt wiki, 2014a). Nxt blocks have a field called the **generation signature**. Active accounts sign the generation signature with their private key and then hash the signature. If the resulting hash is lower than the target, then the active account can generate the next block, obtaining all the fees. Creating blocks is called forging blocks, in contrast with Bitcoin's mining, which requires computational power. The target for every active account is weighted by the amount of funds in that address (thus the proof-of-stake) and increases (doubles) every second until a node in the network forges the next block. This network target is tuned so that new blocks are forged on average every 60 seconds.

If nodes put in common their generation signature hashes at the beginning of a block, the node with the lowest hash will forge the next block. This is called **transparent forging**, because the node that will forge the next block is known beforehand. This can be an advantage as the other nodes will send unconfirmed transactions directly to this node. Transparent forging can also be used to detect which nodes are refusing to forge blocks, in order to exclude them from the forging process.

Transactions are signed with the private key of the issuing address. Some possible transactions in Nxt include sending money, registering an alias, transmitting a message, issuing a digital asset, and submitting/executing an offer for an asset.

As the process of forging blocks is low on computational power, supporters believe full nodes could be run on any device, including mobile devices. Supporters also hope transaction fees will act as a protection against inflation, because fees recirculate to the active accounts.

The specification of the Nxt protocol can be found in Nxt wiki (2014). More information, including the client and other tools, can be found at www.nxtcrypto.org.

12.7.6 Ripple

Ripple is a decentralized financial network which was first proposed by Ryan Fugger in 2004. In the original Ripple network, users establish trust relationships among them. These trust relationships are basically credit lines between the users. Users choose the amount to allocate to each of their lines of credit with other users. Once these relationships are in place, a user can send funds to another user through this web of relations. Figure 12.5 shows how a user, Laura, can send funds to another user, Paula, without a previous relationship. The Ripple protocol routes the funds through the chain of trust, that is the transaction *ripples* through the network until it reaches its destination. In this case, the settlement is done through Beatrice, who has trust relationships with both

---

[24] Nxt uses a different elliptic curve algorithm than Bitcoin. It uses Elliptic-Curve Korean Certificate-based Digital Signature Algorithm (EC-KCDSA) for message signing with Curve25519 for shared secret generation (Nxt wiki, 2014).

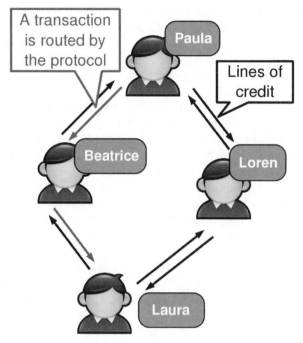

FIGURE 12.5   Ripple protocol

Laura and Paula. Ripple introduces a degree of counterparty risk between users, but users have the ability to control this risk by setting appropriate credit limits.

The modern Ripple network, created by Ripple Labs, can be used to route any asset, not only digital assets or cryptocurrencies. Thus Ripple is a payment system which is agnostic to the currency used. The network can handle assets such as fiat money or precious metals.

The Ripple network maintains a distributed database called the **ledger**. The ledger contains the balances and credit limits of all accounts. This ledger does not contain the whole transaction history as in Bitcoin, making it much more lightweight[25]. Ripple clients do not necessarily have to store a copy of the ledger, as they can receive cryptographic proof from servers that relevant transactions are included in the ledger, similarly to Bitcoin's SPV (section 8.8). However, as keeping a copy of the Ripple ledger is more manageable than keeping a copy of Bitcoin's blockchain, Ripple supporters expect that many users will opt to run a Ripple server, thus keeping a copy of the whole ledger.

The ledger is structured as a **ledger chain**, where each version of the ledger includes a hash to the parent version. A new version of the ledger is created through a process called **consensus**, that decides which information is to be included into the new version of the ledger. Ripple servers poll neighboring servers for new transactions and incorporate them into their new version of the ledger. Faced with a double-spend transaction, Ripple servers choose the transaction deemed correct by the majority of their neighbors. This is

---

[25] The whole Ripple network maintains a copy of the entire transaction history, although individual servers are not required to store it.

similar to the way Bitcoin nodes decide which unconfirmed transaction is the correct in case of a double-spend attempt. The consensus process allows the network to validate a new version of the ledger every few seconds, making settlement of transactions very fast. Ripple uses a combination of Merkle trees and Radix trees to allow servers to update their ledgers efficiently during the consensus process, as well as to provide thin clients with cryptographic proof of their transactions.

To prevent Sybil attacks against the consensus process, Ripple introduces unique node lists. Every user has a **unique node list** of nodes that she believes are not likely to collude against her, say, in a double-spend attack. The nodes in this list are usually geographically dispersed nodes, belonging to unrelated institutions or trusted nodes in the network that are unlikely to collaborate to feed the user false information during the consensus process. An additional advantage of unique node lists is that it makes the network denser, and disagreements in the consensus process faster to settle.

Ripple **accounts** use elliptic curve public-key cryptography to digitally sign trans-actions. Addresses are also derived from the public key[26], but they start with "r" as in "rhaWwMcmP5DehVyuY2Kz38AmfLB9NWr11W".

Ripple creates a new currency, called **ripples** or **ripple credits (XRP)**. A total XRP money supply of 100 billion has already been created (Wikipedia, 2014k). Ripple ac-counts can hold balances in ripples, fiat currencies, and other digital assets (called cus-tom currencies). Most instruments in Ripple are debt-based, except for XRPs and virtual currencies created anew. XRP serves the role of a bridge currency between other digital assets in the Ripple network. Transaction fees are also paid in XRP and are destroyed, preventing spam transactions. The destruction of transaction fees makes the amount of XRP decrease (slowly) over time.

A problem with the original implementation of Ripple was that a new user had to know someone already in the network in order to enter it. This created an artificial bar-rier to entry for new users, and created fragmentation in the network, creating isolated sub-networks. To solve this problem, Ripple created the concept of gateways. **Gateways** are businesses that allow users with no previous relation to other Ripple users to enter the network. Users usually deposit funds with a gateway, and the gateway issues a pos-itive balance to them. Thus users bear counterparty risk to the gateways. Gateways are generally trusted by many users and they allow connecting between otherwise separate parts of the network. There are no barriers to entry to create a new gateway: any estab-lished business can become one, all that is needed is that users trust the business[27]. Users can decide to trust several gateways, which creates some decentralization in the system. Gateways are specially necessary in the early stages, when the network has a sparse to-pology: payments can be routed through gateways connected by lines of trust[28]. In case no lines of trust are available between gateways, payments can be settled using XRPs. Gateways introduce trust in third party organizations, but Ripple supporters expect that, once the network get much denser, the importance of gateways will diminish.

---

[26] Ripple uses the same elliptic curve specification as Bitcoin, secp256k1, so in principle the same Bitcoin private key could be used to generate a Ripple address.

[27] Regulations in most jurisdiction might require new gateways to register as money transmitters and acquire a license.

[28] This settlement of payments between gateways shares some similarities with correspondent banking (Brown, 2013).

The Ripple protocol offers a built-in distributed exchange. Any user can place orders on the ledger and trades are automatically processed by the Ripple protocol. Ripple's distributed exchange can be used to route payments where different currencies are used at both ends. In cases where there is not enough liquidity for the exchange between the desired currencies, XRPs can be used as an intermediate step.

The Ripple protocol supports the issuance of digital assets, such as new virtual currencies. Ripple developers are also working in supporting digital contracts in the protocol (Ripple wiki, 2014a). A good overview of how Ripple works can be found in Buterin (2013c) and Ripple wiki (2014b). More information, including clients and other tools, can be found at ripple.com.

CHAPTER 13

The Privacy Battle

All transactions in Bitcoin are stored in the blockchain and therefore are public. However, transactions do not include information about the users behind them, only the Bitcoin addresses are included. This makes Bitcoin pseudonymous, because users' privacy is hidden behind a pseudonym: the Bitcoin address.

This does not mean, however, that users' privacy is protected. First, the balances held by each address are public and readily available just by querying the UTXO (Chapter 6). Second, addresses can be linked to one another by observing the transactions between them. Thus Bitcoin is sometimes compared to making someone's bank statement available online but blanking out the name.

A consequence of Bitcoin's lack of anonymity is that it opens the possibility for bitcoins not to be fungible. As the origin of the funds can be traced, some funds, such as stolen bitcoins or bitcoins known to have been used for illicit purposes, could be marked as tainted, thus breaking the fungibility. There are already some proposals to register Bitcoin businesses and/or users, and it is believed that the next natural step would be to control the origin of bitcoins. This would fragment the Bitcoin system and it is generally viewed as dangerous by the Bitcoin community (Buterin, 2013d).

This chapter will introduce some known techniques to de-anonymize Bitcoin users, as well as several technologies proposed to enhance privacy. A recent survey of the privacy issues in Bitcoin, and some solutions, can be found in Wood and Vu (2013).

13.1 NETWORK ANALYSIS

The **transaction graph** is a graph where Bitcoin transactions are placed at the vertices, and the edges connect a transaction input with the associated transaction output, see Figure 13.1. As all of the transaction outputs have to be fully expended, the transaction graph is a **directed acyclic graph (DAG)**. Therefore, there can be no cycles in the graph: the output of a transaction cannot be the input of a previous transaction in the blockchain.

Most analyses of the transaction graph assume that all the inputs in the same transaction belong to a single user. This need not be the case, and in Chapter 12 some applications were introduced where a single transaction is passed around to multiple users to sign. However, these applications still occupy a niche and thus the assumption that a single user is signing each transaction is usually correct. This could change in the future if multisignature wallets (section 8.6) or some of the applications described in Chapter 12 take off.

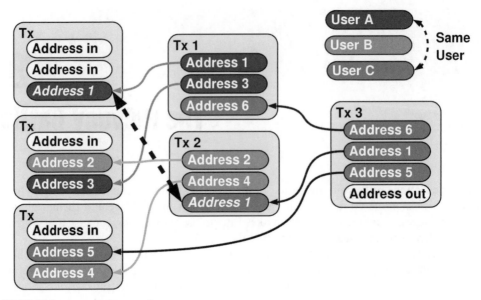

FIGURE 13.1 Transaction graph

Assuming, then, that all input addresses in a single transaction belong to the same user, the transaction graph can be simplified applying the **closure under signing operation** (Buterin, 2013e). The closure of an address is a recursive operation defined as:

- An address belongs to its own closure.
- If there is a transaction with inputs from both address A and address B, then both addresses belong to the same closure. That is, the closure of both addresses is the union of their closures.

In other words, the closure operation groups together all the addresses that have been signed together. This assumes that the user that signs two different addresses controls the private keys of all the addresses, and therefore is the same user.

Reuse of addresses makes analysis of the transaction graph easier. In the example in Figure 13.1, "Tx 2" sends funds to a previously used address, "Address 1". The reuse of this address enables the linking of two sets of addresses that were not previously joined by the closure operation: this is shown by the dotted line in the figure. Many clients still reuse addresses because of the complexity in backing up wallets that generate new random addresses (section 8.1). Transition to new wallet technologies, such as HD wallets (section 8.5) is set to reduce the amount of address reuse in the future.

Change addresses (Chapter 6) can also be included into the closure operation. However, it is somewhat more imprecise to decide which addresses in a transaction are change addresses, and this can lead to errors (Meiklejohn et al., 2013). Change addresses can also leak information about the total funds held in an address.

The result of applying the closure operation to all the addresses in the transaction graph is the **user graph**. The user graph greatly simplifies the transaction graph, condensing the information. Figure 13.2 shows the user graph derived from the transaction graph

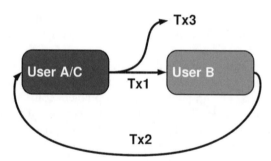

FIGURE 13.2 The user graph corresponding to the transaction graph of Figure 13.1

in Figure 13.1. In the user graph, the vertices represent users and the edges represent transactions between them. This network can be used to distinguish types of users such as hoarders, to identify communities or large operators such as web wallet services or exchanges (Reid and Harrigan, 2013).

Several techniques can be applied to the user graph to further gain information about Bitcoin users:

- **Integrate off-network information.** Attackers can combine the information gained through network analysis with other information, such as the identity of donation addresses, exchange or online wallet services addresses, or vanity addresses (section 8.7).
- **Integrate IP traffic.** If an attacker is able to observe the IP traffic of the Bitcoin network, she can associate Bitcoin users with IP addresses. This attack can be performed by someone able to inspect all internet traffic. But even without access to all internet traffic, an attacker could create a connection to each and everyone of the nodes in the Bitcoin network. When a new transaction is broadcast to the network, the node that broadcasts it first is very likely to be the source of the transaction (Reid and Harrigan, 2013). However, the effectiveness of this approach is declining with the increase usage of SPV clients[1] (section 8.8).
- **Network topology.** Several measures can be inferred from the user graph: graph connectivity, in-degree and out-degree of vertices, concentration of funds and the circulation of bitcoins. These topological metrics can serve to better understand the behavior of Bitcoin users (Ron and Shamir, 2013).
- **Cluster analysis.** A clustering of the behavior of the vertices in the user graph can help further reduce the size of the user graph, by better identifying users (Androulaki et al., 2013).
- **Flow and temporal analysis.** Large flows of funds can be traced through the user network. Users can be singled out if at some point they receive an unusually large flow compared to their balance. Or the most active entities in the network can be

---

[1] The tendency in the network is to running lightweight clients in SPV mode (section 8.8) as the costs of running full nodes increases. This makes this attack somewhat more difficult, as an attacker with connections to all nodes would only see the transactions aggregated by a node servicing SPV clients. This node can, however, retain the IP information of the wallets that connect to it. A sophisticated attacker could create nodes servicing SPV wallets to gain access to this information.

singled out for further study. If a user—for example a competing business—has been already identified, the flows to and from that user can be studied in search for clues about its business.

- **Graph isomorphism with other social networks.** If an attacker has access to the user graph of some other social network, she can try to combine the two graphs to link users in both graphs. The **graph isomorphism problem** consists of deciding whether there is a bijection between the vertices of two graphs that preserves all the edges. Intuitively two graphs are isomorphic if the vertices of the two graphs can be super-imposed, so that they become the same graph, just with different labeling. Although the graph isomorphism problem is concerned with whether the two graphs are ex-actly isomorphic, there are robust algorithms that can exploit internal symmetries in the two graphs to "superimpose" significant portions of them (Backstrom et al., 2007; Narayanan and Shmatikov, 2009). Used this way, a graph where the users are identified—say from a social network—can be superimposed on the Bitcoin user graph and the result used to de-anonymize Bitcoin users.

Aside from the user graph, other information can be used to help de-anonymize Bitcoin users. For instance, the decimal places in the amounts transferred can sometimes be traced back to the matching of an order in an exchange, or to the payment to a merchant whose price has been converted to bitcoins using the exchange rate current at the time.

Active de-anonymizing attacks are also possible. One active attack could inject marked Bitcoins to then trace their course through the network, for example law enforce-ment following the money trail of an illegal activity. Another active attack could be to operate a laundry service, recording the original Bitcoin and IP addresses of its users.

13.2 LAUNDRY SERVICES

Laundry services or **mixing services** allow users to send their funds to a central pool and later retrieve the funds to a different Bitcoin address. These services combine the inputs

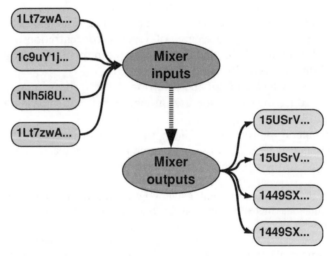

FIGURE 13.3 Laundry service

of many users so that the outputs are difficult to trace back to the inputs. Figure 13.3 illustrates how a laundry service works. First, user's funds are sent to a common address belonging to the operator of the service. The funds in this address are then sent through a layer of internal transactions (only one is shown in the figure) with the purpose of confounding those who try to follow the trail of funds. Finally the funds are returned to their owners through a different address, or better still a number of addresses. The laundry operator keeps a fee as compensation for the service.

The outputs of the laundry cannot be readily linked to the inputs: only the laundry operator has this information. Laundries usually introduce a delay between the deposit and the withdrawal, waiting for enough transactions to accumulate in the meantime.

Laundry services are more efficient when the number of users and the volume of transactions are high. As of the time of writing, these services are only used by a minority of Bitcoin users, and therefore their utility to those willing to use them is limited.

Laundry services are vulnerable to Sybil attacks, where an attacker can create most of the transactions into a laundry, thus giving the false impression to other users that the laundry has enough volume. The attacker can then identify regular users of the laundry more easily. The efficiency of this Sybil attack is somewhat limited by the fact that the attacker incurs transaction fees.

Another problem of laundries is that they require trust in the operator. It is very easy for this operator to steal users' funds, just by receiving inputs into the laundry and never redeeming them.

Laundry services do not provide full anonymity, as they can leak important information, like the fact that a particular input address has used the service or the amount of the funds laundered. Furthermore, the laundry operator can keep records of the transactions that take place, and users have no way to ensure that these records are destroyed. An attacker might even operate her own laundry.

For an analysis of the degree of anonymity achieved by various Bitcoin laundry services, see Möser et al. (2013).

13.3   GREENLISTING

There have been several proposals to create services to register Bitcoin users. Registering Bitcoin addresses is commonly known as **greenlisting**, or **address validation**. Users would register their addresses with the greenlisting provider, going through an identity verification process. The provider keeps these registered addresses in a database. Customers of the service can query this database through an API. The service provider charges its customers—say merchants—for the service. When a user wants to pay a merchant, the merchant can check that the address of the customer is greenlisted and reject the transaction if it is not, as depicted in Figure 13.4.

The central database can readily be extended to keep track of transactions and flag certain funds as tainted. A merchant could refuse to take tainted bitcoins as payment, or ignore the transaction in case it settled in the blockchain, increasing the costs and risks for Bitcoin users. Opponents of greenlisting also point out that if bitcoins were split between clean and tainted, clean bitcoins would demand a premium. Some businesses would have the ability to "clean" tainted Bitcoins and could capture the price differential,

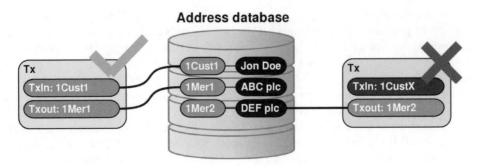

FIGURE 13.4   Greenlisting

raising the cost of using Bitcoin to all users but presumably without reducing Bitcoin-related crime (Buterin, 2013d).

Another consequence of greenlisting is that users in the database could be used to create anchors in the user graph, and the tools introduced in section 13.1 would then be able to de-anonymize large portions of the Bitcoin user graph much more easily.

Greenlisting proposals could have the effect of spurring the community to adopt techniques to increase users' privacy and render greenlisting useless. The rest of this chapter will explore some of these technologies.

13.4   PRIVACY-ENHANCING TECHNOLOGIES

Laundry services require a central provider that can either steal the funds or leak information. Thus there has been considerable interest in the community in finding ways to perform the function of a mixing service in a decentralized way. This section introduces several anonymizing technologies proposed by Bitcoin developers that do not require modifications to the Bitcoin protocol.

13.4.1 CoinJoin

CoinJoin was introduced in Maxwell (2013a). In CoinJoin several users agree to a size of funds to be mixed and then create a transaction with multiple inputs and outputs of the chosen size, one for each participant. This transaction is passed along off-chain to be signed by all the participants. Once signed by everybody, it is published in the blockchain, as shown in Figure 13.5.

CoinJoin is usually implemented using a meet-up server so that not even the participants get to know which outputs correspond to which inputs, except for their own. A decentralized version, where no trust in a central meet-up server is required, is also available.

A limitation of CoinJoin is that all inputs and outputs must be of the same quantity. However, this can also be an advantage as using a single denomination avoids leaking extra information.

CoinJoin has the property of confounding most network analysis strategies proposed so far, because these strategies usually assume that addresses that are input to a

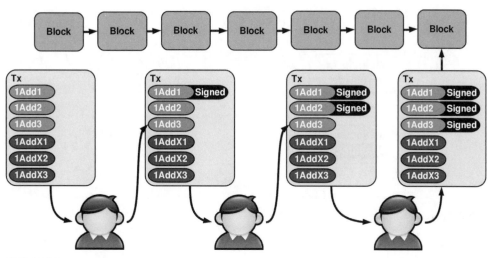

FIGURE 13.5 CoinJoin

single transaction belong to the same user (section 13.1). One additional benefit for users of CoinJoin is that they pay lower transaction fees than other schemes, as only a single transaction is published in the blockchain, irrespective of the number of participants[2].

As was the case for mixing services, CoinJoin is vulnerable to Sybil attacks, where an attacker can control most of the participant addresses in a round of CoinJoin making the identification of other CoinJoin users trivial.

13.4.2 CoinSwap

CoinSwap was introduced in Maxwell (2013b). CoinSwap brings a third party into a transaction, so that the payer and the receiver addresses cannot be linked. This is shown in Figure 13.6 where Alice wants to make a transaction to Bob but does not want her address linked to Bob's address[3]. In CoinSwap, a third party, Carol, is brought to the transaction. Carol agrees to receive Alice's funds and pay Bob. Note that Carol pays Bob with different (unconnected) funds from those received from Alice, so that the two transactions cannot be linked.

CoinSwap makes it impossible for Carol to steal the funds. This is achieved using hashlocked transactions. **Hashlocked transactions** are transactions that require knowledge of the preimage of a hash to unlock, i.e. they are transactions locked by a hash. An example of the *<scriptPubKey>* of a hashlocked transactions is:

```
OP_RIPEMD160 <hash> OP_EQUALVERIFY <pubkey> OP_CHECKSIGVERIFY
```

---

[2] Note, however, that miners usually require bigger transaction fees for transactions of larger size (section 9.3).

[3] This is a highly simplified version of the protocol: see Maxwell (2013b) for a more detailed diagram.

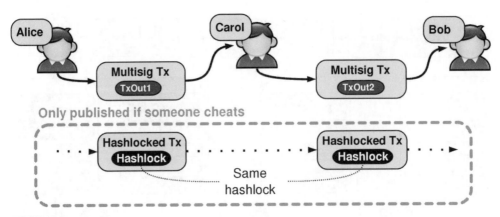

FIGURE 13.6   CoinSwap

To redeem this transaction output, the user must provide both a value that hashes to *<hash>* (the preimage of the *<hash>*) and the correct signature.

The CoinSwap protocol proceeds as follows. First, Alice places the funds in a multisignature transaction output that needs the signatures of both Alice and Carol to spend (TxOut1). Similarly, Carol places the funds in a multisignature output requiring the signatures of Carol and Bob (TxOut2)[4]. If all goes well, Alice and Carol will both sign TxOut1 and send the funds to Carol, and Carol and Bob will sign TxOut2, sending the funds to Bob.

However, the procedure to sign TxOut1 and TxOut2 to unlock the funds can be tricky. For example, assume Alice signs TxOut1 first (Carol will also sign as the funds will be sent to her). Carol could then refuse to sign TxOut2 or require a bribe from either Alice or Bob to unlock them. Similar arguments apply if Carol signs TxOut2 first. Thus neither Alice nor Carol would be willing to unlock first. This is where the hashlocked transactions come into play.

To prevent this gridlock, two **linked hashlocked transactions** are created, following these steps:

- Bob generates a hash, keeping the preimage of the hash (the key to the hashlock) private. He sends the hash to Alice and Carol.
- Alice then creates a hashlocked transaction spending TxOut1 to Carol, signs it and sends it to Carol. Carol could sign this transaction and publish it, but then the funds would be locked in an output requiring both her signature and the preimage of the hash, which she does not know at this stage.
- Carol for her part creates a hashlocked transaction spending TxOut2 to Bob, and sends this transaction to Bob.
- Bob then sends the preimage of the hash to Carol. At this point, either Alice and/or Carol proceed to unlock the original multisignature transactions (TxOut1 and

---

[4] Associated to both TxOut1 and TxOut2 are correctly signed time-locked refund transactions for these outputs that return the funds to their original owners after a certain period (Maxwell, 2013b).

TxOut2) as they are supposed to. Otherwise, the hashlocked transactions would be unlocked with the same effect.

- To proceed, Carol unlocks TxOut2 because she is confident that if Alice does not unlock TxOut2 she can use the preimage of the hash and unlock the hashlocked transaction herself.
- Alice will wait until the funds in TxOut2 are unlocked by Carol to unlock the funds in TxOut1 herself.

The key element in this scheme is that both hashlocked transactions are linked, because if one of them were to be published to the blockchain, the preimage would then be automatically public and could be used to unlock the other.

The hashlocked transactions are kept private and are only published to the blockchain if someone tries to cheat[5]. In case the hashlocked transactions are published, the anonymity of the scheme is lost, because the two hashlocked transactions can be linked together by the value of the preimage.

CoinSwap could also be used to "launder" the funds in an address: in this case Alice and Bob are the same person. CoinSwap assumes there is a private communication channel between all the parties. The specification of CoinSwap can be found in Maxwell (2013b), complete with a detailed diagram.

13.4.3 Stealth Addresses

Stealth addresses were introduced in Todd (2014b). **Stealth addresses** allow receivers to publish a seed to generate addresses that they control. Senders can then make payments to addresses derived from this seed, while attackers cannot associate the final address with the published seed.

Stealth addresses are based on the Diffie–Hellman key exchange protocol. The **Diffie–Hellman key exchange protocol** is a cryptographic method that allows two users to create a common shared secret even in the presence of an attacker who can observe all the communications between them[6]. An often-cited analogy for the Diffie–Hellman key exchange protocol is the following: Alice and Bob wish to agree on a secret shared color. They first agree on a common color (c). Next they each pick a secret color (a for Alice and b for Bob), mix it with the common color (c) and share their mixes, that is Alice would send (c+a) and Bob would send (c+b). Finally, each of them mixes the received mixed color with their own secret color. They both arrive at a secret shared color (a+b+c) because they both mix the same ingredients into it. However, an attacker Trudy observing the communication channel cannot arrive at the secret shared color: if

---

[5] As of the time of writing, hashlocked transactions are non-standard, so an agreement with a miner must be reached to include them in the blockchain (section 6.7).

[6] There has been an increased attention to the Diffie-Hellman key exchange (DHKE) recently, because it is the only protocol included in TLS that provides perfect forward secrecy. **Perfect forward secrecy** is a property of key establishment protocols, such as those in TLS, that guarantees secrecy of the encrypted data even if the private key to the certificate is compromised. In perfect forward secrecy both the server and the client create nonces that they exchange in a DHKE to arrive at a secret shared key for the session. Even if an attacker records all the traffic and is in possession of the private key to the TLS certificate, she will not be able to decrypt the messages because she lacks the knowledge of any of the session keys created in the DHKE.

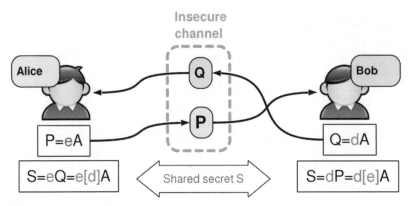

FIGURE 13.7   Elliptic Curve Diffie–Hellman key exchange

Trudy were to mix (a+c) with (b+c) he would arrive at (a+b+2c), i.e. she cannot get the proportions of the colors right.

Diffie–Hellman key exchange can be built on top of several cryptographic primitives. The most common is based on the difficulty of the discrete logarithm problem. The one introduced here is based on the generalized discrete logarithm problem on an elliptic curve, i.e. the **Elliptic Curve Diffie–Hellman** key exchange (**ECDH**).

Figure 13.7 shows the creation of a shared secret key using the ECDH key exchange. First Alice generates a secret key e, computes $P = e \cdot A$ where A is the generator of the elliptic curve[7] (section 5.4) and sends P over to Bob. Bob, for its part, generates a secret key d, computes $Q = d \cdot A$ and sends it to Alice. The shared secret key is simply $S = e \cdot Q = d \cdot P$.

In the stealth addresses protocol, sender and receiver create a ECDH shared secret that they use to derive an address. The private key of this address would only be known to the receiver. Figure 13.8 shows the procedure:

- The receiver, Bob in Figure 13.8, generates a private EC key d and its corresponding public key $Q = d \cdot A$. She publishes the public key, Q, on her website.
- The sender, Alice in Figure 13.8, generates a private EC key e and its corresponding public key P. The shared secret between Alice and Bob will be $c = H(e \cdot Q) = H(d \cdot P)$, where H is a cryptographic hash function (section 7.1). Note that Bob does not know P at this stage, and thus cannot derive the shared secret c yet.
- Alice then creates a transaction sending the funds to the public EC key $Q + (c \cdot A)$. She also includes in the transaction an OP_RETURN transaction output where she places her part of the shared secret key P.
- Bob can then scan the blockchain for new transactions where part of the shared secret is included in an OP_RETURN output. This procedure is explained below.

To receive the payment, Bob must scan all the incoming transactions to the blockchain:

---

[7] Note all elliptic curve operations must be performed modulo p, the order of the prime field.

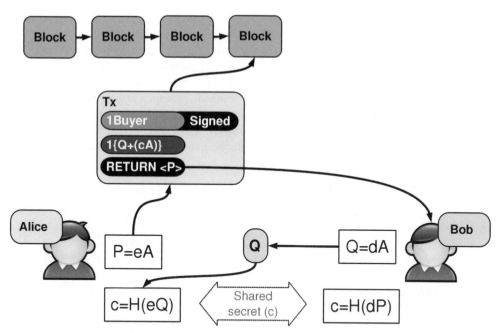

FIGURE 13.8 Stealth addresses

- Filter those transactions that include an OP_RETURN code for further processing.
- Assume the data included in the OP_RETURN transaction output P is as an EC point and compute $c = H(d \cdot P)$.
- Check if the same transaction includes a payment to the address generated by the public key $Q + (c \cdot A)$. If it matches, then the private key associated with that address is given by $d + c$. Note that this private key is not known to the sender, because she does not know d.

There are some proposals in the community to integrate stealth addresses with the Payment Protocol (section 8.9). One disadvantage of stealth addresses is that their processing requires a full node to be able to scan all incoming transactions.

13.4.4 Merge Avoidance

Merge avoidance was proposed in Hearn (2013) with the aim to increase the privacy of Bitcoin transactions. **Merge avoidance** is a protocol whereby a wallet requesting a Bitcoin payment spreads the payment into a large set of addresses and denominations. For instance a wallet requesting a payment of 10 bitcoins could indicate 100 addresses for different amounts ranging from 0.5 bitcoins to 0.0001 bitcoins, such that the sum of all totals 10 bitcoins. The sender of the funds then can either create one big transaction with the 100 outputs or create many small transactions with a few outputs each. In either case, the receiver ends up with many transaction outputs of small denominations. She can then combine these to create payments, leaking much less information that if she only had available a few transaction outputs containing large funds. Thus merge avoidance makes the application of network analysis algorithms (section 13.1) harder.

Merge avoidance could be easily integrated with the Payment Protocol (section 8.9). The many addresses generated by merge avoidance can easily be handled by HD wallets (section 8.5).

The main drawback of merge avoidance is that it increases considerably the transaction fees on the part of the sender. A second smaller drawback is that the creation of many addresses increases the memory requirements of the wallet clients, which could be problematic for memory-constrained wallets, such as those in smartphones.

13.4.5 Committed Transactions

Committed transactions, introduced in Back (2013), solve the fungibility problem even in the presence of powerful miners with the intention to block certain transactions. Committed transactions do not improve the privacy or anonymity of users, only the fungibility of coins. Implementing committed transactions would require changes in the Bitcoin protocol.

A **committed transaction** is a transaction where its creator commits to the input and output addresses without revealing them initially. One way to commit to such addresses is to hash the EC public keys using a different hashing algorithm to that employed in address derivation (section 5.6). The resulting hashed public keys are sometimes called blinded addresses. Despite the addresses being blinded, miners can still check that a transaction is not a double-spend:

- If a committed transaction and a regular transaction try to double-spend the same transaction output, miners would notice because the public key is revealed in the regular transaction and the blinded address could be derived from it. This derived blinded address would match the blinded address of the committed transaction. Note that miners would have to keep a cache with the blinded addresses of all unspent outputs in addition to the regular UTXO.
- If two committed transactions try to double-spend the same transaction output, miners would notice as the two blinded addresses match.

Thus miners could accept committed transactions into the blocks they mine without risk of double-spending. After a committed transaction has been buried by several blocks in the blockchain, the creator of the committed transaction can reveal the blinded addresses, publishing their public keys. At this point miners wishing to block the transaction would have to fork the current blockchain and compete with the rest of the miners to try to make their branch longer. Note that the blockchain would have to be forked at the point where the committed transaction was included, giving the original branch a considerable initial advantage.

The number of blocks lapsed until the committed transaction is revealed can be chosen so that it is uneconomical for miners to engage in this behavior. Furthermore a single user could include intermittent committed transactions and reveal them in a way that ensures that miners wishing to block these transactions never win the race against the rest of miners.

Details for a possible implementation can be found in the comments in Back (2013).

13.5   FULLY ANONYMOUS DECENTRALIZED CURRENCIES

Technologies already exist to create fully anonymous decentralized currencies. These technologies are based on more recent cryptographic primitives such as zero-knowledge proofs, commitments, accumulators, and succinct non-interactive zero-knowledge proofs among others. The disadvantage of these technologies is that they usually require more computational power (per transaction) than Bitcoin, and the storage requirements are also far bigger than those of Bitcoin[8]. However, there is a growing interest in these technologies and efforts are being made to optimize them with promising results.

This section will introduce the cryptographic primitives that underpin these technologies and will summarize some recent proposals. As the material is somewhat mathematically involved, it may be skipped on a first reading.

13.5.1   Zero-knowledge Proofs

Zero-knowledge proofs (ZKP) are proofs that some statement is true that do not reveal any additional information apart from the fact that the statement is true. There seems to be a contradiction in this definition at first glance, but the definition will become clearer after some examples. The beauty of zero-knowledge proofs is that they allow proof that someone is in possession of a piece of information, such as a number with certain properties or the solution to a problem, without revealing that piece of information.

Commitment schemes are widely used in zero-knowledge proofs. A **commitment scheme** is a strategy where someone commits to a value without revealing the value until a later time. A commitment scheme allows two players to play a game of head-or-tails remotely: the first player commits to either heads or tails first, then the second player tosses the coin and communicates the result, and finally the first player reveals the commitment. An straightforward way to create a commitment is to encrypt the value using a symmetric cipher, later revealing the secret key[9].

13.5.2   Zero-knowledge Proof of Graph 3-colorability

This section introduces zero-knowledge proofs for the graph 3-colorability problem. **Computational complexity theory** is a computer science branch concerned with the resources required to solve certain problems (Arora and Barak, 2009). Complexity theory classifies problems according to the computational cost incurred in solving them. If this cost increases polynomially with the size of the problem, it belongs to the polynomial class (P) and is said to be tractable. If the cost increases exponentially, the problem is considered intractable. Intractable problems can be sometimes solved if the size of

---

[8] One recent proposal, Zerocash, achieves storage requirements and verification times comparable to those of Bitcoin (13.5.7).

[9] This is a simplistic commitment scheme, and extra precautions must be taken when using it. For instance, if the committed value is a few bits, it is easy for the prover to brute-force a key that would yield any desired outcome. Another simple commitment scheme could be achieved from a hash function: simply hash the committed value and later reveal the value. Any commitment scheme that uses a symmetric cypher or a hash function must include additional information in the encrypted message to prevent an attacker from brute-forcing it.

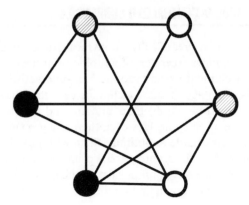

FIGURE 13.9 A 3-colorable graph

the problem is small. What makes these problems intractable is the fact that they are exponentially more difficult to solve the larger they are. In contrast, large tractable (P) problems can be routinely solved.

For some intractable problems a solution can be verified in polynomial time. These problems belong to the NP class. NP stands for **nondeterministic polynomial time** and is one of the most important classes in computational complexity theory. Solutions to NP problems are verifiable in polynomial time by a deterministic Turing machine. In other words, NP problems are problems for which a proposed solution can be verified with a fast algorithm (polynomial time) using a regular computer (deterministic Turing machine)[10]. This does not mean that a solution to an NP problem can be found in polynomial time, only that a solution can be checked to be valid in polynomial time.

An example of an NP problem is the **graph 3-colorability problem**. The vertices of a graph are painted with one of three possible colors. The graph 3-colorability problem is to determine if there exists a way to color the vertices in such a way that none of the edges connects two vertices with the same color. Figure 13.9 shows an example of a 3-colorable graph with a valid solution painted on the vertices.

Graph 3-colorability is an NP problem because given a graph and a proposed coloring of the vertices, it can be decided whether the coloring is valid in polynomial time. The algorithm simply runs through all the edges, checking that the two vertices connected by the edge have a different color. This algorithm is polynomial in the number of edges.

There is an efficient zero-knowledge proof for the graph 3-colorability. That is, given a graph, someone in possession of a solution to the graph 3-colorability problem on that graph—the prover—can show in zero-knowledge that she is in possession of a solution to another person—the verifier. The zero-knowledge proof repeats these steps:

- The prover chooses a random permutation of the colors in the solution. This random permutation is necessary to ensure that the verifier does not gain any knowledge of the solution.
- The prover commits to the permuted colors, without revealing their values.

---

[10] A regular computer as opposed to a quantum computer (section 14.6).

- The verifier chooses one edge of the graph randomly and sends the selected edge to the prover.
- The prover reveals the values of the two vertices connected by the edge to the verifier. Note that the prover does not reveal the values of all the committed vertices, because that would give away the solution to the graph 3-colorability problem. The prover only reveals the committed values of the two vertices requested.
- The verifier checks that the colors revealed for the two vertices are different.

By repeating this procedure many times, the verifier can become convinced that the prover has a valid solution to the graph 3-colorability problem with a confidence as high as she wants. Usually repeating the procedure m^2 times where m is the number of vertices in the graph is assumed to produce an acceptably low probability of cheating. Assume the prover does not know a valid solution to the graph 3-colorability problem, but she knows a coloring which is almost a solution except that the nodes connected by one single edge have the same color. Knowing this "almost" solution is the most favorable situation for a cheater. If she presents this as a valid solution, the verifier has a $1 - 1/m$ provability of accepting the solution, where m is the number of edges. If the procedure is repeated m^2 times, the provability of accepting the invalid solution is $(1 - 1/m)^{m^2} \approx e^{-m}$, which becomes negligible even a for reasonably small number of m. For example, the probability of accepting an invalid solution is in the order of 10^{-9} for $m = 20$.

This procedure is often called **cut-and-choose**, because the verifier chooses the edge whose vertices she wants revealed at each iteration. It is called cut-and-choose in analogy to the fair way of choosing a card from a shuffled deck. The cut-and-choose technique makes zero-knowledge proofs inefficient, because it requires many steps to convince the verifier. In the following sections, some zero-knowledge proofs that do not require a cut-and-choose procedure are introduced.

The graph 3-colorability problem is NP-complete. **NP-complete** is a subset of the NP class: any NP problem can be converted to an NP-complete problem in polynomial time. As the graph 3-colorability problem is NP-complete, any other NP problem can be transformed to a graph 3-colorability problem. Making use of this property, one of the biggest breakthroughs in zero-knowledge proofs was to demonstrate that **a solution to every NP problem can be proven in zero knowledge** with the only requisite that an encryption function, used to encrypt the commitments, must exit (Goldreich et al., 1991).

The proof of this theorem follows these steps: first the NP problem is transformed into a graph 3-colorability problem and then a solution to the 3-colorability problem is proven in zero-knowledge.

13.5.3 Zero-knowledge Proof for the Discrete Logarithm

A **trapdoor function** is a function that is easy to compute in one direction, but it is very difficult to compute in reverse. For instance, $f(x) = g^x \bmod n$ is a trapdoor function under the strong RSA assumption. The **strong RSA assumption** states that for an appropriately chosen n (section 5.3) and given c, it is impossible to find x and y such that $c = x^y \bmod n$ in polynomial time. This trapdoor function can be used to create zero-knowledge proofs of a discrete logarithm, where the prover knows a number x which is the discrete logarithm of a committed value c, that is $c = g^x \bmod n$, where g is the group generator.

A commitment c can always be proved straightforwardly by revealing the committed values. Revealing x to the verifier, allows the verifier to check $c = g^x \bmod n$ and thus proves the commitment. However, this proof is not zero-knowledge, as the verifier obtains knowledge of the committed value x.

There are several possible constructions for zero-knowledge proofs of a discrete logarithm. The most common one is the **Schnorr protocol** (Schnorr, 1991). A zero-knowledge proof using the Schnorr protocol follows these steps:

- The prover selects a random number r, computes $t = g^r \bmod n$, and sends t to the verifier.
- The verifier selects and sends a random value e to the prover.
- The prover computes $u = r + e \cdot x$ and sends u to the verifier. Note that the verifier does not gain knowledge of x, as it is blinded by the random r.
- The verifier accepts if $g^u \bmod n = t \cdot c^e \bmod n$, which holds if the commitment is valid: $g^u \bmod n = g^{r+e \cdot x} \bmod n = g^r \cdot g^{e \cdot x} \bmod n = g^r \cdot (g^x)^e \bmod n = t \cdot c^e \bmod n$.

Another important protocol to prove knowledge of a discrete logarithm in zero knowledge uses the Pedersen commitment scheme introduced in Pedersen (1991). In a **Pedersen commitment scheme**, the prover commits to x by choosing a random r and computing[11]: $c = g^x \cdot h^r \bmod n$, where g is the generator and $h = g^a \bmod n$ is computed from a random value a at the initialization of the scheme. A Pedersen commitment $c = g^x \cdot h^r \bmod n$ can be proved in zero knowledge following these steps:

- The prover chooses two random numbers p, q, computes $d = g^p \cdot h^q \bmod n$, and sends d to the verifier.
- The verifier selects and sends a random value e to the prover.
- The prover computes $u = p + e \cdot x$, $v = q + e \cdot r$ and sends it to the verifier.
- The verifier accepts if $g^u \cdot h^v \bmod n = d \cdot c^e \bmod n$. This assertion holds if the commitment is correct: $g^u \cdot h^v \bmod n = g^{p+e \cdot x} \cdot h^{q+e \cdot r} \bmod n = g^p \cdot h^q \cdot (g^x)^e \cdot (h^r)^e \bmod n = d \cdot (g^x \cdot h^r)^e \bmod n = d \cdot c^e \bmod n$.

Both the Schnorr and the Pedersen protocols can be used to prove knowledge of a value included in a one-way accumulator (13.5.5). Zerocoin (13.5.6) uses a Pedersen commitment to create the coins from a serial number, later proving in zero-knowledge that a coin with that serial number is included in a one-way accumulator.

13.5.4 Non-interactive Zero-knowledge Proofs

All the zero-knowledge proofs presented so far are **interactive zero-knowledge proofs**, because the prover and the verifier must interact during the proof. In particular, the verifier generates a series of random numbers during the verification process to ensure that the prover cannot cheat.

A **non-interactive zero-knowledge proof (NIZKP)** is a zero-knowledge proof that does not require interaction between the prover and the verifier. Non-interactive zero-knowledge proofs are essential to the construction of a fully anonymous decentralized currency,

---

[11] This short description is glossing over many details.

because zero-knowledge proofs underlie the spending of anonymous coins. The owner of the coins should be able to create a NIZKP spend transaction that can later be checked by anyone.

In a NIZKP, the prover creates a proof of knowledge, that can later be verified by anyone. In this sense a NIZKP is similar to a digital signature. The most widely used construction to transform an interactive ZKP to a non-interactive ZKP is the Fiat-Shamir heuristic introduced in Fiat and Shamir (1986). The Fiat-Shamir heuristic replaces the response of the verifier (random values) by the result of the hash of some intermediate results. This non-interactive proof of knowledge assumes that the prover cannot predict the outcome of the hash function, i.e. the hash function acts as a random oracle. Thus it is said the proof of the NIZKP holds in the **random oracle model**.

A prover can create a NIZKP of a Pedersen commitment $c = g^x \cdot h^r \bmod n$ following these steps:

- Choose two random numbers p, q and compute $d = g^p \cdot h^q \bmod n$.
- Compute $e = H(d)$ where H is a cryptographically secure hash function.
- Compute $u = p + e \cdot x$, $v = q + e \cdot r$.
- Publish (d, e, u, v) as the NIZKP.

Anyone can then check the validity of the NIZKP (d, e, u, v) of the commitment c by checking that $e = H(d)$, and that $g^u \cdot h^v \bmod n = d \cdot c^e \bmod n$.

13.5.5 Accumulators

One-way accumulators were introduced in Benaloh and de Mare (1994). **One-way accumulators** are an efficient way of combining multiple elements (numbers) into a data structure of constant size. They also allow for efficient proofs that a particular element is contained in the accumulator. The accumulator proposed in Benaloh and de Mare (1994) is based on the strong RSA assumption and represents the set $\{y_1, y_2, ..., y_m\}$ as:

$$z_m = x^{y_1 \cdot y_2 \cdots y_m} \bmod n$$

where z_m is the accumulator. Note that the accumulator z_m is of the same size than the individual elements y_i: the accumulator compacts the information in the set of elements. For a large n, an appropriately large number of elements y_i can be included in the accumulator.

To prove that a particular element y_i is included in the accumulator, the prover must first compute a **witness** w_i:

$$w_i = x^{y_1 \cdot y_2 \cdots y_{i-1} \cdot y_{i+1} \cdots y_m} \bmod n$$

A zero-knowledge proof that the prover knows a value (y^i) in the accumulator follows the steps:

- The prover selects a random number r, computes $C = w_i^r \bmod n$ and sends both the witness w_i and C to the verifier.
- The verifier selects and sends a random value e to the prover.

- The prover computes $u = r + e \cdot y_i$ and sends it to the verifier. Note that the verifier does not gain knowledge of y_i, as it is blinded by r.
- The verifier accepts if $w_i^u \bmod n = C \cdot z_m^e \bmod n$.

This zero-knowledge proof does not reveal which element of the accumulator (y_i) the prover has a witness for. However, it does reveal the witness w_i and this breaks the anonymity of a digital currency using this zero-knowledge proof. For this reason, practical implementations such as Zerocoin use more involved zero-knowledge proofs that hide both the element in the accumulator y_i and the witness w_i.

A new element y_{m+1} can be efficiently added to the accumulator by computing $z_{m+1} = z_m^{y_{m+1}} \bmod n$. When a new element is added to the accumulator, existing witnesses of the accumulator have to be updated accordingly.

13.5.6 Zerocoin

Zerocoin (Miers et al., 2013) extends the Bitcoin protocol using all the cryptographic tools introduced in this section: commitments, accumulators, witnesses, and non-interactive zero-knowledge proofs. Zerocoin creates a layer on top of Bitcoin that operates as a decentralized mixer. A zerocoin can be minted by spending a bitcoin. Later a ("different") bitcoin can be retrieved from the zerocoin, in a way that makes it impossible to link[12] the mint and redeem operations.

A zerocoin is created following the steps:

- The user generates a serial number S and a random trapdoor number r and uses them to create a Pedersen commitment $C = g^S \cdot h^r \bmod n$. The serial number S is chosen randomly so that the probability of collision with the serial number of an existing zerocoin is negligible. From this point on, the commitment C will be referred to simply as the zerocoin[13].
- The user creates a Zerocoin mint transaction. This is a regular Bitcoin transaction where the user spends a bitcoin to create a zerocoin. The zerocoin C is included in the transaction.
- Nodes in the network update the accumulator that holds all the existing zerocoins z to include the new zerocoin C: $z_{new} = z^C \bmod n$.

At this point the zerocoin is recorded in the accumulator, z_{new}. Note that the user did not reveal the serial number, S, or the random trapdoor, r. The zerocoin can be spent and redeemed for a bitcoin following the steps:

---

[12] Although it is impossible to link the zerocoin mint and the zerocoin spend transactions mathematically, it could be possible to link them by other means, such as observing the origin IP address of both transactions, the timing of the transactions and so on.

[13] The Zerocoin protocol requires that C is a prime number to avoid double-spending of zerocoins. If a user were to create a zerocoin $C' = g^{S_1} \cdot h^{r_1} \cdot g^{S_2} \cdot h^{r_2} \bmod n$, she could then make two zerocoin spends of the coins $C_1 = g^{S_1} \cdot h^{r_1} \bmod n$ and $C_2 = g^{S_2} \cdot h^{r_2} \bmod n$. To avoid this double-spending possibility, the zerocoin C is required to be a prime number. Thus, if after selecting S and r the zerocoin C turns out not to be prime, the user should choose S and r again until a prime C is generated.

- The user creates a non-interactive zero-knowledge proof (NIZKP) that proves she knows of a zerocoin that embeds the serial number S and that this zerocoin is in the accumulator. This zero-knowledge proof is somewhat more involved than the zero-knowledge proofs introduced previously in this section. It is based on the zero-knowledge proof of membership in an accumulator introduced in Camenisch and Lysyanskaya (2002) and it uses zero-knowledge proofs of double discrete logarithms[14] (Camenisch, 1998). It is basically a double proof that the serial number corresponds to a zerocoin and that this zerocoin is included in the accumulator. This proof does not reveal either the zerocoin C, the trapdoor random number r, or the witness to the accumulator w_i.
- The user embeds this NIZKP in a bitcoin transaction where the output returns a bitcoin to a Bitcoin address of her choosing.
- Nodes keep a list of serial numbers spent in previous redeemed transactions, to prevent a zerocoin owner from double-spending. After receiving a zerocoin redeem transaction, nodes check that the serial number S is not included in the list of spent serial numbers, then check the validity of the NIZKP and finally add the serial number S to the list of spent serial numbers.

The bitcoins spent in the mint operations do not go anywhere, they stay on escrow, ready to be redeemed when a zerocoin commitment is revealed. A zerocoin spend could be combined with a zerocoin mint in the same transaction, thus creating a transaction from a zerocoin to a zerocoin directly, without having to convert to a bitcoin as an intermediate step.

Implementing Zerocoin in practice requires an upgrade of Bitcoin Core: all nodes in the network would have to upgrade simultaneously. Once upgraded, nodes running the Zerocoin extension perform the following housekeeping operations:

- They must add new minted zerocoins to the accumulator. It is proposed in Miers et al. (2013) that miners store accumulator checkpoints in the coinbase transaction. Other nodes would then validate that the accumulator is correctly updated with the new zerocoins minted in the block, before accepting the block. This could free lighter nodes from the task of updating the accumulator themselves, while still allowing some nodes to update the accumulators themselves, or at least audit the accumulator checkpoints.
- They must add the serial numbers of the new spend transactions to the spend serial number list. This is specially important for mining nodes, as the inclusion of a double-spent zerocoin redeem transaction in a mined block would invalidate the block.
- They do not need to ensure that the number of bitcoins reserved for zerocoins is correct because this is guaranteed by construction.

Mint transactions use a fixed denomination for the zerocoins, say 1 zerocoin for 1 bitcoin. However, multiple denominations can be created basically by running a different accumulator for each denomination[15].

---

[14] The double discrete logarithm of y to the bases g and a is defined as the value of x that satisfies $y = g^{a^x}$.

[15] Zerocoin developers have proposed some extensions that allow zerocoins of multiple denominations (Garman et al., 2014).

An often-made criticism of Zerocoin is that the accumulator parameters computed during the set-up phase constitute a backdoor. An attacker in possession of these parameters could create zerocoin redeem operations at her wish. However, there are techniques to securely create a trapdoor during the set-up phase. One such technique is multi-party computation, which could be used to create a secure trapdoor even if only one of the participants is honest and discards her inputs.

However, the major drawback of Zerocoin is the size of the NIZKP used to redeem zerocoins, due to its cut-and-choose nature. These NIZKP have a size of approximately 25kB (Garman et al., 2014), which exceeds the current 10kB limit for Bitcoin transactions, making them impractical under current Bitcoin rules. One possible workaround could be storing these NIZKP off-blockchain in a dedicated server or in a distributed hash table (Miers et al., 2013).

Another drawback of Zerocoin is that minting, spending, and verifying operations take from 0.3 to 0.8 seconds (Miers et al., 2013), which can be a problem for nodes verifying the transactions. One proposed solution could be to distribute this computational effort among the nodes, in such a way that security is not compromised.

In a follow-up (Garman et al., 2014), the authors of Zerocoin propose some changes to make the NIZKP smaller and faster to process while preserving anonymity. A proposal similar to Zerocoin is Pinocchio Coin (Danezis et al., 2013). Pinocchio Coin uses elliptic curve accumulators instead of RSA accumulators, which greatly reduces the size of the proofs to approximately 350 bytes. However, Pinocchio Coin suffers from scalability issues, as the coin generation time grows linearly with the number of coins in existence.

13.5.7 Zerocash

Zerocash (Ben-Sasson et al., 2014) is another extension to the Bitcoin protocol that achieves a fully anonymous decentralized currency. The main advantage of Zerocash is that spend transactions are much smaller and faster to verify that in Zerocoin, thus solving one of the practical problems Zerocoin faced. Other advantages of Zerocash are that it does not require fixed denominations, that it hides the transfer amount, and that it hides a payment's origin and destination.

Users can create coins of any value through mint transactions, which create a series of commitments. On the other hand, a **pour transaction** allows two previously minted transactions to be gathered and the resulting amount poured into two new output coins. By connecting several pour transactions, any number of previously minted coins can be gathered and the funds poured into any set of new output coins. Pour transactions allow coins to be split and mixed, without revealing the addresses of the spent coins or the addresses to where the new coins are directed[16]. Neither do they reveal the amounts spent or how the total amount is divided among the destination addresses. Thus pour transactions are conducted in full anonymity. Pour transactions can be used to subdivide, merge, or transfer ownership of anonymous coins. They also allow to make payments in public coins using the funds stored in anonymous coins, as pour transactions can include an amount to be publicly spent.

Pour transactions are checked in a similar way that regular Bitcoin transactions are checked: sums of inputs must match sum of outputs, inputs must be correctly assembled,

---

[16] Note that Zerocash addresses are different from Bitcoin addresses.

and so on. However, the difference is that Zerocash pour transactions are performed in zero-knowledge, not revealing any information about the addresses or the amounts involved in the transaction. To achieve this, pour transactions use an implementation of succinct non-interactive zero-knowledge proofs (succinct NIZKP) called zk-SNARKs[17] (Ben-Sasson et al., 2013). In a regular NIZKP both the proof length and the verification time increase linearly with the size of the statement to be proved. In contrast, in a zk-SNARK proof lengths depend only on the security parameter, thus the name *succinct* NIZKPs. This presents an advantage for Zerocash, because the statement to be proved (in a pour transaction) is relatively complex and using zk-SNARKs allows for compact proofs (i.e. spends) and fast verification times by nodes.

Zerocash stores coins in a Merkle tree, instead of an accumulator as in Zerocoin. Zerocash proofs take up 288 bytes[18], with verification times of 9 milliseconds. Coin generation time range from 1 minute to 3 minutes, depending on the number of cores available in the device. However, the generation time scales logarithmically with the number of coins. The public key used to generate new coins is a somewhat large 0.9 GB, but only one copy of the key has to be saved.

The public key includes a trapdoor, and knowledge of this trapdoor could allow an attacker to mint as many new coins as she wishes. However, knowledge of the trapdoor does not allow an attacker to break anonymity. As in the case of Zerocoin, there are techniques to securely create a trapdoor during the set-up phase.

One disadvantage of Zerocash is that it relies in several new cryptographic primitives, such as pairing-based cryptography or knowledge of an exponent, that have not yet been subject to ample scrutiny by the cryptographic community. Further details about Zerocash can be found in Ben-Sasson et al. (2014).

---

[17] zk-SNARK is an acronym for zero-knowledge Succinct Non-interactive ARgument of Knowledge.
[18] 288 bytes is the size of the zk-SNARK included in a Zerocash transaction. The size of a Zerocash transaction is somewhat larger.

CHAPTER 14

Odds and Ends

This chapter further expands on several topics that have been previously only mentioned briefly.

14.1 OTHER TRANSACTION PROTOCOLS

14.1.1 Micropayment Channels

Some applications require many small transactions to take place, i.e. micropayments. One typical use case for micropayments is paying for an ongoing service, such as network connectivity or content viewing. As Bitcoin transaction fees are reasonably low, micropayments could be performed using multiple transactions of small amounts. This approach, however, has several disadvantages. First, there are fees associated with every transaction (section 9.3). Second, there is a limit to how small a transaction amount can be, the dust limit, created to prevent the bloating of the UTXO (Chapter 6). Third, the receiver is left with many small transactions, which can be costly to spend, as the resulting spending transaction would have a large size.

These disadvantages are overcome by setting up a micropayment channel. A **micropayment channel** is a communication link between two parties—say a client and a server—to create a stream of transactions that is updated frequently but is not published on the blockchain until the end of the relationship. To set up a micropayment channel these steps are followed (Bitcoin wiki, 2014f):

- The client creates a transaction (Tx1) that sends a large amount to a 2-of-2 multisignature address with the addresses of both the client and the server. The client signs the transaction but does not publish it, nor does she send it to the server.
- The client then creates a new transaction (Tx2) spending the funds from the previous multisignature transaction, sending them back to her. This transaction has a time lock set for some time in the future, say 1 hour. The client sends this transaction to the server.
- The server signs this second transaction Tx2. This is a partial sign, as it requires the signature of the client too. The server sends this partially signed transaction to the client. Note that at this point the server has not seen the original transaction Tx1. The only information about this transaction that the server has is the hash, as it is included in Tx2.

- The client checks that the partially signed Tx2 is correct. Then she publishes Tx1, because she can use the partially signed Tx2 to retrieve the funds once the time lock expires. The funds are now locked in the multisignature transaction output of Tx1.
- The set-up phase of the micropayment channel is now complete. Assume that the client uses the service and wants to send a small amount of funds using the channel, say 1 mBTC. To accomplish it, the client creates a third transaction Tx3, spending the output of Tx1 to both the address of the server (the small amount) and his own address (the rest). She signs Tx3 and sends it to the server.
- The server could for its part sign Tx3 and publish it to receive the 1 mBTC, but if the relationship between the server and the client is ongoing, the server might prefer to wait for the client to make further use of the service.
- If the client makes use of the service again, she can update Tx3, increasing the funds sent to the server and decreasing the funds sent back to herself. She signs this updated Tx3 and sends it to the server. This procedure could be repeated many times, updating the amount every time.

Note that during all this procedure, only Tx1 is published to the blockchain. When the relationship between the server and the client ends, the server signs and publishes the latest Tx3 received from the client. Note that at no time can the server access all the funds stored in Tx1, as updating the amounts in the channel is in the hands of the client. Note also that the server cannot keep the funds in Tx1 ransom as the client can use Tx2 to retrieve them, once the time lock expires.

One last detail is that, as the time lock of Tx2 approaches, the micropayment channel should be closed, say by the server publishing the latest Tx3, and a new micropayment channel should be set up. Otherwise, the server runs the risk of the user publishing Tx2 once the time lock expires.

More details on the micropayment channel protocol can be found in Bitcoin wiki (2014f). Details of its implementation in the bitcoinj library can be found in Bitcoinj Documentation (2014).

14.1.2 Atomic Cross-chain Trading

Atomic cross-chain trading solves the problem of safely exchanging funds between two different blockchains. The protocol is called atomic because the two transactions (one in each blockchain) either both take place or none of them takes place, i.e. the transfer of funds is an atomic operation. The protocol uses a special type of transaction called a **chain-trade script** (Bitcoin wiki, 2014f). A chain-trade script is similar to a hashlocked transaction (13.4.2) but with the difference that a chain-trade script transaction can be spent either with two signatures or with one signature and the preimage of a hash. Note that chain-trade script transactions are not standard in Bitcoin.

Two users—Alice and Bob—wish to exchange funds in two different blockchains. For instance, Alice will send funds in the first blockchain to Bob, while Bob will send funds to Alice in the second blockchain. They can use the atomic cross-chain trading protocol as follows:

- Alice generates a random number x, the preimage of the hash, and creates a transaction (Tx1) sending the funds in the first blockchain to a chain-trade script. This script can be redeemed either with the signature of both Alice and Bob, or with Bob's signature and knowledge of the preimage x.

- Alice creates a second transaction (Tx2) spending the funds in the chain-trade script back to herself, and signs it. This transaction is time locked in the future. She passes the partially signed Tx2 to Bob.
- Bob signs Tx2 and sends it back to Alice.
- Alice verifies that the signature for Tx2 is correct and then publishes Tx1 on the first blockchain. At this point Bob does not know x, as this is kept secret by Alice. All Bob can see is $H(x)$ (the hash of x), which is included in Tx1.
- The same steps are now performed on the second block chain symmetrically. First, Bob creates a chain-trade transaction (Tx3) redeemable with the signatures of both Alice and Bob, or with Alice's signature and the preimage of the hash (the same hash $H(x)$ as in Tx1 is used[1]). Then Bob creates a time-locked transaction (Tx4) sending the funds in the chain-trade script in Tx3 back to himself, and gets Alice's signature on this transaction. Finally, Bob publishes Tx3 on the second blockchain.
- At this point the funds are in place in both blockchains, but the exchange is not finalized yet. To finalize it, Alice creates a transaction (Tx5) spending the funds in the chain-trade script in Tx3 to herself. To do so, she provides her signature and the preimage of the hash x. However, once she publishes this transaction the preimage of the hash, x, is made public, and thus Bob can use it to create a transaction (Tx6) sending the funds in the chain-trade script Tx1 to himself. This finalizes the exchange.

Note that transactions Tx2 and Tx4 are not published if the exchange proceeds as planned. These transactions allow Alice and Bob to recover their funds in case something goes wrong and the cross-chain exchange falls apart.

The protocol described here fails if a fork occurs in any of the two blockchains involved. For instance, if Tx5 happened to be involved in a fork of the second blockchain, and the branch where Tx5 sits ended up being orphaned, the preimage x would be revealed without Tx5 being valid. Thus a practical implementation of atomic cross-chain trading would have to take into account blockchain reorganizations. More details on atomic cross-chain trading can be found in Bitcoin wiki (2014f, 2014b) and Tiernan (2014).

14.2   ALTERNATIVES TO PROOF-OF-WORK

Proof-of-work is an elegant solution to the distributed synchronization problem of deciding which transaction should be included in the distributed ledger at each time (section 10.3). However, proof-of-work is not the only scheme that solves this problem. There has been a lot of debate in the Bitcoin community about the merits of proof-of-work compared to other potential schemes. Critics of proof-of-work often cite the following disadvantages:

---

[1] Although Bob does not know the preimage of the hash (x), he does know the hash $H(x)$, as it has been published in Tx1.

- Large investments in specialized hardware, ASICs, with limited use aside from mining and large energy consumption. The difficulty of Bitcoin mining will rise until the block reward equals the cost of running mining equipment, a large part of which is the cost of electricity. Once this equilibrium is reached all mining rewards will go to pay for the cost of mining. Thus mining can be viewed as a tax on bitcoin holders with no social benefits, critics argue. Defendants of mining reply that mining serves a purpose, namely securing the blockchain, and the bitcoins awarded are thus not wasted.
- Concentration of mining power in the hands of a few players. As mining hardware specializes, this tends to concentrate mining in the hands of a few professional miners. Critics argue this concentration of mining power could be dangerous for the network.

This section introduces two alternatives to proof-of-work: proof-of-stake and proof-of-burn. Other schemes are possible, such as the consensus process used by Ripple introduced in 12.7.6. Still many other possibilities have been proposed, such as proof-of-bandwidth, proof-of-storage, proof-of-resource, proof-of-activity, and so on.

14.2.1 Proof-of-stake

In proof-of-work, the probability of mining a block depends on the computational work done by the miner. In **proof-of-stake** users are said to *mint* new blocks, as opposed to mining them. Minting does not require computational power, because the probability of minting a block depends on the *stake* that the user has. Block minting is usually awarded to users in proportion of their holdings, using some metric such as the amount of funds or the coin age hold. Coin age is the product of the funds times the age of these funds (the period since those funds were last spent).

The often-cited advantages of proof-of-stake are:

- **Environmentally friendly.** Proof-of-stake does not employ the large computational resources that proof-of-work does, consuming very little energy.
- **Less centralized**, as all holders of funds can mint new blocks and have an economic incentive to do so.
- **Raises the cost of a 51% attack**, as a successful attacker should have a majority stake in the currency. But an attacker holding such a big stake might not have an incentive to perform an attack detrimental to the currency, and thus to herself. Also, a majority stake in the currency is usually worth more than a majority of the mining investment. This is true of Bitcoin as of the time of writing, where the market capitalization of the currency is around USD 6,000 million but the investment required to achieve the network hash rate, using current technology, is in the order of USD 50 million (roughly 50,000,000 GH/s at a cost of 1 USD/GH/s)[2]. In contrast, an attacker that has 51% of the mining power in a proof-of-work system does not stand

---

[2] Not to be confused with the total cumulative investment in mining equipment, which is much higher because a large portion of it was invested in less efficient technologies.

to lose from her attack, as she could repurpose the hardware to mine another cryptocurrency after a successful attack[3].

- **Lower transaction fees**, as there is little investment in mining equipment and the electricity cost of minting blocks is negligible. However, it can be argued that in a proof-of-stake cryptocurrency, transaction fees would reflect the price of an scarce resource, namely space in a block, and this price could be independent of the cost of producing a block.

The main problem with proof-of-stake systems is their difficulty in solving blockchain forks. In case of a fork, users of a proof-of-stake system have funds in both branches of the fork, and thus have an incentive to keep on minting blocks in both branches. This is not a problem in a proof-of-work system, as miners have to make a decision on which branch of the fork to employ their computational power. This is known as the **nothing-at-stake** problem: fork resolution might be harder to achieve in proof-of-stake systems, because users do not have a stake in either branch of the fork, and thus would choose to support both.

One possible solution might be for any branch of the fork to penalize miners who are also mining for other branches, thus forcing miners to take sides with a branch, thus helping the fork resolve itself. There is one practical problem, however: mining in proof-of-stake is probabilistic, and the probability that a small miner mines a block in both branches is very small (the product of the probabilities of mining a block in each of the branches). Thus small miners still have an incentive to mine all branches in a fork (Buterin, 2014c). Every practical proof-of-stake system has to deal with this nothing-at-stake-problem.

The protocol of a proof-of-stake system awards the next block to be minted to some participant in the network. This process is usually made random and fair, in the sense that participants are "selected"[4] to mint the next block in proportion to their share of the funds.

Another drawback of proof-of-stake systems is that users with few funds might not want to receive funds from a large player, as it is easy for a player with a lot of funds to carry out a double-spend attack.

Another disadvantage is that there is no separation between mining and holding funds. Thus everybody that has funds should be mining too, to avoid losing money. Users that cannot run a full node could be compelled to store their funds with services that do the mining for them, thus increasing counterparty risk for small users.

Some proposed implementations of proof-of-stake are (Bitcoin wiki, 2014t):

---

[3] It is argued in Houy (2014) that a credible attacker that announces her intentions to buy a majority of a proof-of-stake cryptocurrency in order to destroy it would be able to buy such majority of the coins at negligible cost. It is a Nash equilibrium for all coin holders to sell their coins at any price, if the attacker is credible. Critics of this argument respond that users might resist selling at a very low price or form a coalition to fight off the attacker. Furthermore, once the attacker holds a majority of the coins, she would not have an incentive to destroy the currency, thus making her threat less credible.
[4] As the system is decentralized, there is no central entity that "selects" who will mint the block. There is an algorithm that all users run, say a hashing function, and when the result of this algorithm hits a target, that typically depends on the stake of the user, the user is eligible to mint a new block. At this point the user mints the block and publishes it.

- **Peercoin.** Peercoin selects who should mint the next proof-of-stake block based on coin age. It solves the nothing-at-stake problem by using hybrid proof-of-work and proof-of-stake mining. See section 11.2 for more details.
- **Nxt.** Only active Nxt accounts[5] are eligible to forge a new block. Nxt selects who should forge the next block based on the amount of funds held by the account (Nxt wiki, 2014b).
- **Cunicula.** Unlike Peercoin or Nxt, this is a theoretical proposal, not a practical implementation. The focus of Cunicula's proposal is how to incentivize users to participate in the proof-of-stake minting process. This is achieved by taxing inactive users, to the tune of 5% of their funds per year, and dividing the proceeds to the active minting users. This proposal does not directly address the nothing-at-stake problem, arguing that a 51% attack where an attacker mints a new chain privately would not succeed: other users would not have an incentive to accept this branch when it is finally made public, as they would lose their rewards in the legitimate branch. See Bitcoin wiki (2014t) for details of this proposal.
- **Meni.** This is also a theoretical proposal. It proposes a hybrid proof-of-work/proof-of-stake system. Blocks are mined using regular proof-of-work mining. Periodically—say every 100 blocks—a proof-of-stake block is minted. Users sign this block using their private key and collect the rewards proportionally to the funds they hold. In case of forking, users are encouraged to choose a branch to cast their signatures, because signatures on both branches of a fork are ignored[6], depriving the user of the rewards. The goal of the proof-of-stake layer is to increase the security of the system and its resilience against 51% attacks and double-spending. See Bitcoin wiki (2014t) for details of this proposal.
- **Slasher** (Buterin, 2014c). Users have the privilege of signing blocks based on the result of a hash that takes information from many blocks ago, say 2,000. Users receive block rewards for signing blocks. If a fork happens, the same user would be chosen to mint a new block in both branches of the fork, as the "lottery" is carried out using information from old blocks common to both branches of the fork. Slasher tackles the nothing-at-stake issue by punishing users who mint blocks in both branches of a fork. Other users can police the branches of a fork and if they find two blocks in different branches signed by the same account, they can submit a proof to the main blockchain, who will punish the cheating account by depriving it of the reward, and giving a small reward to the policing user. This creates an incentive for proof-of-stake accounts to opt for one of the branches in the fork, the branch whose probability of success is deemed higher.

14.2.2 Proof-of-burn

The idea behind proof-of-burn is that users show that they burned funds to some address that is verifiable unspendable. Several proposed applications of proof-of-burn are:

---

[5] To be active, an account must have an input confirmed by at least 1,440 blocks.
[6] There is a weighting system: addresses that participate in the proof-of-stake see their weight increased over time. If an address signs two proof-of-stake blocks in a fork, its weight is set to 0.

- **Award rights to mint new blocks.** This is similar to a proof-of-stake system, with the difference that minted blocks are awarded proportional to the amount of burnt coins. Burnt coins' privilege to mint blocks can be made to degrade over time, thus giving an incentive to users to burn new coins. The rate of decay of burnt coins can be used to control the monetary supply, as burning new coins decreases the monetary base (Bitcoin wiki, 2014s).
- **Transfer value between different blockchains.** If two blockchains are aware of one another, funds can be transferred to one blockchain by proving that funds have been burned in the other. This way of transferring funds between blockchains has the advantage of preserving the monetary base between the two chains. This procedure is similar to the side-chains proposal (section 14.4), with the difference that in the side-chains proposal, the transfer of value between chains is done through a 2-way peg mechanism.
- **Allocate the initial distribution of a new digital asset.** Some projects, such as Counterparty (12.7.2) have used a proof-of-burn to determine the initial allocation of their coins. Users who participated in the initial allocation burnt bitcoins to a verifiable unspendable address and were awarded a share of the new currency XCP.

14.3 MERGED MINING

Many applications have emerged recently that use the blockchain technology originally introduced in Bitcoin. Examples of these applications are alt-coins (Chapter 11), meta-coins (section 12.7), side-chains (section 14.4), or digital notaries (section 7.2). The blockchains maintained by these applications are often called **alternative chains**.

As the resources invested in securing these alternative chains are usually lower than the investment that has gone into Bitcoin mining, it is desirable for some alternative chains to be able to benefit from the security of Bitcoin's blockchain. Merged mining introduces a way to achieve this goal. In **merged mining** an alternative chain accepts as mined blocks either a regular block from the alternative chain or proof that a block from the alternative chain has been secured in Bitcoin's blockchain. It is called merged mining because regular Bitcoin miners can simultaneously mine Bitcoin's blockchain and the alternative chain.

A miner that is running both the Bitcoin Core Server and the mining server for the alternative chain performs merged mining in the following way:

- The miner creates a valid block from the alternative chain and hashes it. She then includes the hash of this block in the input of the coinbase transaction of the Bitcoin's block she is currently trying to mine[7]. If the alternative chain block gets updated, say because new transactions are added, she computes the new hash of the block and updates the hash in the coinbase transaction of the Bitcoin's block she is mining.
- At some point the miner will find a valid Bitcoin block, which is added to the Bitcoin blockchain. This block includes by construction a copy of the hash of the alternative chain block.

---

[7] Merge mining could be achieved using any other method that inserts data into Bitcoin's blockchain (section 12.6).

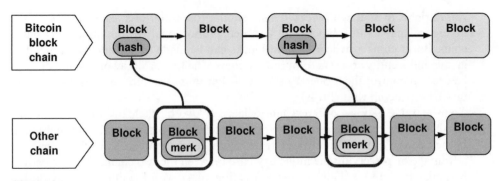

FIGURE 14.1 Merged mining

- The miner then publishes the block to the alternative chain, including the hash of Bitcoin's block where the alternative chain block is included and the Merkle branch from the coinbase to the Bitcoin's block header. The alternative chain protocol is prepared to accept this Merkle branch as proof-of-work that the block was mined.

The alternative chain usually has its own mining mechanism. New blocks can either originate through this regular mining, or they can be blocks that are merge-mined with Bitcoin. This approach is sketched in Figure 14.1. Note how the alternative chain can produce more frequent blocks (or less frequent for that matter), and thus only some alternative chain's blocks will be merge-mined[8]. This is not a problem, as the merge-mining protocol is prepared to accommodate merge-mined blocks at irregular intervals. Merged mining is usually profitable for miners because they receive the block reward and the fees from both chains with the only extra cost of running a full node for the alternative chain.

The biggest drawback of merged mining is that a large miner could decide to attack the alternative chain, and she pays no cost to do so. Some alt-coins have allegedly been attacked this way.

Merged mining can be accomplished without any changes to Bitcoin's protocol: only changes in the alternative chain protocol are required. Merged mining appeared originally as a way for some alt-coins, such as Namecoin, to include a hash of their blocks inside Bitcoin's blockchain to increase the security of their own blockchains. But the concept can be applied to other applications such as distributed notaries.

More details on merged mining can be found in Bitcoin wiki (2014a).

14.4 SIDE-CHAINS

Side-chains are blockchains that share their monetary base with Bitcoin. A side-chain does not create tokens by itself, it receives the tokens from Bitcoin's blockchain. Funds can be transferred between a side-chain and Bitcoin's blockchain back and forth, at a

---

[8] Additionally it cannot be expected that every Bitcoin miner will be doing merged mining with a particular alternative chain. Some Bitcoin miners would prefer not to merged-mine at all.

constant ratio (exchange rate). This process is called **2-way pegging** because the value of the side-chain tokens is pegged to the value of bitcoins.

There was a predecessor to 2-way pegging called 1-way pegging (Back, 2014a). In 1-way pegging bitcoins were burnt to some address. The proof-of-burn then could be used to redeem tokens in the side-chain using a fixed peg. This process is called 1-way pegging because the price of the tokens in the sidechain could never surpass the price determined by the peg, otherwise owners of bitcoins would convert them to the new tokens and sell them, buying bitcoins with the proceeds. This arbitrage would decrease the price of the side-chain tokens to that determined by the peg. However, it is possible in 1-way pegging for the side-chain tokens to be worth less than their peg to bitcoins, as there is no direct way (with a fixed exchange rate) to convert these tokens back to bitcoins. The original application envisioned for 1-way pegging was to allow the transition to a major new version of the Bitcoin protocol through a gradual migration of the existing bitcoins.

The main advantage of side-chains is that they allow testing of innovative ideas, but without diluting the monetary base of Bitcoin. In other words, money supply can be transferred between side-chains and the main blockchain, allowing the creation of new applications while keeping Bitcoin as the transactional currency for all of them.

The specification of how to perform a 2-way pegging is still being worked on, but Bitcoin developers believe it is technically feasible. On a very high level, a possible implementation of 2-way pegging could be (Buterin, 2014a):

- First a user spends some bitcoins to a P2SH address (section 6.6). This P2SH address contains a script that will unlock the bitcoins if given a proof that the tokens in the side-chain were destroyed, i.e. a proof-of-burn.
- The user then submits a transaction to the side-chain containing a cryptographic proof that the transaction in the Bitcoin blockchain took place. This transaction to the side-chain is signed by the same private key that created the P2SH transaction in Bitcoin's blockchain.
- The side-chain verifies the proof and awards new tokens to the corresponding address.
- If in the future the user wishes to convert the tokens back to bitcoins, she first creates a transaction burning those tokens to a special address (a provable unspendable address) and then sends a transaction spending the original Bitcoin P2SH address. This transaction includes a proof that the proof-of-burn transaction took place in the side-chain.

This description has glossed over many important details, such as how to construct proofs that a transaction took place in a different blockchain, how to verify these proofs (possibly in zero knowledge), how to compact the size of the proofs, how the side chains are mined, and so on. As of the time of writing many of the details are still being fleshed out (Buterin, 2014a).

The 2-way pegging mechanism provides a security firewall between the side-chain and the main blockchain. If a bug is found in a side-chain, the damage is confined to that side-chain and to the funds transferred to that side-chain, but the main blockchain or other side-chains are unaffected.

Proponents of side-chains argue that they are much more efficient than creating on-blockchain meta-coins, because they would not clog up Bitcoin's blockchain with metadata.

Mining would only happen in the main blockchain, with side-chains being mere repositories of funds. Miners in the side-chains would presumably be rewarded with transaction fees. Another possibility is that side-chains could be merge-mined with Bit-coin. Critics argue that a blockchain merge-mined with Bitcoin is at risk, as the Bitcoin miners could attack any merge-mined chain without any downside aside for the foregone reward from the merge-mined blockchain (a successful attacker might even profit from the attack).

One possible application of side-chains could be to create a beta version of Bitcoin, say, one version that included significant changes, such as increasing the block size or incorporating contract features available in some meta-coins (section 12.7). Creating a side-chain would allow thorough testing of this new version of Bitcoin, and would smooth the migration process because users wishing to use the new features would have an incentive to migrate their bitcoins and to test-run the new system. Evolving Bitcoin versions to incorporate innovative features in this way could compete with alt-coins and meta-coins in offering new features.

Another proposed application is to create a side-chain with a much higher transac-tion rate, via smaller block intervals and bigger block sizes. This side-chain could enable decentralized exchanges featuring a much higher frequency that could enable new forms of trading, such as high-frequency trading.

Changes in the Bitcoin protocol would have to be made to enable 2-way pegging with side-chains. A proposal that shares some similarities with side-chains, called tree-chains, can be found in Todd (2014a, 2014c).

14.5   OPEN TRANSACTIONS

Open Transactions (OT) is an open source financial cryptography library sometimes described as "PGP for money" (Open Transactions wiki, 2014b). Open Transactions is based on the concept of triple entry accounting (Grigg, 2005), which allows digital assets to be created and transferred between accounts in a server in a cryptographically secure way. Both server and client implementations are readily available.

Users in Open Transactions are identified only by their public keys. Thus users are pseudonymous as in Bitcoin, and can create as many pseudonyms (public keys) as they like. Pseudonyms in Open Transactions are called "**nyms**."

Issuers (any nym can be an issuer) can create their own digital assets—say a curren-cy—by formulating a Ricardian contract and signing it with their private key. **Ricardian contracts**, introduced in Grigg (2004), are digital contracts where a hash (message digest) of the contract is cryptographically signed by the issuer[9]. A Ricardian contract is human and machine-readable, usually using a standard protocol such as XML. Ricardian con-tracts protect against the issuer of the contract changing its contents over time. They

---

[9] An issuer can create a key to specifically sign a contract, but in this case the chain of keys leading to the issuers top level public key must be included in the contract. Thus all the information re-quired to verify a contract is self-contained in it.

are also more efficient to process compared to the current regular contracts as they are machine-readable. Other advantage of Ricardian contracts is that the public key of the issuer is included in the contract: this allows any user in possession of the contract to use this public key to communicate securely with the issuer, send payments, and so on.

Once an issuer (a nym) has created a digital asset contract, she can issue units of the asset to other nyms (users).[10] Every time a new unit of the digital asset is credited to a nym, a unit of the digital asset is debited to the issuer. The issuer then has an obligation over the asset, such as paying coupons and redeeming principal in case of a bond. Digital assets can be transferred between nyms either fully anonymously or pseudonymously. Fully anonymous transfers use a variant of David Chaum's blind signatures[11] and are untraceable (section 10.1). Pseudonymous transfers are similar to bank transfers, but cryptographically signed with the private keys of the nyms (sending and receiving) and the server.

Open Transaction servers play the role of banks, keeping a balance of the assets owned by every user. However, transactions follow the logic of **triple-signed receipts** (Grigg, 2005; Open Transactions wiki, 2014a; St. Clair, 2010), where the server and the user interchange a signed balance agreement in the receipt of every operation. The balance agreement includes the balance of funds and the open positions, say of outstanding transfers requested by the user. The signed receipt is strong enough proof that neither the server nor the user need to keep a history of the transactions: in case of a dispute, only the last signed receipt is relevant. Furthermore, because the receipts are signed by both the server and the user, servers cannot alter the balance of their users. Thus Open Transactions' users do not need to trust that the server does not arbitrarily change their balance. However, they still have to trust the issuers of digital assets that they hold.

Open Transactions can be used to create a federation of servers from which users can choose. Digital assets and their operations (cash withdrawals, transfers, checks, and so on) follow the same Ricardian contract protocol, so assets can be transferred between servers seamlessly. The main advantage of Open Transactions is that it separates the roles of digital asset issuers and transaction servers. This avoids the perverse incentive that a central server playing both roles might have to increase the supply of issued tokens. Other features of the Open Transactions project are:

- Users can operate in "cash-only" mode, i.e. without creating an account in any server. Users operating in "cash-only" mode would still need to contact servers (anonymously) to perform token exchanges (section 10.1).
- Exchanges. Servers can act as exchanges, accepting trading orders, closing trades and settling them.
- Invoicing system. Invoices are signed by the issuer of the invoice.
- Payment plans, which could allow issuers to issue instruments such as bonds. The server would then process payments—say coupons—from the issuer account to the owners of the digital assets automatically.

---

[10] A malicious server cannot issue digital assets by itself. Only the issuer, holding a copy of the private key, can issue them.

[11] Open Transactions uses an implementation of a variant of Chaum's blind signatures called Lucre (Laurie, 2008). Other blind signature schemes such as Chaum (1982) and Brands (1993) have been proposed to be included.

- Private messaging system using the Public Key Infrastructure.
- Integration with Bitcoin. Recent changes allow blockchain-based currencies to be supported without an issuer of a contract.
- Smart contracts through scriptable clauses. Open Transactions implements a scripting language for contracts inspired by Nick Szabo's contract language (Open Transactions wiki, 2014c; Szabo, 2002).

Development of Open Transactions precedes the creation of Bitcoin. The original envisioned application was the issuance of virtual currencies, such as those backed by precious metals. Since the creation of Bitcoin, Open Transactions' developers have been working on integrating it with the cryptocurrencies ecosystem, enabling many interesting applications.

One such application is to create multisignature voting pools for exchanges and web wallets. There has been increasing interest to move away from exchanges and web wallets that hold their user's funds, as these have been shown to introduce points of failure into the ecosystem. Open Transactions' advocates have proposed that exchanges or web wallets could use multisignature voting pools. **Multisignature voting pools**, or multisig voting pools, are a group of independent Open Transaction servers, say one for each web wallet service. When users of a particular web wallet deposit funds, these are stored in a multisignature address (sections 6.3 and 6.6) that requires the collaboration of a majority of the servers to access the funds. After depositing the funds, the user receives a deposit receipt signed by the original server (web wallet). When the user wants to spend the funds, she signs an OT request that includes details of how the transaction should be processed. This request is sent to the servers in the voting pool, who then vote to process the transaction if it is correctly signed by the user.

If the web wallet service provider disappears, the user can still access her funds through any of the other servers in the voting pool. Furthermore, the web wallet cannot steal or lose its users' funds through hacking or malfeasance, as this requires the collaboration of a majority of servers in the voting pool. Members of a voting pool have an incentive to police each other, as the wrongdoings of any of them would negatively affect the rest. A more detailed explanation of multisignature voting pools can be found in Ranvier (2013). For more information on Open Transactions, see <u>opentransactions.org</u>.

14.6   QUANTUM COMPUTING

A quantum computer is a device that directly makes use of quantum mechanics behavior to perform a computation. In contrast, regular computers only make use of classical physics' properties of matter. There has been a lot of research in quantum computing during the last decades, yielding several important results.

The basic unit of information in a classical computer is the bit, which stores either a 0 or a 1. In a quantum computer, the basic unit of information is the qubit or quantum bit[12]. In contrast with a bit, a qubit can be in state $|0>$, $|1>$[13] or any *superposition* of

---

[12] There are many possible ways to physically realize qubits, such as photon polarization, electron spin, or nuclear spin. The basic properties of qubits are similar across these implementations.
[13] The states $|0>$ and $|1>$ are called the computational basis states. The notation $|>$ is called the Dirac notation.

them[14]. Taking a group of n qubits, as any of them can be in any superposition of states |0> and |1>, the whole group is in a superposition of 2^n states. Thus, the amount of information stored in a group of qubits grows exponentially with the number of qubits. In contrast, the amount of information stored in a set of regular bits only grows linearly with the number of bits.

When a qubit is measured all its information collapses to one of the two states 0 or 1 with certain probabilities. Similarly, only when the group of qubits is measured does its state collapse and the exponentially large amount of information is lost. However, the information stored in a group of *unmeasured* qubits can be manipulated using **quantum gates**. Quantum gates can be assembled to perform any computation on a group of unmeasured qubits, much in the same way as Boolean logic gates can be assembled to perform any computation in a classical computer. The power of quantum computing lies in the fact that a group of qubits stores an exponentially large amount of information and this information can be processed using quantum gates. The biggest challenge, however, is how to retrieve the information stored in the qubits after the computation. The most common approach is to create a pattern of interference that would reveal the solution.

A quantum computer can do everything than a regular computer can, with a polynomial time adjustment. Moreover, there are things that a quantum computer can do that a regular computer would have to perform an exponential number of steps to accomplish. Greater detail about quantum computers can be found in Hagar (2011).

Most public key cryptography systems used in practice, such as RSA or elliptic curves, rely on the fact that some mathematical problems are believed to be hard to solve using classical computers. For instance, RSA relies on the fact that factoring large integers is computationally hard, whereas elliptic curve algorithms rely on the fact that computing the discrete logarithm on an elliptic curve is computationally hard. It has not been *proven* that these problems are computationally hard, they are only *believed* to be computationally hard.

The importance of quantum computing for public key cryptography is that there exists a quantum algorithm that can factor large integers in polynomial time. This is Shor's algorithm, and is one of the main achievements of quantum computing theory to date. **Shor's algorithm** reduces the integer factorization problem to finding the period of an integer in a group. This period is related to the factorization of the integer, and thus given the period, the factorization can be computed. For an accessible discussion of Shor's algorithm see Aaronson (2007). Shor's algorithm has been later extended to also break the discrete logarithm problem both on finite cyclic groups (Diffie–Hellman) and on elliptic curves. Thus *all public key protocols used in practice can be broken using quantum computers*[15].

---

[14] The state of a qubit can be interpreted as a vector in a complex vector space, where the states |0> and |1> form an orthonormal basis.

[15] Aside from breaking ciphers, quantum computing researchers also focus on solving other types of problems using quantum computers. **BQP, bounded error quantum polynomial time**, is the quantum computational complexity class that generalizes P. That is, it is the class of problems that can be solved in polynomial time using a quantum computer. An example of a problem in BQP is integer factorization. Whether BQP contains NP is an open question in computational complexity theory, although it is believed to be false.

Another important quantum computing algorithm is Grover's algorithm. **Grover's algorithm** allows searching for a solution in an unsorted problem space in $O(N^{1/2})$. A classical brute-force algorithm can search the problem space in $O(N)$. This algorithm could be used, for example, to find collisions in hash functions or to break symmetric key ciphers. However, as Grover's algorithm only offers a square root speed-up over classical brute-force algorithms, both *hash functions and symmetric key ciphers are considered safe against quantum computers*, as doubling the key lengths would retain the same security level.

It is yet unknown whether powerful enough quantum computers could be built in practice: the most powerful quantum computer so far has only been able to factor the number 21. There are many practical difficulties to building quantum computers, such as isolating the system from decoherence, which is what happens when some external process corrupts the desired evolution of the system.

Turning the attention to the consequences of the advent of practical quantum computers in Bitcoin, addresses are the hash of public elliptic curve keys (section 5.6). Therefore the elliptic curve public key is not revealed until an address is used: a transaction that spends funds from an address must include in its <*scriptSig*> the public key (section 6.1). Therefore, used addresses have a copy of their public keys in the blockchain, while unused addresses do not. Thus unused addresses are more quantum-resistant than used addresses, and this is an argument in favor of not reusing addresses.

However, an attacker equipped with a quantum computer could set up a node and listen for broadcast transactions. Equipped with the public key in incoming transactions, the attacker could use Shor's algorithm to compute the private key and use this key to sign a transaction sending the funds to an address under her control. Therefore, 0% address reusing is not a long-term solution for Bitcoin in a post-quantum world. Fortunately, there already exist several public key schemes that are quantum-resistant (Bernstein et al., 2008), such as hash-based public key signatures (like Lamport signatures—Buterin (2013g)), code-based encryption (like McEliece), lattice-based systems (like NTRU), and multivariate-quadratic systems (like HFE^{v-}).

The problem with all these public signatures schemes is that they are far less efficient than elliptic curve schemes, requiring larger signatures and more computational time for the same security level. As public key cryptography is essential not only to the security of Bitcoin, but to the security of the internet, hopefully these quantum-resistant public key systems will improve their efficiency, or new public key technologies will be developed that could efficiently take on the role of elliptic curve cryptography in Bitcoin, if the need arises. See Buterin (2013g) for a possible path of action to ensure Bitcoin is quantum-safe in case powerful quantum computers are created.

14.7   RECENT ADVANCES IN CRYPTOGRAPHY

This section will briefly cover some of the latest advances in cryptography and how they could be taken advantage of by cryptocurrency applications.

14.7.1   Homomorphic Encryption

Homomorphic encryption refers to a class of encryption that allows performing certain types of operations on the encrypted data. The result of these operations remains encrypted, and can only be decrypted using the decryption key. The main advantage of homomorphic encryption is that the computer that is performing the computation does not need to have access to the original data.

The first homomorphic encryption schemes that were developed allowed only certain types of operations to be performed on the encrypted data, usually only addition or multiplication. An example of a scheme that allows only addition on the encrypted numbers is the Paillier scheme (Paillier, 1999), which has interesting applications such as in electronic voting. More recently, some homomorphic encryption systems have been proposed that allow arbitrary operations on the data (Gentry, 2010b, 2009a). These are called **fully homomorphic encryption (FHE)** systems. FHE allows general computation on encrypted data.

An application of FHE would be to delegate processing of sensitive data to the cloud. Without FHE, the best that can be done is to encrypt the data before sending it to the cloud. But the server on the cloud performing the computation has to decrypt it, and this poses a security risk. With FHE, services could be run in the cloud with confidence that the data will not be leaked. FHE systems are still somewhat inefficient, limiting its applications for cloud computing.

In the cryptocurrencies world, one important practical application of FHE systems is to use them in autonomous agents (section 12.4). Using FHE, autonomous agents could hold an encrypted copy of the private key without the risk that a hostile server that happens to be running the autonomous agent might steal the funds.

14.7.2 Obfuscation

Computer programs are usually distributed as compiled binaries. Their instructions are in a format ready for a computer to execute, rather than for humans to understand and potentially change. An exception to this are open source programs, whose source code is distributed along with the compiled binaries (section 1.2). Often the owners of the software do not wish their users to be able to understand what the program is doing for commercial reasons. Other times the owners put in place restrictions against unauthorized copies, such as DRM protection. In both cases, owners of the software would like to produce copies of the program that are impossible to reverse engineer. There are several techniques that can be used to slow reverse engineering efforts, such as eliminating symbolic information, encrypting the code[16], obfuscating code, deploying anti-debugger techniques, and so on. However, most of these techniques fail against a determined attacker, as witnessed by the ease with which most proprietary DRM-protected computer programs and other media are cracked. A good review of reverse engineering techniques and some anti-reversing techniques can be found in Eilam (2005).

Thus there is a large commercial interest in using cryptographic tools to protect the innards of a computer program against eavesdropping or tampering, while at the same time allowing the program to run on the computer of any potential attacker. Up until recently, cryptographic results on obfuscation have largely been negative. It was

---

[16] Encrypting the binary code is not a definitive solution because for once, the decryption key must necessarily be somewhere in the distributed code, and furthermore, the code must be at some point decrypted and stored in memory for the computer to be able to run it.

demonstrated in Barak et al. (2001) that a **general purpose obfuscator** could not be created[17].

However, recent research has found that under a less general definition of obfuscation, cryptographic obfuscators are indeed possible. The definition under which these obfuscators have been constructed is **indistinguishability obfuscation**. Given two different programs that perform exactly the same function, an indistinguishable obfuscator generates two obfuscated programs such that it is impossible[18] to tell which obfuscated program corresponds to which original program. Researchers have proposed in Garg et al. (2013) a candidate for indistinguishability obfuscation based on what they call **Multilinear Jigsaw Puzzles**. The idea behind multilinear jigsaw puzzles is to mix each piece of a program with random elements chosen in such a way that this randomness cancels out when the program is run in the intended way. This proposal is based on new cryptography that has not yet been fully vetted by the community. Also, in its current form it is still inefficient, as small programs are converted to much larger and more complex programs when obfuscated.

A program obfuscated with an indistinguishability obfuscator can conceal any information, such as a password or a private key. A demonstration of why this is the case, taken from Buterin (2014e), assumes that there are two original programs:

- One program keeps a copy of the password and computes the hash of this password every time it is executed. It then outputs the hash.
- The second program stores a copy of the hash directly and outputs this value when invoked.

When the indistinguishable obfuscator is applied to the two programs, it is not possible to tell the two resulting obfuscated programs apart. The first obfuscated program cannot leak the password: if it were to leak it, this obfuscated program could be distinguished from the second obfuscated program that cannot leak the password as it does not hold a copy of it. Therefore indistinguishability obfuscation does indeed conceal the private information of a program.

In a sense, obfuscators are the holy grail of cryptography: an obfuscator could be used to build public key schemes from symmetric ciphers by simply obfuscating a program with a symmetric encryption key. Or it could be used to create a fully homomorphic system (Barak et al., 2001).

Obfuscators could allow autonomous agents to hold internal passwords, such as login information for any website. They could also allow the creation of autonomous agents that perform proprietary computations: a company could release autonomous agents in the wild without fear that their design could be copied by its competitors.

---

[17] In fairness, the definition of a general purpose obfuscator was too stringent, as it included programs that were specifically designed not to be obfuscated (Green, 2014a).
[18] Impossible in the sense that it is not computationally feasible.

Bibliography

Aaronson, S. (2007) *Shor, I'll do it.* www.scottaaronson.com/blog/?p=208

alp (bitcointalk.org user) (2013) *Implementing External State Contracts.* bitcointalk.org/index.php?topic=260898.0

Antonopoulos, A. (to be published, 2014) *Mastering Bitcoin—Unlocking Digital Crypto-currencies.* O'Reilly Media.

Ametrano, F. (2014) *Hayek Money: The Cryptocurrency Price Stability Solution.* papers.ssrn.com/sol3/papers.cfm?abstract_id=2425270

Andresen, G. (2011) *BIP 11, M-of-N Standard Transactions.* github.com/bitcoin/bips/blob/master/bip-0011.mediawiki

Andresen, G. (2012) *Brainwallet Braindump.* gist.github.com/gavinandresen/3840286

Andresen, G. (2013a) *The Macro-economics of Alt-coins.* gavintech.blogspot.com/2013/08/the-macro-economics-of-alt-coins.html

Andresen, G. (2013b) *BIP 50, March 2013 Chain Fork Post-Mortem.* github.com/bitcoin/bips/blob/master/bip-0050.mediawiki

Andresen, G. (2013c) *BIP 70, Payment Protocol.* github.com/bitcoin/bips/blob/master/bip-0070.mediawiki

Andresen, G. (2013d) *BIP 72, URI extensions for Payment Protocol.* github.com/bitcoin/bips/blob/master/bip-0072.mediawiki

Andresen, G. (2013e) *Core Development Update #5.* bitcoinfoundation.org/blog/?p=290

Andresen, G. (2014) *Floating Fees for 0.10.* bitcoinfoundation.org/2014/07/07/floating-fees/

Androulaki, E., Karame, G., Roeschlin, M., Scherer, T., Capkun, S. (2013) *Evaluating User Privacy in Bitcoin.* In Financial Cryptography and Data Security. *Lecture Notes in Computer Science,* 7859: 34–51.

Arora, S., Barak, B. (2009) *Computational Complexity: A Modern Approach.*

Assia, Y., Buterin, V., Hakim, L., Rosenfeld, M. (2014) *Colored Coins—BitcoinX,* retrieved July 2014, docs.google.com/document/d/1AnkP_cVZTCMLIzw4DvsW6M8Q2JC0lIzrTLuoWu2z1BE

Babaioff, M., Dobzinski, S., Oren, S., Zohar, A. (2012) *On Bitcoin and Red Balloons.* research.microsoft.com/pubs/156072/bitcoin.pdf

Back, A. (2002) *Hashcash—a Denial of Service Counter-measure.* www.hashcash.org/papers/hashcash.pdf

Back, A. (2013) *Blind Symmetric Commitment for Stronger Byzantine Voting Resilience.* bitcointalk.org/index.php?topic=206303.0

Back, A. (2014a) *2-way Pegging (Re: is there a way to do bitcoin-staging?).* In Bitcoin-development mailing list. sourceforge.net/p/bitcoin/mailman/message/32108143/

Back, A. (2014b) *Fungibility, Privacy and Identity.* www.youtube.com/watch?v=3dAdI3Gzodo

AnonCoin (2014) *About the Coin,* retrieved July 2014. anoncoin.net/index.php/the-coin

Backstrom, L., Dwork, C., Kleinberg, J. (2007) *Wherefore Art Thou r3579x?: Anonymized Social Networks, Hidden Patterns, and Structural Steganography.* In Proceedings of the 16th International Conference on World Wide Web, pp. 181–90. ACM.

Bank for International Settlements (2013) *Triennial Central Bank Survey. Foreign Exchange Turn-over in April 2013: Preliminary Global Results.* www.bis.org/publ/rpfx13fx.pdf

Barak, B., Goldreich, O., Impagliazzo, R., Rudich, S., Sahai, A., Vadhan, S., Yang, K. (2001) *On the (Im)possibility of Obfuscating Programs.* www.wisdom.weizmann.ac.il/~oded/PS/obf4.pdf

Baric, N., Pfitzmann, B. (1997) *Collision-free Accumulators and Fail-stop Signature Schemes Without Trees.* In EUROCRYPT '97, *Lecture Notes in Computer Science,* 1233: 480–94.

Belshe, M. (2013) *P2SH Safe Address.* www.bitgo.com/p2sh_safe_address

Benaloh, J., Michael de Mare (1994) *One-way Accumulators: A Decentralized Alternative to Digital Signatures.* In EUROCRYPT '93, *Lecture Notes in Computer Science,* 765: 274–85. www.cs.stevens.edu/~mdemare/pubs/owa.pdf

Bennenbroek, N. (2014) *Bitcoin 101: A Primer.* UBS.

Ben-Sasson, E., Chiesa, A., Garman, C., Green, M., Miers, I., Tromer, E., Virza, M. (2014) *Zero-cash: Decentralized Anonymous Payments from Bitcoin.* In IEEE Symposium on Security and Privacy (Oakland). zerocash-project.org/media/pdf/zerocash-extended-20140518.pdf

Ben-Sasson, E., Chiesa, A., Genkin, D., Tromer, E., Virza, M. (2013) *SNARKs for C: Verifying Program Executions Succinctly and in Zero Knowledge.* In Proceedings of the 33rd Annual International Cryptology Conference, CRYPTO '13: 90–108. eprint.iacr.org/2013/507.pdf

Bernstein, D. (2014) *Irrelevant Patents on Elliptic-curve Cryptography,* retrieved July 2014, cr.yp.to/ecdh/patents.html

Bernstein, D., Buchmann, J., Dahmen, E. (2008) *Post-Quantum Cryptography.* Springer.

Bloom, B. (1970) "Space/Time Trade-off in Hash Coding with Allowable Errors." *Communications of the ACM,* 13(7): 422–6.

The Bitcoin Foundation (2014a) *Bitcoin Developer Guide,* retrieved July 2014, bitcoindev.us.to/en/developer-guide

The Bitcoin Foundation(2014b) *Bitcoin Developer Reference,* retrieved July 2014, bitcoindev.us.to/en/developer-reference

Bitcoinj Documentation (2014) *Working with Micropayment Channels,* retrieved July 2014, bitcoinj.github.io/working-with-micropayments

Bitcoin wiki (2014) *Agents,* retrieved July 2014, en.bitcoin.it/wiki/Agents

Bitcoin wiki (2014a) *Alternative Chain,* retrieved July 2014, en.bitcoin.it/wiki/Alternative_chain

Bitcoin wiki (2014b) *Atomic Cross-chain Trading,* retrieved July 2014, en.bitcoin.it/wiki/Atomic_cross-chain_trading

Bitcoin wiki (2014c) *Base58Check Encoding,* retrieved July 2014, en.bitcoin.it/wiki/Base58Check_encoding

Bitcoin wiki (2014d) *Bitcoin Improvement Proposals,* retrieved July 2014, en.bitcoin.it/wiki/Bitcoin_Improvement_Proposals

Bitcoin wiki (2014e) *Comparison of Mining Pools,* retrieved July 2014, en.bitcoin.it/wiki/Comparison_of_mining_pools

Bitcoin wiki (2014f) *Contracts,* retrieved July 2014, en.bitcoin.it/wiki/Contracts

Bitcoin wiki (2014g) *Dominant Assurance Contracts,* retrieved July 2014, en.bitcoin.it/wiki/Dominant_Assurance_Contracts

Bitcoin wiki (2014h) *Double-spending,* retrieved July 2014, en.bitcoin.it/wiki/Double-spending

Bitcoin wiki (2014i) *Getblocktemplate,* retrieved July 2014, en.bitcoin.it/wiki/Getblocktemplate

Bitcoin wiki (2014j) *Hardware Wallet,* retrieved July 2014, en.bitcoin.it/wiki/Hardware_wallet

Bitcoin wiki (2014k) *List of Alternative Cryptocurrencies,* retrieved July 2014, en.bitcoin.it/wiki/List_of_alternative_cryptocurrencies

Bitcoin wiki (2014l) *List of Address Prefixes,* retrieved July 2014, en.bitcoin.it/wiki/List_of_address_prefixes

Bitcoin wiki (2014m) *Mining Hardware Comparison,* retrieved July 2014, en.bitcoin.it/wiki/Mining_hardware_comparison

Bitcoin wiki (2014n) *Mini Private Key Format*, retrieved July 2014, en.bitcoin.it/wiki/Mini_private_key_format

Bitcoin wiki (2014o) *Paper Wallet*, retrieved July 2014, en.bitcoin.it/wiki/Paper_wallet

Bitcoin wiki (2014p) *P2Pool*, retrieved July 2014, en.bitcoin.it/wiki/P2Pool

Bitcoin wiki (2014q) *Pooled Mining*, retrieved July 2014, en.bitcoin.it/wiki/Pooled_mining

Bitcoin wiki (2014r) *Prohibited Changes*, retrieved July 2014, en.bitcoin.it/wiki/Prohibited_changes

Bitcoin wiki (2014s) *Proof of Burn*, retrieved July 2014, en.bitcoin.it/wiki/Proof_of_burn

Bitcoin wiki (2014t) *Proof of Stake*, retrieved July 2014, en.bitcoin.it/wiki/Proof_of_Stake

Bitcoin wiki (2014u) *Scalability*, retrieved July 2014, en.bitcoin.it/wiki/Scalability

Bitcoin wiki (2014v) *Script*, retrieved July 2014, en.bitcoin.it/wiki/Script

Bitcoin wiki (2014w) *Smart Property*, retrieved July 2014, en.bitcoin.it/wiki/Smart_Property

Bitcoin wiki (2014x) *Splash*, retrieved July 2014, en.bitcoin.it/wiki/Splash

Bitcoin wiki (2014y) *Thin Client Security*, retrieved July 2014, en.bitcoin.it/wiki/Thin_Client_Security

Bitcoin wiki (2014z) *Transaction fees*, retrieved July 2014, en.bitcoin.it/wiki/Transaction_fees

Bitcoin wiki (2014aa) *Transaction Malleability*, retrieved July 2014, en.bitcoin.it/wiki/Transaction_Malleability

Bitcoin wiki (2014ab) *Wallet Import Format*, retrieved July 2014, en.bitcoin.it/wiki/Wallet_import_format

Bitcoin wiki (2014ac) *Why a GPU Mines Faster than a CPU*, retrieved July 2014. en.bitcoin.it/wiki/Why_a_GPU_mines_faster_than_a_CPU

Bradbury, D. (2014a) *Developers Battle over Bitcoin Block Chain*. CoinDesk. www.coindesk.com/developers-battle-bitcoin-block-chain/

Bradbury, D. (2014b) *Bitcoin Core Development Falling Behind, Warns BitcoinJ's Mike Hearn*. CoinDesk. www.coindesk.com/bitcoin-core-development-falling-behind-warns-mike-hearn/

Brands, S. (1993) *Untraceable Off-line Cash in Wallets with Observers*.

Brito, J., Castillo, A. (2013) *Bitcoin—A Primer for Policymakers*. Mercatus Center, George Mason University. mercatus.org/sites/default/files/Brito_BitcoinPrimer_embargoed.pdf

Brito, J., Shadab, H., Castillo, A. (2014) *Bitcoin Financial Regulation: Securities, Derivatives, Prediction Markets, and Gambling*.

Brown, R. (2013) *A Simple Explanation of How Money Moves around the Banking System*. gendal.wordpress.com/2013/11/24/a-simple-explanation-of-how-money-moves-around-the-banking-system/

Brown, R. (2014a) *How I Explain Bitcoin and Cryptocurrencies to New Audiences*. gendal.wordpress.com/2014/03/27/how-i-explain-bitcoin-and-cryptocurrencies-to-new-audiences/

Brown, R. (2014b) *A Decentralized Securities Trading and Settlement System is Being Built Hidden in Plain Sight*. gendal.wordpress.com/2014/06/10/a-decentralized-securities-trading-and-settlement-system-is-being-built-hidden-in-plain-sight/

Brown, R. (2014c) *Who Will Decide the Future of Retail Payments?*. IBM Insights on Business. insights-on-business.com/banking/who-will-decide-the-future-of-retail-payments/

Bruce, J.D. (2013) *Purely P2P Crypto-Currency with Finite Mini-Blockchain*. www.bitfreak.info/files/pp2p-ccmbc-rev1.pdf

Buterin, V. (2013a) *Bitcoin Network Shaken by Blockchain Fork*. Bitcoin Magazine. bitcoinmagazine.com/3668/bitcoin-network-shaken-by-blockchain-fork/

Buterin, V. (2013b) *Critical Vulnerability Found In Android Wallets*. Bitcoin Magazine. bitcoinmagazine.com/6251/critical-vulnerability-found-in-android-wallets/

Buterin, V. (2013c) *Introducing Ripple*. Bitcoin Magazine. bitcoinmagazine.com/3506/introducing-ripple/

Buterin, V. (2013d) *Why The Bitcoin Greenlist is Structurally Dangerous to the Bitcoin Ecosystem*. bitcoinmagazine.com/8204/why-the-bitcoin-greenlist-is-structurally-dangerous-to-the-bitcoin-ecosystem/

Buterin, V. (2013e) *Trustless Bitcoin Anonymity Here at Last*. Bitcoin Magazine. bitcoinmagazine. com/6630/trustless-bitcoin-anonymity-here-at-last/

Buterin, V. (2013f) *Primecoin: The Cryptocurrency Whose Mining is Actually Useful*. Bitcoin Magazine. bitcoinmagazine.com/5635/primecoin-the-cryptocurrency-whose-mining-is-actually-useful/

Buterin, V. (2013g) *Bitcoin is Not Quantum-Safe, and How We Can Fix it when Needed*. Bitcoin Magazine. bitcoinmagazine.com/6021/bitcoin-is-not-quantum-safe-and-how-we-can-fix/

Buterin, V. (2013h) *In Defense of Alternative Cryptocurrencies*. Bitcoin Magazine. bitcoinmagazine. com/6926/in-defense-of-alternative-cryptocurrencies/

Buterin, V. (2013i) *Deterministic Wallets, Their Advantages and their Understated Flaws*. Bitcoin Magazine. bitcoinmagazine.com/8396/deterministic-wallets-advantages-flaw/

Buterin, V. (2013j) *Bootstrapping An Autonomous Decentralized Corporation, Part 2: Interacting With the World*. Bitcoin Magazine. bitcoinmagazine.com/7119/bootstrapping-an-autonomous-decentralized-corporation-part-2-interacting-with-the-world/

Buterin, V. (2013k) *Mastercoin: A Second-Generation Protocol on the Bitcoin Block-chain*. Bitcoin Magazine. bitcoinmagazine.com/7961/mastercoin-a-second-generation-protocol-on-the-bitcoin-blockchain/

Buterin, V. (2014a) *Side Chains: The How, The Challenges and the Potential*. Bitcoin Magazine. bitcoinmagazine.com/12349/side-chains-challenges-potential/

Buterin, V. (2014b) *Ethereum: A Next-Generation Cryptocurrency and Decentralized Application Platform*. Bitcoin Magazine. bitcoinmagazine.com/9671/ethereum-next-generation-cryptocurrency-decentralized-application-platform/

Buterin, V. (2014c) *Slasher: A Punitive Proof-of-stake Algorithm*. blog.ethereum.org/2014/01/15/slasher-a-punitive-proof-of-stake-algorithm/

Buterin, V. (2014d) *Multisig: The Future of Bitcoin*. Bitcoin Magazine. bitcoinmagazine.com/11108/multisig-future-bitcoin/

Buterin, V. (2014e) *Cryptographic Code Obfuscation: Decentralized Autonomous Organizations Are About to Take a Huge Leap Forward*. Bitcoin Magazine. bitcoinmagazine.com/10055/cryptographic-code-obfuscation-decentralized-autonomous-organizations-huge-leap-forward/

Buterin, V. (2014f) *The Question of Mining*. Ethereum blog. blog.ethereum.org/2014/03/20/the-question-of-mining/

Buterin, V. (2014g) *On Mining*. Bitcoin Magazine. bitcoinmagazine.com/14282/mining-2/

Caldwell, M. (2013) *BIP 38, Passphrase-protected Private Key*. github.com/bitcoin/bips/blob/master/bip-0038.mediawiki

Camenisch, J. (1998) *Group Signature Schemes and Payment Systems Based on the Discrete Logarithm Problem*. ftp.inf.ethz.ch/pub/crypto/publications/Cameni98.pdf

Camenisch, J., Lysyanskaya, A. (2002) *Dynamic Accumulators and Application to Efficient Revocation of Anonymous Credentials*. CRYPTO '02: 61–76.

Camenisch, J., Hohenberger, S., Lysyanskaya, A. (2006) *Compact E-Cash*. cs.brown.edu/~anna/papers/chl05-full.pdf

Cawrey, D. (2014) *Auroracoin Airdrop: Will Iceland Embrace a National Digital Currency?*. Coin-Desk. www.coindesk.com/auroracoin-airdrop-iceland-embrace-national-digital-currency/

Charlon, F. (2013) *Open Assets Protocol (OAP/1.0)* github.com/OpenAssets/open-assets-protocol/blob/master/specification.mediawiki

Chaum, D. (1982) *Blind Signatures for Untraceable Payments*.

Chaum, D., Fiat, A., Naor, M. (1990) *Untraceable Electronic Cash*.

Coase, R. (1937) "The Nature of the Firm." *Economica* 4(16): 386–405.

CureCoin (2014) *What IS CureCoin?*, retrieved July 2014. curecoin.net/index.php/en/knowledge-base/14-knowledge-base/about-curecoin/19-what-is-curecoin

CryptoCorp (2014) *Securing Wallets by Integrating a Third-party Oracle*, retrieved July 2014. cryptocorp.co/technology.htm

CryptoNote (2014) *Untraceable Payments*, retrieved July 2014. cryptonote.org/inside.php

Dai, W. (1998) *b-money*. www.weidai.com/bmoney.txt

Danezis, G., Fournet, C., Kohlweiss, M., Parno, B. (2013) *Pinocchio Coin: Building Zerocoin from a Succinct Pairing-Based Proof System*. In Proceedings of the First ACM Workshop on Language Support for Privacy-Enhancing Technologies, ACM.

Dashjr, L. (2011) *BIP 20, URI Scheme*. github.com/bitcoin/bips/blob/master/bip-0020.mediawiki

Decker, C., Wattenhofer, R. (2013) *Information Propagation in the Bitcoin Network*. www.tik.ee.ethz.ch/file/49318d3f56c1d525aabf7fda78b23fc0/P2P2013_041.pdf

Decker, C., Wattenhofer, R. (2014) *Bitcoin Transaction Malleability and MtGox*. arxiv.org/abs/1403.6676

Demian Lerner, S. (2013) *The Well Deserved Fortune of Satoshi Nakamoto, Bitcoin Creator, Visionary and Genius*. bitslog.wordpress.com/2013/04/17/the-well-deserved-fortune-of-satoshi-nakamoto/

Derek de Vries, Crutchley, J.P., Hwang, J., Jevremovic, I. (2014) *Bitcoins and Banks. Problematic Currency, Interesting Payment System*. UBS.

Devcoin (2014) *How Devcoin Works*, retrieved July 2014. devcoin.org/how-devcoin-works.html

Diffie, W., Hellman, M. (1976) "New Directions in Cryptography." *IEEE Transactions on Information Theory*, IT-22: 644–54.

Dourado, E. (2014) *Here's How Cryptocurrencies Could Replace the US Dollar*. elidourado.com/blog/bitcoin-dollar/

The Economist, February 22, 2014, *The Great Hiccup*.

The Economist, July 3, 2014, *Crypto Crowd*.

Eilam, E. (2005) *Reversing: Secrets of Reverse Engineering*. John Wiley & Sons.

Elwell, C., Murphy, M., and Michael Seitzinger (2013) *Bitcoin: Questions, Answers, and Analysis of Legal Issues*. www.fas.org/sgp/crs/misc/R43339.pdf

Ersek, H. (2014) *Western Union CEO: What Digital Currencies are Missing*. finance.fortune.cnn.com/2014/03/18/western-union-ceo-what-digital-currencies-are-missing/

Ethereum (2014) *Ethereum White Paper*, retrieved July 2014. github.com/ethereum/wiki/wiki/[English]-White-Paper

Ethereum wiki (2014) *Dagger*. github.com/ethereum/wiki/wiki/[English]-Dagger

European Central Bank (2012) *Virtual Currency Schemes*. www.ecb.europa.eu/pub/pdf/other/virtualcurrencyschemes201210en.pdf

Eyal, I., Gun Sirer, E. (2013) *Majority is not Enough: Bitcoin Mining is Vulnerable*. arxiv.org/pdf/1311.0243v5

Ferguson, N., Schneier, B., Kohno, T. (2010) *Cryptography Engineering: Design Principles and Practical Applications*. John Wiley & Sons.

Fiat, A., Shamir, A. (1986) *How to Prove Yourself: Practical Solutions to Identification and Signature Problems*. In CRYPTO '86, *Lecture Notes in Computer Science*, 263: 186–94.

Finney, H. (1993) *Detecting Double-Spending*, retrieved April 2014. www.finney.org/~hal/chcash2.html

Finney, H. (2004) *RPOW—Reusable Proofs of Work*, retrieved April 2014. www.finney.org/~hal/rpow/

Freicoin (2014) *FAQ*, retrieved July 2014, freico.in/faq/

Friedenbach, M., Timón, J. (2013) *Freimarkets: Extending Bitcoin Protocol with User-specified Bearer Instruments, Peer-to-peer Exchange, Off Accounting, Auctions, Derivatives and Transitive Transactions*. freico.in/docs/freimarkets-v0.0.1.pdf

Garg, S., Gentry, C., Halevi, S., Raykova, M., Sahai, A., Waters, B. (2013) *Candidate Indistinguishability Obfuscation and Functional Encryption for all circuits*. eprint.iacr.org/2013/451.pdf

Garman, C., Green, M., Miers, I., Rubin, A. (2014) *Rational Zero: Economic Security for Zerocoin with Everlasting Anonymity*. hms.isi.jhu.edu/images/bitcoin14.pdf

Garzik, J. (2013a) *StorJ, and Bitcoin Autonomous Agents*. garzikrants.blogspot.com/2013/01/storj-and-bitcoin-autonomous-agents.html

Garzik, J. (2013b) *"Solution" to Bitcoin Volatility*. garzikrants.blogspot.com/2013/11/solution-to-bitcoin-volatility.html

Gentry, C. (2009a) *A Fully Homomorphic Encryption Scheme*. crypto.stanford.edu/craig/craig-thesis.pdf

Gentry, C. (2010b) "Computing Arbitrary Functions of Encrypted Data." *Communications of the ACM*, 53(3). crypto.stanford.edu/craig/easy-fhe.pdf

Goldreich, O., Micali, S., Wigderson, A. (1991) "Proofs that Yield Nothing but their Validity." *Journal of the ACM*, 38(3): 690–728.

Goodin, D. (2012) *Why Passwords have Never been Weaker—and Crackers have Never been Stronger*. Arstechnica. arstechnica.com/security/2012/08/passwords-under-assault/

Graf, K. (2013) *On the Origins of Bitcoin: Stages of Monetary Evolution*. konradsgraf.com/storage/OntheOriginsofBitcoinGraf03.11.13.pdf

Green, M. (2012a) *The Future of Electronic Currency*. blog.cryptographyengineering.com/2012/05/future-of-electronic-currency.html

Green, M. (2012b) *The Crypto Dream*. blog.cryptographyengineering.com/2012/10/the-crypto-dream.html

Green, M. (2013) *The Many Flaws of Dual_EC_DRBG*. blog.cryptographyengineering.com/2013/09/the-many-flaws-of-dualecdrbg.html

Green, M. (2014a) *Cryptographic Obfuscation and "Unhackable" Software*. blog.cryptographyengineering.com/2014/02/cryptographic-obfuscation-and.html

Green, M. (2014b) *Attack of the Week: OpenSSL Heartbleed*. blog.cryptographyengineering.com/2014/04/attack-of-week-openssl-heartbleed.html

Greenberg, A. (2014) *Nakamoto's Neighbor: My Hunt For Bitcoin's Creator Led To A Paralyzed Crypto Genius*. Forbes. www.forbes.com/sites/andygreenberg/2014/03/25/satoshi-nakamotos-neighbor-the-bitcoin-ghostwriter-who-wasnt/

Grigg, I. (2004) *The Ricardian Contract*. In First IEEE International Workshop on Electronic Contracting (WEC'04). iang.org/papers/ricardian_contract.html

Grigg, I. (2005) *Triple Entry Accounting*. iang.org/papers/triple_entry.html

Grigg, I. (2014) *A Quick History of Cryptocurrencies BBTC—Before Bitcoin*. Bitcoin Magazine. bitcoinmagazine.com/12241/quick-history-cryptocurrencies-bbtc-bitcoin/

Grossman, R., Mitropoulos, A., Boise, J. (2014) *Sizing Up Bitcoin*. FitchRatings. thewhyforum.com/articles/sizing-up-bitcoin

Güring, P., Grigg, I. (2011) *Bitcoin and Gresham's Law—the Economic Inevitability of Collapse*. iang.org/papers/BitcoinBreachesGreshamsLaw.pdf

Haber, S., Stornetta, S. (1991) "How to Time-stamp a Digital Document." *Journal of Cryptology*, 3(2): 99–111.

Hagar, A. (2011) *Quantum Computing*. The Stanford Encyclopedia of Philosophy. plato.stanford.edu/entries/qt-quantcomp/

Hajdarbegovic, N. (2014) *Bitcoin Miners Ditch Ghash.io Pool Over Fears of 51% Attack*. CoinDesk. www.coindesk.com/bitcoin-miners-ditch-ghash-io-pool-51-attack/

Hearn, M. (2012) *BIP 50, Connection Bloom Filtering*. github.com/bitcoin/bips/blob/master/bip-0037.mediawiki

Hearn, M. (2013) *Merge Avoidance. A Note on Privacy-enhancing Techniques in the Bitcoin Protocol*. medium.com/bitcoin-banter/7f95a386692f

Heilman, E. (2014) *One Weird Trick to Stop Selfish Miners: Fresh Bitcoins, A Solution for the Honest Miner*. eprint.iacr.org/2014/007.pdf

Houy, N. (2014) *It Will Cost Nothing to "Kill" a Proof-of-Stake Crypto-currency*. ftp.gate.cnrs.fr/RePEc/2014/1404.pdf

Howden, D. (2014) *Bitcoin Bank Run*. bastiat.mises.org/2014/02/bitcoin-bank-run/

Hughes, E. (1992) *A Cypherpunk's Manifesto*. www.activism.net/cypherpunk/crypto-anarchy.html

Irwin, N. (2013) *Bitcoin Needs a Central Banker.* www.washingtonpost.com/blogs/wonkblog/wp/2013/11/19/bitcoin-needs-a-central-banker/

Kaliski, B. (2000) *PKCS #5: Password-Based Cryptography Specification. Version 2.0.* IETF RFC 2898. tools.ietf.org/html/rfc2898#page-9

Katz, J., Lindell, Y. (2007) *Introduction to Modern Cryptography: Principles and Protocols.* Chapman and Hall/CRC.

King, S. (pseudonym), Scott Nadal (pseudonym) (2012) *PPCoin: Peer-to-Peer Crypto-Currency with Proof-of-Stake.* peercoin.net/assets/paper/peercoin-paper.pdf

King, S. (pseudonym) (2013) *Primecoin: Cryptocurrency with Prime Number Proof-of-Work.* http://primecoin.io/bin/primecoin-paper.pdf

Koning, J.P. (2013) *Separating the Functions of Money—the Case of Medieval Coinage.* jpkoning.blogspot.com/2013/09/separating-functions-of-moneythe-case.html

Krawisz, D. (2013) *The Problem with Altcoins.* themisescircle.org/blog/2013/08/22/the-problem-with-altcoins/

Krawisz, D. (2014) *The Coming Demise of the Altcoins (And What You Can Do to Hasten It).* themisescircle.org/blog/2014/03/14/the-coming-demise-of-the-altcoins/

Krebs, B. (2014) *New Clues in the Target Breach.* krebsonsecurity.com/2014/01/new-clues-in-the-target-breach/

Kurose, J., Ross, K. (2012) *Computer Networking: A Top-down Approach*, 6th Edition. Pearson Education.

Lamport, L., Shostak, R., Pease, M. (1982) "The Byzantine Generals Problem." *ACM Transactions on Programming Languages and Systems*, 4(3): 382–401. research.microsoft.com/en-us/um/people/lamport/pubs/byz.pdf

Larimer, S. (2013) *Bitcoin and the Three Laws of Robotics.* Let's Talk Bitcoin blog. letstalkbitcoin.com/bitcoin-and-the-three-laws-of-robotics/

Laurie, B. (2008) *Lucre: Anonymous Electronic Tokens v1.8.* anoncvs.aldigital.co.uk/lucre/theory2.pdf

The Law Library of Congress, Global Legal Research Center (2014) *Regulation of Bitcoin in Selected Jurisdictions.* www.loc.gov/law/help/bitcoin-survey/regulation-of-bitcoin.pdf

Levy, S. (2001) *Crypto: Secrecy and Privacy in the New Code War.* Allen Lane.

Litecoin wiki (2014) *Comparison between Litecoin and Bitcoin*, retrieved July 2014. litecoin.info/User:Iddo/Comparison_between_Litecoin_and_Bitcoin

Lubin, J. (2014) *The Issuance Model in Ethereum.* blog.ethereum.org/2014/04/10/the-issuance-model-in-ethereum/

Luria, G., Turner, A. (2014) *Digitizing Trust: Leveraging the Bitcoin Protocol Beyond the "Coin."* Wedbush Securities.

Maidsafe (2014) *MaidSafe.net Announces Project SAFE to the Community*, retrieved July 2014. github.com/maidsafe/Whitepapers/blob/master/Project-Safe.md

Mankiw, G. (2003) *Macroeconomics*, Fifth Edition. Worth Publishers.

Marion, F. (2014) *Satoshi Nakamoto Quotes.* crypt.la. crypt.la/2014/01/06/satoshi-nakamoto-quotes/

Massias, H., Serret Avila, X., Quisquater, J.-J. (1999) *Design of a Secure Timestamping Service with Minimal Trust Requirements.* 20th Symposium on Information Theory in the Benelux, May 1999.

MasterCoin wiki (2014) *FAQ*, retrieved July 2014. wiki.mastercoin.org/index.php?title=FAQ

Maxwell, G. (2011) *Deterministic Wallets.* bitcointalk.org/index.php?topic=19137.0

Maxwell, G. (2013a) *CoinJoin: Bitcoin Privacy for the Real World.* bitcointalk.org/index.php?topic=279249.0

Maxwell, G. (2013b) *CoinSwap: Transaction Graph Disjoint Trustless Trading.* bitcointalk.org/index.php?topic=321228.0

May, T. (1992) *The Crypto Anarchist Manifesto.* www.activism.net/cypherpunk/crypto-anarchy.html

Mc, R.Millan (2014) *The Inside Story of Mt. Gox, Bitcoin's $460 Million Disaster*. Wired. www. wired.com/2014/03/bitcoin-exchange/

Meiklejohn, S., Pomarole, M., Jordan, G., Levchenko, K., McCoy, D., Voelker, G., Savage, S. (2013) *A Fistful of Bitcoins: Characterizing Payments Among Men with No Names*. Proceedings of the 2013 Conference on Internet Measurement Conference, ACM. cseweb.ucsd.edu/~smeiklejohn/files/imc13.pdf

Menn, J. (2010) *Fatal System Error*. PublicAffairs.

Merkle, R. (1980) *Protocols for Public Key Cryptosystems*. Proceedings of the 1980 Symposium on Security and Privacy, IEEE Computer Society: 122–33.

Miller, A., Shi, E., Kosba, A., and Jonathan Katz (2014) *Nonoutsourceable Scratch-Off Puzzles to Discourage Bitcoin Mining Coalitions*. cs.umd.edu/~amiller/nonoutsourceable.pdf

Miers, I., Garman, C., Green, M., Aviel D. Rubin (2013) *Zerocoin: Anonymous Distributed E-Cash from Bitcoin*. IEEE Symposium on Security and Privacy (Oakland). spar.isi.jhu.edu/~mgreen/ZerocoinOakland.pdf

Mizrahi, A. (2013) *The Theory of Colored Coins*. github.com/bitcoinx/colored-coin-tools/wiki/colored_coins_intro

Möser, M., Böhme, R., Breuker, D. (2013) *An Inquiry into Money Laundering Tools in the Bitcoin Ecosystem*. Proceedings of the 2013 eCrime Researchers Summit. maltemoeser.de/paper/money-laundering.pdf

Nakamoto, S. (2008a) *Bitcoin: A Peer-to-Peer Electronic Cash System*. bitcoin.org/bitcoin.pdf

Nakamoto, S. (2008b) *Bitcoin P2P e-cash paper*. www.mail-archive.com/cryptography@metzdowd.com/msg09959.html

Nakamoto, S. (2009) *Re: Bitcoin v0.1 Released*. satoshi.nakamotoinstitute.org/emails/cryptography/17/

Narayanan, A., Shmatikov, V. (2009) *De-anonymizing Social Networks*. Proceedings of the 30th Symposium on Security and Privacy: 173–87. IEEE.

Natham, A. (editor) (2014) "All About Bitcoin." *Goldman Sachs, Top of Mind*, 21.

National Institute of Standards and Technology (2001) *Descriptions of SHA-256, SHA-384, and SHA-512*. csrc.nist.gov/groups/STM/cavp/documents/shs/sha256-384-512.pdf

Normand, J. (2014) *The Audacity of Bitcoin*. J.P. Morgan.

Nxt wiki (2014a) *Whitepaper:Nxt*, retrieved July 2014. wiki.nxtcrypto.org/wiki/Whitepaper:Nxt

Nxt wiki (2014b) *Introduction: What is Nxt?*, retrieved July 2014. wiki.nxtcrypto.org/wiki/Nxt_Wiki

Nxt wiki (2014c) *FAQ*, retrieved July 2014. wiki.nxtcrypto.org/wiki/FAQ

Olson, P. (2013) *We Are Anonymous*. William Heinemann.

Open Transactions wiki (2014a) *Triple-Signed Receipts*, retrieved July 2014. opentransactions.org/wiki/index.php?title=Triple-Signed_Receipts

Open Transactions wiki (2014b) *About*, retrieved July 2014b. opentransactions.org/wiki/index.php?title=About

Open Transactions wiki (2014c) *Smart Contracts*, retrieved July 2014c. opentransactions.org/wiki/index.php?title=Smart_contracts

Oppliger, R. (2009) *SSL and TLS: Theory and Practice*.

Paar, C., Pelzl, J. (2010) *Understanding Cryptography: A Textbook for Students and Practitioners*. Springer.

Paillier, P. (1999) *Public-Key Cryptosystems Based on Composite Degree Residuosity Classes*. Advances in Cryptology—EUROCRYPT '99. Lecture Notes in Computer Science, 1592: 223–38.

Paul, R. (2011) *Oracle Gives Up on OpenOffice after Community Forks the Project*. Arstechnica. arstechnica.com/information-technology/2011/04/oracle-gives-up-on-ooo-after-community-forks-the-project/

Pedersen, T. (1991) *Non-interactive and Information-theoretic Secure Verifiable Secret Sharing*. Advances in Cryptology—CRYPTO '91. *Lecture Notes in Computer Science*: 576: 129–40.

Percival, C. (2012) *Stronger Key Derivation via Sequential Memory-hard Functions.* www.tarsnap. com/scrypt/scrypt.pdf

Percival, C. (2013) *Colin Percival on #litecoin-dev 02.* bitbin.it/E68HeKkM

PhantomPhreak (alias) (2014) *The Counterparty Protocol*, retrieved July 2014. github.com/ PhantomPhreak/Counterparty

Poulsen, K. (2014) *Behind iPhone's Critical Security Bug, a Single Bad "Goto."* Wired. www.wired. com/2014/02/gotofail/

Provos, N., Mazières, D. (1999) "A Future-Adaptable Password Scheme." *Proceedings of 1999 USENIX Annual Technical Conference*: 81–92.

QixCoin (2014) *What is QixCoin?*, retrieved July 2014. qixcoin.com/

Ranvier, J. (2013) *Voting Pools: How to Stop the Plague of Bitcoin Heists, Thefts, Hacks, Scams, and Losses.* bitcoinism.blogspot.com/2013/12/voting-pools-how-to-stop-plague-of.html

Raymond, E. (2001) *The Cathedral and the Bazaar.* O'Reilly Media.

Reid, F. and Harrigan, M. (2013) *An Analysis of Anonymity in the Bitcoin System.* In *Security and Privacy in Social Networks*, pp. 197–223. Springer New York.

Reiner, A. (2012) *Ultimate Blockchain Compression.* bitcointalk.org/index.php?topic=88208.0

Ripple wiki (2014a) *Contracts*, retrieved July 2014. ripple.com/wiki/Contracts

Ripple wiki (2014b) *How It Works*, retrieved July 2014. ripple.com/wiki/How_it_works

Rivest, R., Shamir, A., Adleman, L. (1978) "A Method for Obtaining Digital Signatures and Public-Key Cryptosystems." *Communications of the ACM*, 2: 120–6.

Rivest, R., Shamir, A., Tauman, Y. (2001) "How to Leak a Secret." Advances in Cryptology— ASIACRYPT 2001. *Lecture Notes in Computer Science*, 2248: 552–65.

Rizzo, P. (2014a) *Why Bitcoin Faces an Uphill Battle in the Remittance Market.* CoinDesk. www. coindesk.com/why-the-future-of-bitcoin-remittance-businesses-isnt-certain/

Rizzo, P. (2014b) *FinCEN Declares Bitcoin Miners, Investors Aren't Money Transmitters.* Coin-Desk. www.coindesk.com/fincen-bitcoin-miners-investors-money-transmitters/

Rochard, P. (2013) *The Bitcoin Central Bank's Perfect Monetary Policy.* themisescircle.org/ blog/2013/12/15/the-bitcoin-central-banks-perfect-monetary-policy/

Ron, D., Shamir, A. (2013) "Quantitative Analysis of the Full Bitcoin Transaction Graph." Financial Cryptography and Data Security. *Lecture Notes in Computer Science*, 7859: 6–24.

Rosenfeld, M. (2011) *Analysis of Bitcoin Pooled Mining Reward Systems.* bitcoil.co.il/pool_analysis.pdf

Rosenfeld, M. (2012) *Overview of Colored Coins.* bitcoil.co.il/BitcoinX.pdf

Rosenfeld, M. (2013) *Multi-PPS.* bitcointalk.org/index.php?topic=281180.0

Sander, T., Ta-Shma, A. (1999) *Auditable, Anonymous Electronic Cash.* www.cs.tau.ac.il/~amnon/ Papers/ST.crypto99.pdf

Santori, M. (2014) *IRS Guidance Further Legitimizes Bitcoin and Provides Clarity, but Demands Unrealistic Reporting.* bitcoinfoundation.org/2014/03/26/irs-guidance-further-legitimizes-bitcoin-and-provides-clarity-but-demands-unrealistic-reporting/

Schneider, N. (2012) *BIP 21, URI Scheme.* github.com/bitcoin/bips/blob/master/bip-0021.mediawiki

Schnorr, C. (1991) "Efficient Signature Generation by Smart Cards." *Journal of Cryptology*, 4(3): 161–74.

Shamir, A. (1979) "How to Share a Secret." *Communications of the ACM*, 22(11): 612–13.

Shirriff, K. (2014a) *Bitcoins the Hard Way: Using the Raw Bitcoin Protocol.* www.righto.com/ 2014/02/bitcoins-hard-way-using-raw-bitcoin.html

Shirriff, K. (2014b) *The Programming Error that Cost Mt Gox 2609 Bitcoins.* www.righto.com/ 2014/03/the-programming-error-that-cost-mt-gox.html

Singh, S. (2000) *The Code Book: The Science of Secrecy from Ancient Egypt to Quantum Cryptography.* Fourth Estate.

Smiling Dave (pseudonym) (2013) *Why Gresham's Law Means the Death of Bitcoin.* smilingdavesblog.wordpress.com/2013/10/18/why-greshams-law-means-the-death-of-bitcoin/

SolarCoin (2014) *FAQs*, retrieved July 2014. solarcoin.org/faq-frequently-asked-questions/

Sompolinsky, Y., Zohar, A. (2013) *Accelerating Bitcoin's Transaction Processing. Fast Money Grows on Trees, Not Chains.* eprint.iacr.org/2013/881.pdf

Sourceforge (2014) *Bitcoin*, retrieved July 2014. sourceforge.net/projects/bitcoin/

St. Clair, B. (2010) *Truledger in Plain English.* truledger.com/doc/plain-english.html

Šurda, P. (2012) *Economics of Bitcoin: is Bitcoin an alternative to fiat currencies and gold?.* dev. economicsofbitcoin.com/mastersthesis/mastersthesis-surda-2012-11-19b.pdf

Šurda, P. (2014) *Mt. Gox and Fractional Reserve Banking.* www.economicsofbitcoin.com/2014/02/mt-gox-and-fractional-reserve-banking.html

Swanson, T. (2014) *Great Chain of Numbers.* www.ofnumbers.com/the-guide/

Szabo, N. (1998a) *Bit Gold.* unenumerated.blogspot.com/2005/12/bit-gold.html

Szabo, N. (1998b) *Secure Property Titles with Owner Authority.* szabo.best.vwh.net/securetitle.html

Szabo, N. (2002) *A Formal Language for Analyzing Contracts.* szabo.best.vwh.net/contractlanguage.html

Szabo, N. (2005) *Shelling Out—The Origins of Money.* szabo.best.vwh.net/shell.html

Tabarrok, A. (1998) *The Private Provision of Public Goods via Dominant Assurance Contracts.* eprint.iacr.org/2013/451.pdf

TAGCoin (2014) *Technical Specifications*, retrieved July 2014. tagcoin.org/technical.php

Tanenbaum, A., Wetherall, D. (2013) *Computer Networks*, 5th Edition. Pearson.

Taylor, M. (2013) *Bitcoin and The Age of Bespoke Silicon.* cseweb.ucsd.edu/~mbtaylor/papers/bitcoin_taylor_cases_2013.pdf

Tiernan, N. (2014) *Atomic Cross Chain Transfers.* github.com/TierNolan/bips/blob/bip4x/bip-atom.mediawiki

Todd, P. (2014a) *Disentangling Crypto-Coin Mining: Timestamping, Proof-of-Publication, and Validation.* sourceforge.net/p/bitcoin/mailman/message/31655380/

Todd, P. (2014b) *Stealth Addresses.* sourceforge.net/p/bitcoin/mailman/message/31813471/

Todd, P. (2014c) *Tree-chains Preliminary Summary.* sourceforge.net/p/bitcoin/mailman/message/32142133/

Varian, H. (2003) *The Economics of Information Technology.*

Velde, F. (2013) *Bitcoin A Primer.* Chicago Fed Letter. www.chicagofed.org/digital_assets/publications/chicago_fed_letter/2013/cfldecember2013_317.pdf

Washington, L. (2008) *Elliptic Curves: Number Theory and Cryptography*, Second Edition. Chapman and Hall/CRC.

Wikipedia (2014a) *Advanced Encryption Standard*, retrieved May 2014. en.wikipedia.org/wiki/Advanced_Encryption_Standard

Wikipedia (2014b) *Auroracoin*, retrieved July 2014. en.wikipedia.org/wiki/Auroracoin

Wikipedia (2014c) *Bitcoin*, retrieved May 2014. en.wikipedia.org/wiki/Bitcoin

Wikipedia (2014d) *BitTorrent*, retrieved July 2014. en.wikipedia.org/wiki/Bittorrent

Wikipedia (2014e) *Darkcoin*, retrieved July 2014. en.wikipedia.org/wiki/Darkcoin

Wikipedia (2014f) *Dogecoin*, retrieved July 2014. en.wikipedia.org/wiki/Dogecoin

Wikipedia (2014g) *Digital Signature Algorithm*, retrieved July 2014. en.wikipedia.org/wiki/Digital_Signature_Algorithm

Wikipedia (2014h) *E-gold*, retrieved May 2014. en.wikipedia.org/wiki/E-gold

Wikipedia (2014i) *Liberty Reserve*, retrieved July 2014. en.wikipedia.org/wiki/Liberty_Reserve

Wikipedia (2014j) *Peercoin*, retrieved July 2014. en.wikipedia.org/wiki/Peer_to_Peer_coin

Wikipedia (2014k) *Ripple (payment protocol)*, retrieved July 2014. en.wikipedia.org/wiki/Ripple_(payment_protocol)

Wile, R. (2013) *927 People Own Half Of All Bitcoins.* Business Insider. www.businessinsider.com/927-people-own-half-of-the-bitcoins-2013-12

Wile, R. (2014) *Think Fees On Normal ATMs Are Expensive? Check Out What It Costs To Use A Bit-coin ATM*. Business Insider. www.businessinsider.com/using-a-bitcoin-atm-is-actually-pretty-expensive-2014-3

Willett, J.R., Hidskes, M., Johnston, D., Gross, R., Schneider, M. (2014) *The Master Protocol/ Mastercoin Complete Specification*, retrieved July 2014, github.com/mastercoin-MSC/spec

wizkid057 (2014) bitcointalk.org/index.php?topic=441465.msg7282674#msg7282674

Wood, C. and Vu, C. (2013) *An Exploration of Bitcoin Anonymity*. christopher-wood.com/docs/ WoodVu_BitcoinPrivacy_Survey.pdf

Woo, D., Gordon, I., Iaralov, V. (2013) *Bitcoin: a First Assessment*. Bank of America Merrill Lynch.

Wood, G. (2014) *Ethereum: a Secure Decentralized Generalised Transaction Ledger*. gavwood.com/ Paper.pdf

World, T. Bank (2014) *Remittance Prices Worldwide*. 9 (March). remittanceprices.worldbank.org/ sites/default/files/RPW_Report_Mar2014.pdf

Wuille, P. (2012) *BIP 32, Hierarchical Deterministic Wallets*. github.com/bitcoin/bips/blob/master/ bip-0032.mediawiki

Wuille, P. (2014) *Proposed BIP for Dealing with Malleability*. gist.github.com/sipa/8907691

Zetter, K. (2011) *How Digital Detectives Deciphered Stuxnet, the Most Menacing Malware in History*. Wired Magazine. www.wired.com/threatlevel/2011/07/how-digital-detectives-deciphered-stuxnet/all/

Index